US AND THE

A study of group conscious

D0834833

LIBRARIES
WITHDRAWN FROM

US AND THEM

A study of group consciousness

W A ELLIOTT

ABERDEEN UNIVERSITY PRESS

First published 1986
Aberdeen University Press
A member of the Pergamon Group

© W A Elliott 1986

British Library Cataloguing in Publication Data

Elliott, W A
 Us and them: a study of group consciousness
 1. Group identity
 I. Title
 302.3   HM131

 ISBN 0 08 032438 X

PRINTED IN GREAT BRITAIN
THE UNIVERSITY PRESS
ABERDEEN

Contents

Preface   **vii**

1 Introduction   **1**
The subject of study, 1; The terminology to be used, 3; The
characteristics of group consciousness, 6; Identification at
different levels, 10; All types of group consciousness are
capable of transforming into others, 11; The group
attachment trait is probably inborn, 12.

2 The Social Attachments of Children   **16**
First attachments, 16; Wider attachments and allegiances, 19;
Artificial juvenile identities, 24.

3 Tribal and Racial Consciousness   **29**
How tribesmen identify, 29; Racial group consciousness, 32;
Social attachments among the higher social animals, 39;
Loyalty to the whole human species, 42.

4 Mother Tongues   **44**

5 Faith and Nation   **54**
Islamic identities, 55; The orthodox of Cyprus, 63; Irish
Protestants and Catholics, 70.

6 Esprit de Corps   **79**
The Gurkha Brigade, 81; British Indian Regiments, 83;
British Regiments and higher formations, 86.

7 Group Identity and Warfare   **96**
Group antagonism, 96; Marx's views on warfare, 97;
Freud's views on warfare, 100; Identification with people or
territory, 105

8 States and Nations   **110**
Positive and negative aspects of group consciousness, 110;
Multinational states, 113; Greater and lesser national
names, 121.

9 Imperial and International Identities   **128**
Imperial levels of identity, 128; The International Working
Class, 135; International organisations, 142; The right of
self-determination, 146; Towards international law and
order, 148.

Epilogue   **151**
References   **157**
Index   **161**

Preface

This book results from experiences creating a desire to understand group consciousness that continues to shake the world in which we live. During the second world war I became acutely aware of the importance of esprit de corps at different levels; and not only how to nurture but even how to create it. Immediately after the war I found myself in Germany with a large and loyal staff of ex-enemies. This gave food for thought that national consciousness might represent the same phenomenon.

I have since tried to keep up with such literature as exists on human identities starting with the now outdated Trotter's *Herd Instincts in Peace and War* through to more recent works by European socio-psychologists. For a time, due to pressure of other professional work, this study had to be temporarily abandoned; but never entirely so. For even a lawyer becomes aware that the workability of national as well as international law ultimately depends on consensus and group consciousness.

Any study of the latter involves historical as well as contemporary examples. Both have been aided by foreign travel to get the feel of local loyalties. In the course of such travel I have become ever more convinced that the group identification of individuals and the resultant loyalties we experience provide the clue not only to the nature of national consciousness itself but also to other forms of social identification of which the national is but one example.

Seton-Watson's book *Nations and States* provided me with a mine of national information from all round the world; but it did not seek to explore the psychological basis of national identities nor provide any general explanation of group consciousness. For examples of other forms of identity from which general conclusions might be attempted to be drawn I built up a box-file of cuttings from newspapers and periodicals including excerpts from broadcasts published in 'The Listener'; also of personal statements by various persons of how and by what names they call themselves. The extent of such direct contemporary evidence is surprising once one is alerted to its presence.

To enable a lawyer to write a book of this nature, however, has also required expert assistance. In this regard I was fortunate in having the initial advice and assistance of the late Margaret Manning, zoologist turned child psychologist, who advised me on books to read. She also impressed upon me that explanations of the present subject were still anyone's guess. But she did not live to see the final text. I am also indebted to Professor Aubrey Manning and Professor David Wood Gush for their assistance on animal social behaviour and its evident connection with the human. Also to several other friends upon whom, from time to time, I have inflicted argumentative views or even portions of the text. Among these I must mention Professors Murdoch and Rosalind Mitchison as well as Gerald and Allison Elliot. But as none have seen the complete text mention of their names carries no indication of any agreement with the conclusions. I am grateful to the *Observer* newspaper for permission to publish an excerpt from an article by the late Arthur Koestler, and also to the *Scotsman* newspaper for permission to publish another by Chris Baur. Also to Sir Karl Popper for permission to publish an extract from his *Conjectures and Refutations*.

Book references in the text have been kept to a minimum to ensure a more readable result even at the risk of displeasing some specialists.

For editorial assistance I am indebted to the professional guidance of Peter Cochrane. He is himself the author of a book of wartime experiences revolving round the esprit de corps of an infantry company and has proved friend and adviser as well as editor. When it came to publication too I could not have been more fortunate than to have Colin MacLean of Aberdeen University Press. The subject happened to be in direct line with seminars he organised at St Andrews University in 1978 on the subject of national identity.

So both editor and publisher have been personally involved in the same line of thinking.

It is customary for an author to end by thanking his wife for checking page proofs and exercising forbearance. But here such mere acknowledgement would never do. For this book was thought about and its several drafts written in what should have been *her* time for which a husband's gratitude can never be adequately expressed.

1

Introduction

THE SUBJECT OF STUDY

The phenomenon of group consciousness has for too long been disregarded. For proof of its importance one need turn no further than the pages of the daily newspapers with their constant reference to identities of different kinds, as well as to conflicts caused by rival identifications. We therefore need to know more about underlying human attitudes and, in particular, why civilisation cannot be better ordered so as to allow expression of the more humane, rather than of the more hostile side of human nature.

Hence the title of this book, *Us and Them*—a popular expression, but nevertheless appropriate to emphasise the dual aspects of group consciousness involving a sense of *we-ness* and *they-ness* which appears to run through all human societies.

This inquiry is thus into certain aspects of human psychology conducted by a lawyer acting with professional advice on the various specialist topics which such a study requires. While the interest of the subject to a lawyer may not at first be apparent, social identity and consensus are nevertheless vital to the working of the law, and, above all, to the ultimate acceptance of a system of international law which has yet to be achieved. This requires a clearer understanding of what causes group consciousness and, in particular, national consciousness, which is the essence of nationhood itself. It also involves the study of lawlessness.

There have been several conferences in recent years as well as books written, groping for a suitable definition of national identity or nationhood. Perhaps the historians are best placed to define the concept. Thus Taylor (1979): 'The simplest definition of a nation is a community who thinks it is a nation.' And Seton Watson (1977): 'A nation exists when a significant number of people in a community consider themselves to form a nation, or behave as if they have formed one. It is not necessary that the whole of the population should so feel, or so behave, and it is not possible to lay down dogmatically a minimum percentage of population which must be so affected. When a significant group holds this belief, it possesses national consciousness.'

But what causes national consciousness in the first place? To provide something more than an *ex post facto* definition one needs to go behind

1

national consciousness itself to consider other equally important forms of group consciousness, and indeed to keep an open mind on whether there may not be psychological processes involved, universal to the human species.

The subject of inquiry is therefore into all forms of group consciousness, whether national, racial, class or linguistic; and, above all, into what gives rise in individuals to feelings of belonging to particular peoples. Little help has been drawn from orthodox sociology, once regarded as the all-embracing science of society, or from social anthropology. For each lays too much stress upon the social structure of particular societies, viewed as totalities in themselves which in reality they seldom are. The main difference indeed between sociology and social anthropology today is that the former seeks to draw inferences from the study of single contemporary urban societies and the latter from primitive rural ones. But neither can throw much light on group consciousness as such which tends to manifest itself through a sense of distinctiveness from others. Nevertheless some social anthropological studies do illuminate primitive kinship ties as well as different types of tribal identification.

In recent years, however, social science has at last begun to take a real step forward through the child psychologists and social psychologists. From them positive work is now beginning to emerge in the vital field of human social attachments. Child psychologists have revealed the importance of early attachments and of the discerned familiar from the unfamiliar. Social psychologists have observed the importance of in-group and out-group behaviour patterns, and the very facility with which social identification can be artificially induced. So, it may be added, have some sociologists but only by straying into what was once regarded as the psychologist's preserve.

Tajfel and Turner have conducted experiments in Bristol under laboratory settings using schoolboys or students as their subjects. In his contribution to *Inter-group Behaviour* (1981), Tajfel lays stress on social preferences and discriminations as a basis for social identity. Similarly, in his *Social Identity and Inter-group Relations* (1982) and also in Turner's *Social Comparison, Similarity and In-group Favouritism* (1979), the authors conclude that the most relevant aspect of group identity is the maintenance of a sense of positive distinctiveness of one's own group from others. From this they derive a theory of social distinctiveness. Tajfel, in particular, emphasises the phenomenon of social categorising and the concept of self in relation to other selves. He also regards stereotyping as providing a clue to social categorising whether by race, class or nationality. These sociopsychological experiments also reveal the extraordinary facility people have for spontaneous identification with groups to which individuals are simply told they belong, without such groups apparently having any wider meaningful purpose. They thus reveal a ready human faculty to identify collectively.

The author, however, only became aware of these studies when this book was practically completed. The present thesis links with them. But it derives from an entirely different approach or perspective. For the present study, in contrast, began with the observation of wider groups at different levels of identification, leading back to the individual. Indeed the author's original interest in these matters arose from contemplation of contrived military esprit de corps and the facility with which soldiers could be induced to experience such collective feelings. This also seemed to indicate a parallel with the national consciousness of recently created nations in which individuals have been placed.

While this was the original order of approach it is not the method of presentation now adopted. It seems preferable to start the other way round with the social attachments of children and proceed from there to the allegiances of juvenile and adult groups.

The conclusions reached by this approach to some extent coincide with current sociopsychological theories particularly those relating to distinctiveness. But there are also pronounced differences. These are in the terminology to be used; the emphasis now placed on feelings of loyalty and allegiance as evidence of attachment and belonging; and the different levels or strands of identification. To observe these requires a wider and indeed historical survey. Loyalties are barely referred to in textbooks owing to the necessarily confined nature of sociopsychological experiments under laboratory conditions in a social vacuum. A final difference is with regard to the recognition of a probable biological trait or faculty for group identification.

In this opening chapter a brief outline of the main features of group consciousness will be given first with the supportive evidence following in subsequent chapters.

THE TERMINOLOGY TO BE USED

The words ethnic, ethnicity and ethnocentrism found in so many textbooks are thought to be too ambiguous and even misleading.

The word ethnic derives from the Greek word ethnos for people, leading later to ethnikoi or people of other religions. In the course of the nineteenth century, ethnology came to mean the study by ethnologists of other peoples or races—hence the modern meaning of the words ethnic, ethnicity and even ethnic art all of which still tend to have racial connotations.

The word ethnocentrism appears to have been introduced by Sumner (1906) who used it to describe the self-regarding attitudes of ingroups in relation to outgroups very much along the lines of Spencer's (1892) dual code of amity and enmity.

These dual attitudes are now examined under a different terminology more in line with what actually happens and what people actually feel.

The word ethnic has now come to be used in British and other national legislation. The meaning of the phrase 'ethnic origins' appearing in the Race Relations Act 1976 required to be interpreted in the case of *Mandla v Dowell Lee* 1984 2 A C 548. This was a case brought by a Sikh father at the instigation of the Race Relations Board against the headmaster of a school who had denied admission to his son for refusing to abandon his Sikh turban and comply with school uniform regulations. The boys were expected to wear the same uniform to identify them, while wearing a turban over the unshorn hair is regarded by orthodox Sikhs as a principal mark of their separate identity.

Under the Race Relations Act 1976, it is made an offence to discriminate unjustifiably against any person on racial grounds which are defined to include discrimination on grounds of 'ethnic origins'.

The issue was therefore whether the Sikhs are an 'ethnic group'. The County Court judge held, on the evidence, that although they are a self-conscious group they are not a racial one. This view was unanimously upheld by three judges of the Court of Appeal under Lord Denning who concluded, under reference to various dictionary definitions, that 'ethnic' still meant racial and that the Sikhs were a religious rather than a racial group. As Lord Justice Oliver put it, there required to be 'the concept of something with which the members of the group were born; or some fixed or inherited characteristic'. This the Sikhs, who started as a religious sect, never were.

On Appeal, however, to the House of Lords, three judges unanimously reversed this decision on the ground that while the word ethnic might still have a racial flavour—this was not the meaning intended by parliament when passing the 1976 Act. For it could not have intended positive proof to be given of biological pedigree. As one judge observed: 'Racial is not a term of art, either legal, or I surmise scientific. I apprehend that anthropologists would dispute how far the word "race" is biologically at all relevant to the species amusingly called *Homo sapiens*.'

The House of Lords were not therefore tied to precise dictionary definitions. In their opinion the word ethnic was now intended by parliament to be used in a more extended sense. All that was required to constitute an ethnic group, in terms of the Act, was that it regard itself, and be regarded by others, as a distinct community by virtue of certain characteristics. These, Lord Fraser listed as a long-shared history of which the group were conscious as distinguishing it from other groups, and the memory of which it kept alive: a cultural tradition of its own, including family and social customs and manners, often but not necessarily associated with religious observance. Other characteristics were a common geographical origin or descent from a small number of common ancestors; a common language not necessarily peculiar to the group; a distinctive literature; and a common religion different from that of neighbouring groups or from the general community. Provided a person who joined the group felt himself or herself to be a member of it, and was accepted by other members, then he was, for the purposes of the Act, a member. It was possible for a person to fall into a particular ethnic group either by birth or by adherence. It made no difference so far as the 1976 Act was concerned, by which route he found himself there.

Lord Fraser added that he had been guided by a similar interpretation by Mr Justice Richardson in the New Zealand Court of Appeal in *Kingansell v Police* (1979) where the judge had said:

> The real test is whether the individuals or the group regard themselves and are regarded by others in the community as being a particular historical identity in terms of their colour or their racial, national or ethnic origins. That must be

based on a belief shared by members of the group ... a group is identifiable in terms of its ethnic origin if it is a segment of the population distinguished from others by a sufficient combination of shared customs, beliefs, traditions and characteristics derived from a common, or presumed common past, even if not drawn from what in biological terms is a common racial stock. It is that combination which gives them an historically determined social identity in their own eyes and in the eyes of those outside the group. They have a distinct social identity based not simply on group cohesion and solidarity but also on their belief as to their historical antecedents.

So here are some recent judicial attempts at defining the words 'ethnic origins', in terms of an acquired sense of social identity and social distinctiveness much along the same lines as the social psychologists. It will be noted, however, that the New Zealand decision also imports the concept of a segment of a national population with its own established identity. If that be so, the word ethnic cannot be applied to the nation viewed as a whole, but only to a lesser segment with its own sense of distinctiveness; but apparently not to a separate social class unless also racially distinctive.

Where exactly then can one draw the line?

The present study is concerned with national consciousness viewed as a whole as well as other forms of social identity including class consciousness. As it concerns human collective feelings it is better to use the words group or collective consciousness to describe them rather than ethnicity. The expression 'group consciousness' will therefore be used as more apt to include not just minorities but all social identity types including national, racial, religious, class and linguistic varieties. Not only will the words ethnic and ethnocentrism therefore be avoided as too ambiguous, but also all other 'isms', including that suffix attached to the words nation, community, society or race. For these tend to signify political movements or beliefs and hence often a bias on the part of the investigator. All such emotive words will therefore be avoided where possible, although, in the religious sphere, it may be difficult to avoid using such words as Hinduism or Judaism.

Even the problem of racism or racialism, so prevalent today, is better described as racial identity importing a sense of racial pride with accent on the positive as well as the negative sides of this form of group consciousness, so giving a clearer view of how ordinary people come to share such feelings. Likewise, the words national identity are to be preferred to nationalism in describing actual situations and comparing, for instance, the Frenchness of the French with the Britishness of the British, rather than writing disapprovingly about nationalism in the abstract.

So it is preferred to avoid the words ethnic, ethnocentrism and all words having the suffix 'ism'.

Words and their meanings are not only vital to the interpretation of statutes, like the Race Relations Act 1976, but also when testing any verifiable proposition by proof or disproof. For no theory can be properly tested if too ambiguous to understand. Everyone knows what is meant by national identity but not so many by ethnocentrism.

Henceforth the term social identity, already used by the social psychologists and now endorsed by the law courts, will be used to cover all identity types. A particular social identity, whether national or otherwise, signifies the end-product of social identification in a sufficient number of individuals. Group consciousness or awareness will also be used to describe the same phenomenon.

The actual process of identity formation or social identification in individuals, however, poses a problem in that the word 'identification' imports two meanings. The Shorter Oxford English Dictionary states that it means 'the action of identifying or fact of being identified'. In this book, however, both meanings may be involved at once. For instance, in the chapter on 'esprit de corps', the placement or designation of recruits in particular military units will be described as also their own identification with them. The latter will be seen as the end-product of social identification and indeed, in microcosm, shows how national identity itself can be fabricated. To avoid ambiguity therefore the word identification will, so far as possible, be used to describe the process of identifying on the part of the individual; and the word designation to describe the fact of being identified collectively by others.

The reason for the choice of title to this book may now be clear. Group consciousness involves dual feelings of *us* and *them*. Such words are not to be disparaged because they are so commonplace. On the contrary they well describe the collective feelings or attitudes of individuals who regard themselves as belonging to nations, subnations, social classes, religious sects or any other identity types with a sense of distinctiveness of their own.

THE CHARACTERISTICS OF GROUP CONSCIOUSNESS

Group consciousness thus imports a sense of *us* or of *we-ness* with a corresponding sense of distinctiveness from others regarded as *them*. One cannot begin to understand how this comes about until one comprehends how collectively identified persons feel about themselves in relation to others. In extreme cases, this may involve all exclusion of self or selfishness and through group consciousness even the making of the supreme sacrifice. It involves the substitution of the collective *we* for the personal *I*. Just as the individual acquires an individual identity under his own name or patronym in relation to other selves, so too social identity requires the awareness of belonging to a distinctively named group in contrast to other groups. The individual then becomes aware of *what* he is in group terms. From such group awareness also stem particular examples such as national, racial, class or religious group consciousness. These are all the end-product of the collective identification of individuals.

Group names are thus important for signifying *what* people are and for serving as labels or symbols of identity, like the name Sikh. The absence of suitable collective names may even inhibit social identification, as with social classes—usually nameless, except in the case of 'the workers'. Collective names, however, are only labels of distinctiveness, designating *us* or *own* people from others. They do not usually cause identification in the first place.

The words 'my' or 'own' people also import a sense of belonging which is crucial to *we-ness* and *they-ness*. So are such familiar words as homeland, motherland or fatherland in different languages: likewise, one's own mother-tongue. Separate languages not only allow intercommunication but also cause excommunication from others and emphasise the familiar from the strange. One's own people are regarded as kith and kin or own kind in the language of the family or tribe. Great leaders too are often called Fathers or Mothers of their People. A respected Royal Family too can assist the sense of being a national family.

Another characteristic of group consciousness is the use of the definite article in relation to the group or groups to which people feel they belong. *The* means one's own. There is frequent reference to the Nation, or the People, or the Faith, with accent on the definite article, as meaning one's own in con-trast to others, without using the proper name which is then taken for granted. A related characteristic is to describe certain individuals as true People, as in the expression a true Frenchman or true Catholic. Likewise those who strongly identify on a class basis as workers, tend to regard true people as being only those of their own class. Even an upper class, within a nation, may prefer not to regard those of different class as true nationals. They may see themselves as lovers of France but not of the French, or of Scotland but not of Scots, so demonstrating a degree of separate class aware-ness. The Frenchness of the French means the distinctive French variety of group consciousness.

None of these attitudes are of course properly comprehended in the concept of ethnic or ethnocentrism.

This concept of the people—the Roman *populus* or Greek *ethnos*—has a long pedigree. Those living in the first kingdom/state of ancient Egypt (2500 BC) viewed themselves simply as *The* People in their own language as opposed to foreigners. So too, at the present day, the Eskimos call themselves Inuit, again meaning people in their own language as opposed to their alien nickname. The Acua tribe of South America bears a nickname given them by Europeans meaning savages, but now prefer to be known simply as Waoranai, again meaning people in their mother-tongue. For some primitive peoples, there is indeed no word for human beings at all in their own language other than that of the lineal names of their particular tribe. The racial name of Bantu derives from AbaNtu being simply the plural for man. So does Deutsch in old High German. Many national names too are really nicknames given by outsiders to those regarded as other people. In old English the name of Welsh meant other people whereas the Welsh name Cymru means 'our-selves'. Such names all indicate feelings of *we-ness*.

Most peoples nowadays, however, have a proper name ascribed to them by which individuals call themselves to signify *what* they are and how they identify collectively. Some such national names derive from ancient tribal ones like those of the immigrant English (Angles) which still remain labels of national identity and distinctiveness.

The new African national names were mostly chosen quite recently by committees. In response to their choice, different peoples have now had to learn to re-identify as Zambians, Malawians, Zimbabweans and so forth which no-one had ever heard of before. They have to come to regard these names as their own or *what* they are in relation to other nationals and in addition to the names of family, clan or tribe.

Separate national names, like personal ones, in one's own language may not be the same as those used by foreigners. Germans thus identify among themselves as Deutschen in their own language, but are known as Germans in Britain or America but in France as Allemandes. Those known as Spaniards in English themselves answer in their own language to the name of Espagnoles. Egyptians do not use that old Greek name but refer to themselves in Arabic as Misri. Moroccans answer to the Arabic word for Westerners.

Even the names of religious adherents, such as Christians, Jews or Muslims all started as nicknames given by outsiders. In each case, however, the particular name has become the hallmark of a strong and widespread social identification.

In the same category of aids to identification come national flags or emblems, as well as national anthems used on state occasions even in the Soviet Union and Communist China. Anthems are played at the International Olympic Games to honour the successful national athletes. Even social classes may have their symbolic colours, like red or blue.

Group names and symbols of identity thus seem to indicate a need on the part of individuals for collective symbols to respect and answer to as being their own. Indeed for any large group this is probably essential where the members cannot all be personally known. This tendency is as prevalent in advanced as in primitive tribal societies. Indeed the message now beginning to come back from the new breed of field anthropologists, prepared for the first time not only to live among and observe but actually to live as and temporarily to identify as primitive tribesmen, appears to be that so-called savages are emotionally not all that different from ourselves. The dividing line between history and prehistory therefore appears to be of little significance in so far as group consciousness is concerned.

Social attachments in the sense now used signify more than mere personal ties and go beyond mere mother and child or other individual attachments. Group consciousness or awareness imports a sense of *us* in relation to others; and hence the interest of social psychologists and some sociologists in ingroup and outgroup behaviour. But the latter cannot be viewed as an entirely separate behaviour pattern. In terms of group consciousness there is indeed no meaningful division between the two. People only display attitudes of *us* due to an acquired sense of *we-ness* determined largely by a sense of *they-ness* in relation to others. So-called ingroup and outgroup behaviour therefore merely reflects the two sides of group consciousness.

So group consciousness involves social attachments going beyond personal ones and immediate relatives and friends to embrace unknown individuals conceived to be own kind whom one may not know personally at all—except that they are conceived to be own people to whom one belongs, by virtue of shared language, accent, religion or nation. To such people, or the country where they live, one feels a sense of attachment of even greater intensity than for single individuals on whose behalf one would rarely be prepared to die. Group attachment, therefore, imports loyalty and allegiance to *us* in the face of outsiders. Again one notes the correlation of *us* and *them* and the prevalence of both ingroup and outgroup behaviour at the same time.

It is fundamental to the present thesis that social attachments on a wider scale can only be expressed through such feelings of loyalty and allegiance. This indeed is how the individual's attachment to his group or its symbols is expressed. As face-to-face relationships are no longer involved, loyalty and allegiance become the very mechanism of group attachment and symbols become important as those of group allegiance. They appear to follow automatically from the fact of social identification and the merging of self consciousness into group consciousness.

In the various examples of group identity, both contemporary and historical, about to be given, the touchstone to be used for discerning whether group consciousness exists, will therefore be where the loyalties are seen to lie. A corresponding test will be the presence of disloyalty or of failing to identify with those expected to be regarded as one's own. In a situation of heightened group feeling with the stereotyping of strangers this can lead to heartless cruelty. Here one sees the typical occlusion of humanitarian feelings towards other kind including traitors who are not regarded as true people or proper human beings at all.

In his studies of stereotyping, Tajfel regards this as a crude propensity for exaggerating the conformities and discomformities of *us* and *them*. Such stereotyping is most evident in the heightened group consciousness of wartime causing people to see all enemies as sinister in their differences. It may also account for their nicknaming. The names and nicknames used by nationals for outsiders of every description whether foreigners, barbarians or gentiles tend to be uncomplimentary. This was even so of the Han and non-Han (barbarian) Chinese. Each language too has its own words for the enemy and frequently in wartime its nicknames for the national foe. With the heightened group consciousness and social antagonism of the Second World War, various nicknames were used by the Allies for their wartime enemies such as Krauts, Nips, Wops, Wogs and Gooks—intermarriage with whom was completely taboo. Wartime comrades, in contrast, were seen as more homogeneous and friendly than perhaps they really were, or, as soon after the war, they again began to appear.

Perhaps this indicates some primitive form of defence mechanism linked to basic feelings of *us* and *them* and designed to exaggerate the conformities and discomformities as benign or malign.

Another way of testing the link between loyalty or allegiance and social identity is in those difficult circumstances where identities (and hence loyalties) are divided with two peoples claiming as their own the same piece of territory, or where one group regards the other as disloyal through wishing to separate. At one time or another this has been the British, American and

Irish experiences, with each identity situation in turn being capable of being tested by where the rival loyalties lay.

The touchstone of social identification, therefore, will henceforth be taken to be where the relevant loyalties lie at any given time. It is difficult indeed to see how collective, as opposed to personal, attachments could work or be expressed in any other way. One cannot identify with single individuals as being an extension of oneself, but one can with fellow nationals or other kindred types with whom one shares a sense of belonging.

IDENTIFICATION AT DIFFERENT LEVELS

A main feature of the human faculty for identification is that individuals can become conscious of belonging to several groups at one and the same time. This is yet another reason for discarding the word ethnic as inappropriate when the same person might be called ethnic at one level, but not at another.

Multiple identities can also be experienced not only by the same persons at several levels but also at different strengths, depending on the degree or direction of their arousal. Probably, however, too many levels cannot be involved at once, for then the necessary sense of distinctiveness becomes too vague for a sufficient sense of *us* and *them* to develop. Different levels of identification with sufficient distinctiveness also coincide with Tajfel's theory of social categorisation, i.e. of individuals classifying themselves in relation to other selves.

National identification of one type or another nowadays appears to be universal. It is usually fostered in a nation–state in which children are brought up under a national educational system. Even national identities, however, may comprise several identity strands such as those of shared language, race, culture or religion, all of which can combine to form a composite national whole if sufficiently distinct from those of other nations. These are really shared conformities. If there are several shared strands at the same level the sense of national identity (as among the Poles) is likely to be profound. But there may also exist vertical identities to lesser and greater nations or a sense of *us* and *them* at higher and lower levels of distinctiveness. Thus a sense of Britishness can exist alongside a sense of being distinctively Scots or Welsh, even in the absence of a Scots or Welsh nation–state, so long as each lesser identity remains sufficiently distinctive not to be engulfed in the greater. A sufficiently distinctive language or territory helps.

The essence of nationhood is therefore not the state itself, but a defined sense of group consciousness at a national level attached to a particular national territory and its inhabitants. Class consciousness on the other hand attaches to a group within a nation regardless of territory. It is usually, however, combined with national allegiance at a higher level—except when induced to regard itself as 'international'. Bi-national nations stand particularly at peril if lacking a sufficiently strong enclosing identity to generate loyalty and allegiance in their support. This is also the case with bi-class nations where the social differences have been allowed to become too profound.

Loyalty and allegiance are therefore clear signs of group consciousness. Disloyalty likewise indicates its absence. Hence the value of wider identities and shared names and symbols for holding diverse peoples together.

ALL TYPES OF GROUP CONSCIOUSNESS ARE CAPABLE OF TRANSFORMING INTO OTHERS

At first sight this may seem a startling proposition, for it seems to run counter to much that is taken for granted and even to call into question current attitudes to class and race, let alone the concept of ethnicity already mentioned. Yet it accords with actual historical and even contemporary transformations.

The Jews for instance provide a clear example of a people who have run the whole gamut of transformation through all social identity types. Under the name first of Israelites or Hebrews, then of Jews (a nickname for the men of Judah), their history has been one of continuing metamorphosis. First a tribal kingdom, then after the Captivity a tribal kingdom again. Later as the rebellious Province of Judaea; then during the Diaspora as the Jews of Jewry with a religious identity that has continued throughout the whole 3,000 years of human recorded history. And *pace* that great Jew, Karl Marx, who thought the Jewish question could be solved by economics, the Jewishness of the Jews has been neither caused nor maintained by economic factors at any point. Latterly, flying in the face of all economic advantage, a new Jewish nation-state has been formed in Israel, causing the religious strand of identity to become less important there for its continuance.

The Sikhs, already mentioned, display a similar metamorphosis while maintaining their social identity under different guises. They started as a religious community founded by Guru Nanalk in the fifteenth century as a casteless Hindu sect. Later they evolved into a separate people who regarded themselves as a distinctive nation, defeating the Moghuls in the Punjab where they established a separate Kingdom ruling over the local Hindus. Then they were defeated by the British who regarded them with respect as a martial race fit to man the Sikh regiments of the British Indian Army. Finally, since the independence of India, and with a separately developed language, there has arisen a movement to transform the Indian Punjab state into a separate nation-state of Khalistan or 'land of the pure' with its own separate capital. A provincial capital has now been conceded together with other demands but not before the Indian Prime Minister was assassinated in revenge for the Indian sacking of the Golden Temple of Amritsar.

So here again is a complete metamorphosis of identity types originating with a religious one. This result is not so peculiar if one realises that group consciousness or a sense of *we-ness* simply springs from the individual's identification with familiars as opposed to strangers. So religious, national, racial, class or any other kind of group consciousness is merely an example of the same underlying phenomenon assuming different cultural guises according to circumstances. Hence, any one type should indeed be capable of transforming into another depending on the different strengths or orientation of the particular identity strands. For everyone is still merely experiencing a sense of *we-ness* and recognising his own *us* as opposed to *them*.

Numerous examples will be given in subsequent chapters not only of religious but also of racial or linguistic groups turning into nations, and even of social classes so doing. Indeed there is no collectively conscious group which is not capable of such transformation.

This very capability provides strong evidence in support of a theory that the essence of *societas* is the sense of *we-ness* which, however, need not be a totality in itself, but may be expressed at different levels and at different strengths.

It is easier then to comprehend how rival religious sects, endeavouring to maintain their separate identities, can be more antagonistic to each other than to the adherents of an entirely different faith; how such sects can, in effect, become classes; or how such classes can come to have their own particular faith. Or that a separate class (not necessarily a ruling one) can become the kernel of a new nation or recreate an old one; that a linguistic group can do the same; or that Black racial consciousness can become transformed over a short period into separate Black African nations; or that the Sikhs can perplex the British law courts as to whether they are a religious group, a race or almost a nation; or that professed British loyalists in Ulster or Rhodesia can at the same time express hostility to the British people and Government.

Theirs is really a level of loyalty, largely to themselves; and all are basically expressing attitudes of *we-ness*.

THE GROUP ATTACHMENT TRAIT IS PROBABLY INBORN

An ability to experience group consciousness is displayed by members of all races and appears moreover to have existed throughout the whole of human history and prehistory. As this process of identification, involving group feelings of attachment and belonging, is psychological it is therefore probably inborn. But it is only an innate faculty or trait capable of arousal in different directions and still subject to social and moral control. As numerous examples will presently show, all actual identities are externally induced and not therefore inherited. Each social identity is merely the end-product of social identification and involves a combination of inborn faculty and external stimulation.

Most developmental and child psychologists and all biologists now recognise the presence of inborn traits in man, as in other animals, whose actual expressions are subject to social control. Some sociobiologists, however, go too far in claiming complex behaviour patterns as innate when they are more often cultural.

A group attachment trait however is not preprogrammed in any way nor is it a fixed instinct or 'drive' like a sexual one which, according to Freudian psychology, requires 'release'. It is only a faculty, but a very valuable one for promoting those necessary feelings of loyalty and allegiance in situations where such are required. Without it, people could not readily be induced to cooperate and be conscious of social duties as well as individual rights. Indeed, so valuable is the group attachment trait that, if it did not exist so-to-speak readymade by being inborn, it would have to be implanted everywhere by culture which might be much more difficult to achieve.

The examples given in subsequent chapters will show how tractable the group attachment trait really is. It is difficult, therefore, to see why even social psychologists fight shy of a biological dimension or why there should exist such a dividing line between individual and social psychology when group consciousness so clearly concerns both. Perhaps this has been due to premature demarcation within university departments. Tajfel in his contribution to the *Context of Social Psychology* (1972 p. 88) states: 'My concern is with the large and crucial areas of social conduct which are uniquely characteristic of the socio-psychological *homo* in the sense that they present empirical discontinuities with his biological background, with his non-social psychological functioning and with the conception of him being fully accounted for by the social system of which he is a part.'

Hence Tajfel precludes consideration of a biological base and of evolutionary factors. Yet sociopsychological processes do not originate solely outside the individual, tending to have him at their mercy. They also involve the individual's own feelings of loyalty and allegiance and his capacity to identify.

The main objection, however, to a biological base really comes from traditional sociology defined in Durkheim's *Rules of Sociological Method* as concerned only with 'social facts' external to the individual, the individual being regarded as falling only within the scope of individual psychology. But this can hardly be so of national or class consciousness involving a majority of like-minded individuals whose loyalties and allegiances are stimulated not only from without but also from within. It is a question of *us* and *them*. The very essence of *societas* is thus psychological. While a social structure can help to arouse group consciousness within its confines, if it fails to generate any loyalty or allegiance on the part of its component individuals, it will disintegrate. In studying group consciousness one is therefore concerned to keep to actual examples and to bear in mind the difference between social structure (the State) and nationhood (national consciousness). Also to try to avoid references to Human Society in the abstract. For, as a social fact, the latter simply does not exist.

It is difficult indeed to see why there should be such objection to the suggestion of an inborn group attachment trait. Most basic aptitudes are inborn, and why not psychological as well as physical ones? It seems unlikely that such a universal phenomenon evident even among children and everywhere expressed in a sense of belonging is likely to be entirely cultural—especially in places where there was once no means of intercommunication.

The ready facility too with which humans can be induced to identify with groups in which they happen to be placed, seems at least to indicate an existing proclivity in this direction, as does the often unintentional transformation of social identity types from one into another. The psychological phenomenon of stereotyping looks biological. There is even some evidence from the higher social animals, divorced from human culture, that they too display feelings which in the human context would be called loyalty and allegiance.

Hence, the difference between humankind and other social animals may only be one of degree.

The study of *societas* needs therefore to be concerned with the group attachment trait and psychological feelings of *us* and *them* which are everywhere displayed. Its expression in national consciousness, while by no means unique, at least suffices to demonstrate that group consciousness is not external to the individual but, on the contrary, is also internal giving rise to feelings of loyalty and allegiance. When a majority of individuals experience such feelings the end-product is national identity—but this still depends on an individual's sense of *we-ness* or, in particular cases, his Frenchness, Britishness or the like. The suffix 'ness' indicates group consciousness.

Nevertheless, any group attachment trait is still subject to social and moral control. Indeed the question of its control is ultimately what this book is all about. But first one needs to know what are our basic inclinations so that institutions and laws are not devised which run too much against the human grain.

The present conclusions, however, do not entirely stand or fall on proving the presence of an inborn faculty for group attachment, inclining people to identify with discernible groups to which they feel they belong. It is only claimed that, upon the balance of probabilities, the inclination to identify with other selves is more likely to be inborn than not. Whether inborn or everywhere culturally implanted, the starting point must surely be an acceptance of the situation as it is, namely, with the universal presence of identities requiring to be accommodated. We all have to live with or within nations which are one type of identity. The contention nevertheless remains that the worst results of group consciousness and antagonism will be that much easier and not more difficult to resolve by recognising and using group consciousness itself.

The basic theory and derivative propositions having now been set out we proceed to consider the evidence from which they derive. As already remarked the preceding propositions were really reached the other way round with most of the evidence first and then the conclusions. But faced with the present wide spectrum of enquiry, readers might have found themselves at a loss to comprehend what is being attempted to be proved, unless the main theoretical outline were first advanced. It is hoped, however, that by so doing, one will not be thought to be matching pieces of evidence to bolster a theory, while deliberately disregarding evidence pointing the other way.

Any would-be objective theory must always of course be verifiable and be open to proof or disproof in whole or in part.

Large-scale controlled experiments, however, are not available in this field so one must rely on other forms of contemporary or historical 'tests'. In so doing, contemporary examples will be preferred to historical, and also direct preferred to indirect evidence of how people identify and how they describe *what* they are. If group consciousness is essentially an expression of human feelings leading to group attachment and a sense of belonging, the best evidence must surely be of how individuals regard themselves at the time; not the subsequent opinion of others viewing them with hindsight. So even the historical examples will be directed to the question of contemporary loyalties and allegiances as indicative of group identification. Here one runs the risk of criticism for writing 'potted history' or of taking too superficial a view of historical situations. But this is only to discover the essential loyalties and identities beneath. It is not to try to gauge, as the historian must, all that happened at a particular time; still less to make any prediction of what may in the future occur. Indeed, this study of group consciousness serves to show that there are no discoverable laws for the development of human society or distinct phases in human history from which any firm predictions can be drawn. But that does not mean one cannot seek to civilise or control group consciousness, or, to this end, seek to probe objectively into its origins and characteristics.

Proof of scientific propositions is by controlled experiment which is usually impracticable in the sphere of human social relations. So the lawyer's looser standards of proof will be adopted, the highest being that of proof beyond reasonable doubt. Such, however, can rarely be proffered in this field. The more usual proof will therefore be according to the lesser standard of proof upon a balance of probabilities. And for some propositions only the lowest standard of all will be advanced, namely as a mere possibility.

2

The Social Attachments of Children

In studying the nature of group consciousness, the best starting point is to see if it is manifested among young children. For if there is an inborn group recognition and attachment trait one would expect it to reveal itself, at least in rudimentary form, even in infancy. Our purpose is therefore to discern with whom infants form their first attachments; thereafter gradually acquire their own sense of personal identity in relation to others; and later a growing sense of collective awareness or recognition of own kind as opposed to other kind.

Studies on infants have the advantage over the study of social behaviour among adults in that infants can be observed without any 'acting up' to their observers. Hence, no subterfuges are necessary to mislead them as to the purpose of the experiment or observation.

For convenience, the word 'culture' will henceforth be used to signify all external social influences, although at this stage hardly 'cultural' in the ordinary sense of that word. That enables certain situations to be described as 'culture-free'.

FIRST ATTACHMENTS

Experiments or observations conducted by child psychologists now indicate the presence of various rudimentary traits even at the earliest stages of human life. Psychological research now reveals the surprising degree to which the infant brain is fully operational at birth. To describe a baby as 'senseless' is to mistake the very nature of infant perception, for it at once begins to react to its social surroundings using all the finely tuned capacities and perceptions at its disposal. As indicated by Schaffer (1971), the infant appears to have a recognition system at work reacting to visual, tactile, auditory and even olfactory signals—perhaps even before birth. One function relevant to the present study, that of auditory perception, appears designed to produce a close and reciprocal clinging attachment between a child and its mother whose voice it can at once recognise—so vital for survival at this helpless stage of the infant's life and later during the child's long maturation period.

This is as important today as it was for our primitive ancestors during the evolutionary period.

In *Attachment and Loss* (1969), Bowlby has demonstrated how the baby reacts at once to the person who cares for and cuddles it which, under most circumstances, is its natural mother. It may also however (under unnatural conditions) be its adoptive mother or some other mother figure. Bowlby's theory is based upon biological inclinations. Other child psychologists' experiments reveal that the infant here plays an active role in cementing these early attachments. A mother too has her own emotional responses consequent upon childbirth and many of these reciprocal reactions appear to be biologically inclined. For instance, a baby's voice or the tone of its crying or chuckling will evoke its mother's sympathy the whole world over. Mexican mothers have been demonstrated to be capable of distinguishing the hunger and pain cries even of Finnish babies. Ainsworth (1967, 1969) has shown in his corresponding works on attachment how black infants in Uganda behave in the same way. All infants, of whatever race, laugh or cry to indicate pleasure or distress and pain, even if born deaf and blind.

These reactions, however, appear to be the only forms of social behaviour which can be proved, beyond reasonable doubt, to be inborn in the sense of being entirely culture-free and displayable even in the absence of prior experience or learning. Infants born deaf and blind are thus observed to smile or laugh at appropriate moments, when they cannot see other people to copy. They also cry although they cannot hear themselves doing so. One can therefore be certain that these particular emotional expressions at least are not cultural in origin, unlike most later developments.

From recent psychological tests on children, it now appears that the new born baby can also recognise individual features like human eyes looking at it. Initially there is a tendency to smile at all humans alike. Carpenter (1975) claims that two-week old infants will look longer at their mother than at a female stranger. Schaffer (1971) has also shown that there is full recognition and preference for the mother by three to four months of age. By the age of eight months this attachment is sufficiently cemented to be the cause of severe mental harm if the child is later fostered out, or placed for adoption or even removed to hospital thereby being deprived of its natural mother's presence. This also accords with the experiments of Harlow (1958) on parentally deprived infant rhesus monkeys with nothing to cling to. If experimentally reared in isolation, these monkeys likewise betray withdrawal symptoms which are quite irreversible. When they later grow up they prove incapable of properly relating to or making normal social relationships with other adult monkeys.

By about their eighth month, infants appear phased to grow frightened of strangers and to prefer familiars and, in particular, their own mothers. There is also some indication (matched by animal evidence) that babies prefer others of their own sex who they can identify by the type of clothing they wear—so providing an early example of social identification using gender as its hallmark. This pattern of preference for observed familiars has again been found around the world with similar phasings found by Dennis (1940) among infants in East Africa and infant Hopi Indians in America. Schaffer (1971) describes the growth of social development as involving proximity-seeking and proximity-avoidance, with resultant social attachments. He says that the development of fear of strangers also indicates the ability to see strangers as different. He concludes that heredity as well as early learning play an important role in the development of specific attachments as well as the fear of strangers.

From quite early in life the human infant is thus seen to display a capacity for recognising conformities and disconformities. This appears to be the first human display of a sense of own kind and other kind; with own kind, under natural circumstances, being of course its natural parents or near relations. At this point too we may already be seeing evidence of human stereotyping with fear tending to exaggerate the conformities and disconformities.

From an early age vocalising with others becomes rapid. The child's ability to vocalise in reply to speech even at the age of a few months is astounding in range, quite unlike any other kind of animal. Its vocabulary runs into scores of words—always, of course, in the language of its parents or familiars. Following Chomsky's proposition about the nature of language acquisition, there has been much debate about what children have to learn about language and what must be innate. However, human infants certainly inherit a ready capacity, above that of the higher social animals, for complex speech, and thus a greater capacity than other animals for handing on culture over the generations. Humans also have much larger brains, relative to body size, to enable them to do so. Language development is regarded by many child psychologists as the true basis of civilisation and culture. It is also a main link in collective identification and social distinction due to its role of excommunication as well as intercommunication.

By now, all attachment behaviour of human infants displays a strong social as well as a biological element. Such attachments are communicated through the language and within the social milieu in which each child is brought up. The totally deaf child tends to keep voicing until about the tenth month and then its voice begins to degenerate, thus demonstrating a clear biological element over which the social eventually predominates. One cannot of course, ascribe a precise proportion to the influence of each and even to try to do so is a pointless exercise.

First attachments are to the family and particularly to the mother. The advantage of such early attachments has been repeatedly stressed by child psychologists and, as a corollary, the harm that is likely to result from the absence of a stable family background and the warmth of a recognisable home to which the infant feels it belongs. Indeed, the importance of such a stable background and affectionate parents is well known to those who have to deal with the consequences of its absence. Without a normal mother-and-child attachment due to bereavement or abandonment, the human child, like the infant rhesus monkey, is likely to grow up displaying neurotic or even withdrawal symptoms that are difficult to reverse or eradicate.

WIDER ATTACHMENTS AND ALLEGIANCES

Charles Darwin wrote in *The Descent of Man* (1871 p. 161): 'The feeling of pleasure from society is probably an extension of parental or filial affection, since the social instinct seems to be developed by the young remaining for a long time with their parents; this extension may be attributed in part to habit, but chiefly to natural selection.'

Infants not only develop attachments to parents or substitute parents and come to distinguish between strangers and familiars, but as they grow older they socialise with wider familiars of their own kind. In this context, Darwin's emphasis on the child's long growing-up process has to be kept in mind. A human child is dependent on its family until at least the age of 16 out of a biologically phased life span of about 70–80 years. Sexuality has by then developed, designed towards procreation followed later by phased bodily decline with dependence again on others. These are all biological phasings. In comparison, chimpanzees live to about 40 and have a proportionate growing-up period of about seven years, before which, if orphaned, they will inevitably die under natural circumstances. They have, therefore, to keep together in reasonably stable family nurture groups.

As the human infant matures, child play begins to be switched from immediate familiars to wider groups and indeed such play now appears to be vital to the process of socialisation, so helping to change the solitary into the sociable child. As children grow up they appear to play quite spontaneously by interaction with their peers and the older they grow the more they tend to do so in association. This need for play, as observed by Robertson (1962), can be stultified at a sensitive period if a young child comes to be hospitalised. Hence the importance of keeping children playing while in hospitals.

In playgroups children are seen to display, in a rudimentary way, some sense of social distinction. In groups containing mixtures of social types, even toddlers seem able to recognise subtle distinctions of race or class through variations in appearance, clothing, behaviour, accent or even tone of voice. It seems that strangers fail to give the familiar recognition signals of own kind, many of which, however, are doubtless learned or copied at the mother's knee.

At this age, the reactive behaviour to strangers, already seen to operate at eight months, is more obvious in the reaction to strange grown-ups. Children also seem to feel warmer and more secure with groups of child familiars from whom they know what to expect. In contrast they tend to distrust strange children as well as grown-ups, in particular the strangeness of people of different colour who not only behave but also look different. In their presence children feel insecure, not knowing what to expect.

These then appear to be the first signs of wider group attachments and the social recognition of *us* and *them*, appearing even in the absence of parental inducement. Indeed, children at the stage of puberty (itself a clear biological phasing) seem to prefer to escape from parental control into peer groups of their own age or sex.

If an inborn group attachment faculty is involved one might expect such an inherited capacity to differ in degree from person to person. This indeed may well be so as individuals do seem to differ in their gregariousness. But it is not within the scope of this book to explore any such differences; on the contrary, it is to try to discern the basic similarity in these human attitudes of *us* and *them*.

A child's capacity for social recognition and social distinction can of course only manifest itself in societies where children are brought up in proximity to those with observable differences of behaviour or appearance as, for instance, where there are different classes, races or other distinctive types within the child's own particular environment. From experiments conducted as far apart as New Zealand and New York, it has been proved that even by 3 years of age, most White children have grown conscious of others as Blacks or Browns distinct from themselves. These experiments were conducted using black or brown dolls from which the 3-year-olds were asked to recognise own kind from other kind, and further to indicate their preferences for one type over the other. White children in the 1960s, whether in New York or New Zealand, mostly preferred white to black dolls as being the 'right' colour. Curiously, however, Black children also knew that Black was the 'wrong' colour to be; doubtless influenced by their parents. Now in the 1980s, with greater Black self-assurance, this has percolated through to the 3-year-olds with their preferences beginning to be reversed and indeed to turn round the other way towards a preference to own colour. There is however some controversy among child psychologists whether the earlier inverted preferences may not have been influenced by the presence of White interviewers. Be that as it may, it nevertheless appears that even Black 3-year-olds now seem to prefer their own kind. So even by that age strong social preferences are being displayed, with some degree of stereotyping: see generally Hartley *et al.* (1948) and Radke *et al.* (1949).

Young children also show a recognition of own kind and other kind in a number of other ways, based upon observable differences in language, religious practice or class. In one study in the Bronx district of New York, described by Pushkin *et al.* (1973), 60 per cent of Jewish children observed between the ages of 4½ and 6½ were already aware of themselves as Jews, answering to that name, and up to 80 per cent in the age group 6½ to 8½. To other (Gentile) children, being Jewish was simply understood to mean 'talking Jewish or going to the Synagogue or not eating bacon'. A more recent London study revealed a corresponding and quite voluntary tendency on the part of young Jews to keep their social distance from others. Religious and family upbringing also inclined them towards social preferences for Jews rather than for those they were taught to regard as impure. Most of their social activities were thus carried on with other Jews for whom the Barmitzvah ceremony was the high point of early life.

The Bronx study similarly revealed religious distinctions between Protestant and Catholic infants in New York and a similar tendency towards social distancing, doubtless encouraged here by parents. In Boston, which has the largest Irish immigrant population in the United States, the two religious groups of Protestants and Catholics tended even in childhood to keep socially apart as they also do in Northern Ireland where this situation is enhanced by separate religious schooling.

Early distinctions of class, as perceived by children, give rise to class awareness and seem to follow the same pattern of proximity or distancing. While children in nursery playgrounds can be seen to play quite happily with children from other classes, they are nevertheless still aware of rudimentary distinctions by observable differences in manner, dress, or tone of voice, all of which signify strangers as opposed to familiars.

For such class awareness to arise, however, the child must be brought up in a society where class distinctions exist and where the unfamiliar or strange can be readily discerned by accent, manners, gait and so forth. In a classless society, like Israel, it is impossible for young children to be aware of being members of a particular social class, for Judaism has always discouraged class distinctions, both within the Synagogue as well as outside. While lacking other classes, however, young Israelis are nevertheless still conscious of themselves as distinct from Palestinians whom they are brought up to regard as second rate and not 'true' Israelis at all. A class identity is therefore fundamentally no different from a national or racial one as both are simply examples of group distinctiveness.

In the British context, class distinctions are exaggerated by the English public (really private) school system of boarding schools, whereby many English children have hitherto been separately educated from the ages of 8 to 18. This helps to stimulate class distinctions in the same way as separate religious schools stimulate religious ones. Children in these schools even acquire a different accent and manner of speaking. Similarly there are a number of private schools in France and Western Germany devised to provide a Catholic as opposed to a state secular education.

A study of 14-year-old working class boys made in east London in 1950 showed that even by that age the boys observed were strongly conscious, and in some cases resentfully so, of being working as opposed to middle class. About the age of puberty they tended to form peer groups of their own age, and sex. It is pertinent here to note that such an awareness of belonging to a distinctive class can only spring indirectly at this age from what are usually called economic factors, and then only when these affect the child's own life style, upbringing and who are its friends. Children themselves do not have income or capital, it is only their parents who do so; but in a country like the United States where personal fortunes may be made and inherited these can be used to fund the sending of children to exclusive private schools which do then tend to create or perpetuate class distinctions.

While evidence on such sensitive matters is hard to obtain it seems reasonable to infer that young children depend here on their family milieu and parents' social preferences. One may be able then to interpolate backwards from adult to juvenile class distinctions however rudimentary the latter may be in comparison.

A survey conducted in Scotland by Market & Opinion Research International was described by Baur (1984) in an analysis worth quoting for the light it throws on how some people, if pressed, are prepared to admit that they identify on a class basis:

> It is a survey which is perhaps more interesting for what it illustrates about the communion of feelings across perceived class frontiers than for what it betrays about the attitudes which are supposed to separate the social classes.
>
> In the first place, the very idea of social class itself appears to be highly subconscious. Perhaps this makes it an instinctive thing. No matter. The truth is that it is not at the front of people's minds. When asked whether they ever thought of themselves as belonging to a particular social class, the great majority of our respondents (66 per cent) simply said 'No.'
>
> Given a choice of ascribing themselves to a particular class, however, people divided themselves into working class (68 per cent) middle class (24 per cent) and upper class (1 per cent). Of our respondents, 7 per cent said they did not know to which class they belonged.
>
> In fact, this compares in some respects quite closely with the official designations of status used in socio-economic analysis. On this criterion, our sample of respondents is divided between the working class (67 per cent) and the middle class (33 per cent). The difference in the size of the middle-class figure may be due partly to the number who told us they did not know to which class they belonged.
>
> It is not quite as simple as that, however. Nearly half (47 per cent) of those people who are officially designated as middle class described themselves to us as working class. Conversely, of those officially designated working class, only 15 per cent claimed to be middle class. What this suggests quite simply is that there are a lot of people whose life-style has moved them firmly into the middle class, but who continue to cling to a working-class identity for themselves.
>
> But what leads people to make this judgment both of their own class and, just as important, the class of others? There are certainly intriguing variations of emphasis in the things people of different classes consider in defining membership of a social class. But the most striking feature of the survey is its demonstration that people use broadly the same criteria regardless of their own class.
>
> What a man earns, where he lives, the job he does—these are the main yardsticks for judging his class. A middle-class person is identified mainly by his neighbourhood (41 per cent) and his job (38 per cent); but in the identification of a working-class person the job (46 per cent) is more important than his neighbourhood (36 per cent). The earning capacity in each case counts about equally.
>
> A middle-class person, on the other hand, attaches more importance to the way someone talks as the determinant of his working class status (32 per cent). This is a much less important signal to the working-class person himself (23 per cent). Conversely, education for the working-class person is a far less important attribute of middle-class status (27 per cent) than it is to the middle-class person himself (39 per cent).

A visible contrast in Scotland tending to foster a sense of working-class distinctiveness is that those who identify as such mostly live in council housing estates giving a clear physical demarcation of *us* and *them*.

Class distinctiveness may also be transmitted culturally from parents to children if not already acquired through such observable differences.

That an awareness of social class is not foremost in children's or adult's minds does not mean that, it may not, on occasions, be aroused. Group consciousness is the reverse of subconscious and again involves an attachment trait which can be readily stimulated.

A child's acquisition of national consciousness usually occurs later in life and is much less due to economic factors. It occurs when he or she becomes nationally aware of himself or herself as a member of a distinct nation or people in relation to other nations or peoples regarded as different. This again requires an ability to comprehend *what* one is, in national terms, and also what the nation signifies in terms of boundaries, constituent peoples, history and culture. Possibly this also needs an ability to read maps on which the national boundaries are delineated so causing a visual impression to spring to mind whenever one thinks of one's own country. Such wider identification thus tends to occur in later adolescence and, in response to national culture and schooling, and also to become conceptualised. It could not arise earlier except in relation to sub-national groups within the larger national one, for there are usually no other nationals living within the child's immediate circle to be distinguished from. The late President Sadat of Egypt in his autobiography *In Search of Identity* (1980) mentioned his early sense of family attachment to his native village in the Egyptian Delta; but emphasised that it was not until later that he and other youths like him ever became conscious of the constitutional position of Egypt as a nation or of himself as an Egyptian in contrast to the occupying British.

When children are taken abroad on holiday too they are able to perceive, many for the first time, their distinction from the children of other nations, speaking different languages and looking different. In foreign holiday camps young children may be observed seeking out their own national kind (often signified by national flags on tents and caravans) as opposed to foreign kind with whom to play, for it is only the former who speak the same language.

From surveys carried out in Geneva in 1951, it was found to be not until the age 10–11 that any clear concept emerged among the children studied of being Swiss. From other studies conducted by Lambert *et al.* (1959) and involving children up to 14 years of age selected from London, Louvain, Amsterdam and Montreal (both French- and English-speaking) the tendency to identify nationally was seen to increase, as one might expect, progressively with age, and also with the knowledge of particular national boundaries. This corresponds to the average age found in a Glasgow study by Jahoda (1962) when local children came to regard themselves as Scottish, with some confusion in that case, however, as to whether 'their' nation was really Scotland or Britain. However, it certainly was not England.

In 1982 a boatload of 12- to 17-year-old English public schoolboys cruising on holiday around the Mediterranean found their vessel suddenly commandeered by the British Government for use in the Falklands campaign. The children all had to be hurriedly off-loaded in mid-holiday. They nevertheless all displayed extreme excitement and a strong patriotic feeling as British against the Argentinians.

Nowadays it appears that national comprehension and awareness among young children may become earlier induced due to television. When watching football or athletic competitions on television children tend to identify with their own national team or national athletes as opposed to foreign ones and to feel a sense of personal pride in their country's achievements.

By now such children have acquired strong attachments of various kinds even if these are only the loyalties of young football supporters with their flags and anthems and tribal antagonisms against rival supporters on the other side. In Scotland these may also reflect the rival identities of Protestants and Catholics seen in groups of 'Billies' and 'Tims' centred around the Protestant Rangers and Catholic Celtic football teams of Glasgow. Such feelings can be stimulated to run as high as they do in the streets of Belfast and have this much in common, namely, that they are essentially working class and masculine. They are part of the British working class ethos dating from the first industrial revolution reflecting family loyalties handed down from father to son and focused on the Home Team and the hallowed Home Ground on which the supporter's ashes may finally be scattered.

These young bloods also display their allegiances to national football teams and therefore exhibit, if only temporarily, a degree of national consciousness which interestingly enough induced a sense of *English* national consciousness in support of an English football team in the 1982 World Cup with the waving of the English national flag—in contrast to the British or Scottish—for the first time in centuries. English tribal supporters, on the rampage, have caused numerous casualties, even deaths; and, in 1985, caused all English teams to be banned, for a spell, from International football.

ARTIFICIAL JUVENILE IDENTITIES

These early surveys on child attachments and identities may now be summarised as confirming the obvious, namely, that generations of children come gradually to identify first with family and then with wider familiars as opposed to unfamiliars; and, later still with co-members of wider distinguishable groups. No actual identities therefore, are ever culture-free, although some are more artificial than others.

Such identities appear to be induced in children by early learning and upbringing within a particular social environment. This may also include adoptive children from a completely different background who are nevertheless induced to feel they belong. Switch the child in infancy and one also switches its attachments and identities, for an infant's brain at birth is a *tabula rasa* insofar as any actual identities are concerned.

It is only the ability to form social attachments which is probably inborn. For even inborn distinctions of appearance, including colour, are not in themselves identities so much as marks of identity available to attract identification.

Dr Garrett Fitzgerald, the Premier of the Irish Republic, in his Dimbleby Lecture on Irish identities (1982) gave the example of the divisive force of upbringing upon two identical female twins, the children of a political colleague, who in infancy had lost their mother, victim of a stray sniper's bullet, during the 1916 Easter Rising. They were Catholics, but a friendly Presbyterian aunt from Belfast offered to take them in while their Catholic father remained in Dublin. One daughter, however, refused to move. She was, therefore, brought up within a Catholic Irish background while the other was nurtured in a Protestant Ulster one. The one identical twin brought up in Belfast quickly adopted the British allegiance and identity of the north, while the other became Catholic and firmly Irish Republican.

While identical twins display similar genetic tendencies in later life (including for instance any proneness to schizophrenia), they only share a proneness to identify. They do not share the same actual identities unless brought up in the same milieu subject to the same parental influences.

So it may be concluded, beyond reasonable doubt, that all actual identities are externally induced and some quite deliberately so. But due to the universal presence and characteristics of group consciousness there nevertheless probably exists among all human races an inborn basic tendency for social identification.

Experiments on young children and students have been carried out in recent years by social psychologists seeking artificially to create such in-group and out-group social behaviour. These are then observed in the hope of trying to deduce what caused such social, as opposed to individualistic, reactions with preference for one's own group as opposed to others. None of these controlled experiments, however, yet appear to have led the investigators to suggest the presence of an *inborn* faculty for group attachment and social recognition. Nevertheless, some seem to come fairly close to so doing. The experiments at least indicate the strong possibility of such a faculty seen in the ready tendency of young human 'guinea pigs' to identify with quite artificial groups they had never heard of before, but into which they had been temporarily placed. That this should be the result of such random placings seems to indicate a pre-existing faculty that is unlikely to be entirely cultural.

One such experiment is described by Tajfel (1978) using 14- to 15-year-old boys who were deceived as to the purpose of the experiment and were assigned to one of two randomly named groups without at first knowing to which the other boys belonged. They were then each given tasks to perform, success in which led to rewards being assigned to the different groups with actual money at stake. The results showed a pronounced bias to each boy's group.

Similar experiments have been conducted by Muscovici with similar results of readily induced bias among students towards their own artificial group with its own random name.

Other experiments carried out by Turner and others are described in *Inter-group Behaviour* (1981), *Differentiation between Social Groups* (1978) and *Social Identity* (1983). In Turner's contribution to *Inter-group Behaviour* he states:

> Other studies illustrate that social categorisation *per se* also causes perceptual and attitudinal biases and differential attraction to in-group and out-group members [Brewer and Silver 1978, Brown and Turner 1979, Doise *et al.* 1972, Turner 1978(a)]. The experiments cited at the beginning of this section report findings similar to those of Tajfel in different settings. Since they were published there has been a continual flow of research results all tending to confirm the initial implications. Thus far, the more carefully researchers have examined whether social categorisation *per se* or in-group/out-group membership is sufficient for inter-group discrimination, the more the answer has been clearly in the affirmative. The conclusion must be that there are *social psychological processes* intrinsic to or stimulated merely by in-group/out-group divisions which tend to create discriminatory social relations. (our italics)

None of these researches, however, go so far as to suggest the presence of an inborn attachment trait as the basis of group consciousness. Perhaps, however, the expression 'social psychological processes' may imply a genetic base. Yet probably not, for most social psychologists still appear to regard the social aspects of their study as a process operating entirely apart from the individual.

In the last decade many social psychologists have begun to concentrate on the problem of social identity and social identification while still avoiding the subject of group consciousness and, above all, the feelings of loyalty and allegiance thereby engendered. Yet loyalty is the individual's expression of social attachment in practice. Mere personal attachment or affection for particular individuals could never hold large groups together. But loyalty to the group and to its symbols or marks of identity is the expression of group consciousness on the part of individuals. When a sufficient number have acquired such mutual feelings through social identification this leads to the end-product of social identity.

Small-scale experiments on handfuls of schoolchildren or students cannot reveal the operation of loyalties in the world at large. They do nevertheless show the importance of social comparisons and distinctions of which Tajfel was among the first to recognise the importance. As Muscovici (1978) too has written

> This change of interest has been particularly clear in the last three or four years; the central problem in the study of intergroup relations has become that of the identification with a group. When and why is one identified with oneself: with one's own group, with another group?... The concept of identity is as indispensable as it is unclear. This is why no attempt will be made to define it and we shall keep it in a zone of shaded obscurity. But the phenomena of identity, mysterious though they may be underlie certain realities which can be defined and circumscribed. The first step towards their elucidation—and it was a step in the right direction—has been to emphasise their dependence on social comparison ... it seems impossible to study relations between groups or between

individuals without taking into account some kind of a notion of social recognition.

So some social psychologists are now firmly directed on to the study of group consciousness.

An important experiment involving the artificial creation of social identification over a short space of time was conducted some years ago in the United States by Muzafer and Carolyn Sheriff (1953) of the University of Oklahoma. Their experiment was carried out in an isolated campsite on twenty-four 12-year-old boys all selected from Protestant families in the lower-middle income group in the Newhaven area. All were checked as being mentally normal and with similar IQs and none of them knew each other beforehand. It was unavoidable that they knew their conduct at the youth camp was about to be observed by staff, but the successful strategem was adopted of leading them to think that it was only in connection with improving camping techniques. Hence, by this simple device, they were prevented from 'acting up' to their outside observers.

The camp area covered about 125 acres with natural recreational facilities like woods and a stream. The precinct also contained two bunk houses, an open mess hut and related facilities.

The experiment was carried out in three distinct stages. The short timing of the last two is important as tending to demonstrate the presence of a proneness towards identification without which what happened could not have occurred.

In the first stage, all activities were camp-wide, involving each individual's personal inclinations and interests. The activities thus provided the reverse of any stimulus towards group identification. Indeed, some individual attachments, though incipiently formed, would traverse the two distinctive group identities about to be created. This initial stage was almost as counter-productive to group formation as would have been the case if the boys had been shut up in individual cells.

Stage 2, which lasted only five days, involved the formation of two groups similar in number and composition. The individual friendships formed in stage one were now deliberately broken up. One group was christened 'The Bulldogs' and was ascribed the colour blue; and the other 'The Red Devils' was ascribed the colour red. Neither of these random names or colours meant anything to the boys beforehand, although the names themselves might be regarded as suggestively aggressive. In this second stage all activities were conducted on a Bulldog or Red Devil basis and were chosen, not for their appeal to the boys as individuals, but for their involvement in team work within their separate groups. All rewards given in this period were made on a group basis and not to particular individuals. Each group too, occupied its own bunkhouse. Spontaneously, each group of boys now began to develop, without further inducement, their own internal social structures. The blue and red colours became recognised as badges of identity and the boys came spontaneously to refer to each other as *we* and *they* restricting their friendships almost entirely to those conceived to be *us*. Three members of the Red

Devils were even branded as 'traitors' and treated so as to ensure they saw less of the boys with whom they had been friendly in Stage 1—but who had since become *them*.

Stage 3, which also only lasted five days, was occupied with intergroup relations between the Red Devils and Bulldogs in a series of competitive activities and situations; and also in mildly frustrating situations so arranged that the actions of the Red Devils were frustrating the Bulldogs and vice versa. This had the immediate and surprising effect of arousing marked social antagonism between the two groups of 12-year-old boys who formerly had no social distinctions whatsoever, whether of class, race, religion or nationality.

It took the initial form of mild quarrels and the erection of hostile Red Devil or Bulldog posters stuck on walls and directed against the other side.

The sequel involved staff trying desperately to re-encourage a degree of amity by mixing up the seating arrangements at meals in the common mess hall. It seems that this was not an original part of the experiment. Seating and friendship preferences however continued to persist on previously contrived Bulldog or Red Devil lines. Finally (and to the distress now even of some of the observers) actual physical fighting amounting almost to a miniature 'civil war' broke out between the two groups over the trivial complaint of what the Bulldogs were supposed to have done to the Red Devils' mess table and cutlery. A general melee ensued which the staff were only able to quell with difficulty. Next day there followed a revenge fight tantamount to what is now commonplace among young football supporters.

The conclusion of the authors of *Groups in Harmony and Tension* was that their experiment might indicate what they chose to call a 'generic norm' with a need to investigate further the human phenomenon of '*we-ness*'. The Sheriffs' conclusions, however, appear to have been taken no further, nor have they subsequently pursued the phenomenon of *we-ness* through group consciousness. They did nevertheless succeed in this important experiment in creating temporary loyalties to Bulldogs and Red Devils which the youthful participants had never even heard of before. They even managed to do so although all the participants looked exactly alike and came from the same social milieu but were nevertheless turned into competitive and even antagonistic social groups. Social recognition of 'own kind' was stimulated by an entirely artificial creation of 'other kind'—of Reds versus the Blues—almost akin to class or racial antagonism.

It is now contended that the most probable 'generic norm' common to the human species is a genetic one and that such underlying psychological processes are probably inherited. But none of the resultant identities are inborn. The process of identification in individuals, whether among children or adults, comes in all cases from without and is therefore capable of transformation.

It is now intended to investigate further this phenomenon of group consciousness and how it comes to occur 'naturally' in the world at large. Also how it is capable of quick and quite artificial fabrication.

3

Tribal and Racial Consciousness

HOW TRIBESMEN IDENTIFY

The group attachment trait may also be observed to operate in tribal societies still surviving to the present day. While culturally isolated from each other, all nevertheless share tribal feelings of loyalty and allegiance.

Anthropological field studies carried out by Morgan (1977) on the Iroquois, Rivers (1910) on the Todas and later by Evans Pritchard (1930) on the Nuer, all show marked cultural differences. But they also reveal a similar pattern of identification centred around tribal names at different levels of identification. These studies were directed more to finding a typology of kinship patterns or social structures—and any general conclusions to be drawn therefrom—rather than in trying to discern how and why primitive man identifies collectively. The identification patterns are nevertheless still sufficiently revealed. Leinhardt (1964) has written 'The geneological tree of a clan or tribe is thus a guide to the political loyalties of its members and their place in society.' Likewise Leach (1982): 'The crucial point is that, in most cases, group identity is expressed by the people concerned in the language of kinship. Whatever else "we" may be, "we" are kinsmen.' Radcliffe-Brown and Malinowski also regarded blood relationships as being the origin and model of every kinship tie, but including adoptive kinsfolk.

Where the loyalties lie in relation to tribe or race will now be used as the yardstick both of tribal and racial consciousness; for that is how the individual attaches to his group and is prepared to cooperate and even die on its behalf. Tribal man is prepared to cooperate only with actual kinsfolk and to die only on behalf of those he conceives to be his own; never on behalf of outsiders or strangers and, least of all, potential enemies. Most social relations are indeed with actual relations.

It may be presumed that, unless there exists clear evidence to the contrary, such confined feelings of kinship or supposed kinship, still universal today, were also those of our primitive ancestors. There is, however, no positive evidence for the existence of any sense of loyalty towards other kind or humankind as a whole. How could there be? Everywhere tribal cooperation is seen to be with those regarded as own people, with social distancing from others. This behaviour seems quite universal, whether observed among tribes still at the hunter–gatherer stage or among more developed pastoralists or agriculturalists. Alterations indeed in farming modes seem to have made little difference in so far as human identification is concerned.

Evans Pritchard's field studies among the Nuer were among the most detailed of social anthropology. They show that the Nuer consisted of a number of tribes each divided territorially into primary, secondary and tertiary sections. To quote Pritchard:

> There is always contradiction in the definition of a political group, for a man is a member of it in virtue of his non-membership of other groups of the same type outside, and he is likewise not a member of the same community in virtue of his membership of the segment of it which stands in opposition to its other segments. Hence, a man counts as a member of a political group in one situation and not as a member of it in a different situation. The outstanding structural characteristic of Nuer political groups is their relativity.

It may be added that these tribal groups, despite the absence of tribal chiefs, engaged in frequent tribal warfare against the Dinka, their traditional opponents.

The surviving hunter–gatherers may literally be called prehistoric in that they have no recorded history; but this is insignificant insofar as human identification is concerned. Current studies of the few remaining hunter–gatherers, however, have the drawback that most have become somewhat dispirited and confined to isolated groups. So each tends to exist as a totality in itself without any inter-relationship (including warfare) with other tribes. They are now perforce pacific.

Cogent evidence of primitive identifications comes from contemporary observations on the Australian Aboriginals when first encountered by the White man in the nineteenth century. Observations on the Walbiri and Waringari showed a pattern of intertribal reaction at different levels of identity answering to different tribal names in a highly complex system of lineal identification. While warfare was never total, it was nevertheless endemic between tribes when members trespassed on tribal hunting grounds or water holes. These Aboriginals identified by family groups and tribes as they had probably done in unbroken sequence of habit for the last 40,000 years since the Australian Continent was first colonised before being cut off by the rising oceans as the ice caps melted. They cannot have identified as Australians. For this is a recent name given to the continent by Dutch explorers to indicate the southern land or Terra Australis. Even today many Aboriginals prefer not to answer to the name Australian as signifying *what* they are.

The cooperative behaviour of primitive man appears therefore to have been confined to own people defined by actual or supposed lineage. But it also included those adopted or captured in childhood by a particular clan with whose name they were thereafter brought up to identify. That was how a small clan of 1,500 Amazulu in Southern Africa in 1800, claiming their mythical descent from 'the Son of Heaven', came to include many others induced to identify as Zulus. The biological clan was simply enlarged by warfare under King Chaka into the esprit de corps of a large fighting Zulu nation which, in the process, became partly de-tribalised. Their descendants in South Africa, still strongly identifying as Zulus, now number about 6 million who share a great warrior tradition that once held the British at bay and who still regard themselves as distinct from other Blacks.

The Bushmen of the Kalahari Desert and the Eskimos of the Antarctic are sometimes cited as proof of the benignity of man before he became a settled agriculturalist with private property to defend or fight about. Yet the primitive Bushmen and Eskimo hunter–gatherers do not identify with mankind as a whole. On the contrary, they identify only with their own clans or tribes and their particular tribal names. While they may nowadays, in their isolation, have little cause for external antagonism or distinctiveness, the Kung are very conscious of own people and once fought fiercely against the Hottentots as may be seen from their cave paintings. The Eskimos too used to fight the Crow Indians as celebrated in many a saga. They also exterminated the immigrant Vikings before Greenland was later recolonised by the Danes. While the Eskimos never had a strong warrior tradition, like the Scottish Highlanders or the Iroquois, they could be provoked into fighting when the occasion demanded. Others like the Celtic tribes of Western Europe were described by contemporaries as mad about warfare which their bards celebrated in great epics the equivalent of Homer's *Iliad*.

In most tribal societies, whatever their stage of development, it is still the custom for a young man, on attaining puberty, to become a potential warrior for his tribe.

None of this proves, however, that warfare as such is encoded in the human genes; only that human beings on a group basis can be drawn into fighting each other for the good of their group. Paradoxically warfare is then seen to bring out, not only the worst, but also the best in individuals with group consciousness and loyalty overriding self-preservation. The emotional attachments indeed and enmities of tribal warfare, including the admiration of valour expressed in all the sagas, appears identical to attitudes displayed in national warfare at the present day.

Palaeontologists and primitive archaeologists are unable to indicate the social behaviour of our proto-human ancestors now known to have existed in Africa at least four million years ago. Their evidence consists of little more than artifacts or fossilised bones, together with traces of dwellings. From such scant and remote evidence it can only be deduced that our progenitors lived in stable family groups of hunter–gatherers collecting food as well as predating on other animals — including some very large ones. Also that they were skilled in the manufacture and use of tools and hunting weapons. No fewer than 450 stone cleavers, for instance, were found in the disarticulated remains of a hippopotamus dating from the upper Pleistocene of over 1½ million years ago.

It seems therefore reasonable to infer that our proto-human ancestors were keen hunters, and like ourselves, very cooperative creatures. But *pace* Rousseau, there is no positive evidence that they were ever coopertive with other than their own immediate kith and kin. Palaeontology and archaeology, however, can tell us little in this regard and provide no firm evidence, either way, of proto-human identifications or conflicts. Weapons fashioned from stone or bone are primarily hunting ones. Complete proof that these were also used against tribal opponents cannot with certainty be derived from evidence of cracked human skulls and widespread primitive cannibalism. The latter could be due to the ritualistic eating of own kind as opposed to other kind, but less likely so before the advent of rituals. Only shields or body armour can indicate warfare, and the only surviving examples are from the later Iron and Bronze Ages when human warfare was endemic.

We are not so concerned, however, with whether these proto-humans frequently fought each other, except insofar as this may suggest identification on a group basis. More convincing proof of social distancing between different groups of early humans, excluding general cooperativeness, comes from the presence today of thousands of separate tribal languages developed for cultural communication with own kind, but likewise indicating excommunication from other kind. There are, for instance, 700 separate tribal languages among the recently warring tribes of Papua/New Guinea—almost a language for every valley. The same proliferation occurs in West Africa from where so many of the American slaves derived. When captured from different tribes they were found to be incapable of intercommunication which hardly indicates general cooperativeness in their homelands. At the end of last century there were indeed some 2000 separate languages within the African continent only one of which (Amharic) was written.

The existence of separate languages for each tribal group therefore provides convincing evidence, stretching back into prehistory, to indicate that primitive socialisation was only upon a tribal basis and tends to confirm that most public relations were with actual relations. For obviously one cannot socialise with those who do not speak the same language.

Such separate languages may go further and demonstrate a cultural connection between language groups like Celts, Slavs and Bantus, and biological or sub-races proper.

RACIAL GROUP CONSCIOUSNESS

Tribal man does not appear to have identified by complete race or subspecies for the obvious reason that there were no circumstances enabling him to do so. His group attachment trait operated rather at the level of family and tribe—just like some of the higher social animals.

Why then, in recent times, have so many tribal peoples, not formerly racially conscious, suddenly become racially aware? The evidence again points to group consciousness taking physical distinctiveness this time as its hallmark in circumstances of racial juxtaposition. For individuals cannot become conscious or aware of themselves as being Black or White except in relation to groups of different colour with whom they come into contact. This was seen in the case of 3-year-old children, and also appears to be so among adults. While differences in colour or physiognomy are genetic, they need not give rise to group antagonism. Humans of different colour can, albeit with difficulty, be induced to share a single group identity, and so regard themselves collectively as *us*.

That racial identity is simply group consciousness happening to focus on physical distinctions as marks of identity, is proved by the very interchange-ability between tribal, racial and national consciousness. Tribal conscious-ness, as already noted, is group consciousness focused upon the level of the tribe. If such identification however becomes supra-tribal through many tribesmen from different tribes becoming collectively conscious together of being *us*, this wider group attachment, if directed against humans of other colour, becomes racial consciousness. But, as soon as racial consciousness centres upon a wider territory to which individuals come to feel they belong, and hence become territorially attached, their racial consciousness promptly turns into national identity.

Basically, therefore, these transformations still reflect the group attach-ment trait and the collective identification of individuals. Physical dis-tinctions of colour among different biological races are simply akin to separate 'uniforms' and represent uniformities and disconformities which may be exaggerated by stereotyping.

The principal biological races of mankind are really subspecies that are separately classified by the taxonomists or systematic biologists by physical distinctions, including colour, which are indicative of separate genotype. There is now only one species of living man, namely *Homo sapiens*. Our principal biological races or subspecies include the Caucasoid, Mongoloid, Negroid and Amerindian. Possibly the small race of Australasids with certain *Homo erectus* features could turn out to have a slightly different pedigree. The Caucasoid includes not only White Europeans but also black Indians and Ethiopians. Many of the subspecies are of course becoming increasingly difficult to classify due to constant cross-breeding, particularly in modern cities where different racial peoples are often thrown together. Nevertheless there remains a tendency even there, to continue to marry own kind, so maintaining the separate genotype.

Darwin in his *Origin of Species* (1859), followed later by *The Descent of Man* (1871), fails fully to explain the formation of human sub-species or their separate genetic maintenance; and in certain passages appears to regard tribes and races as interchangeable.

Some systematic biologists like Eaton (1970) now recognise as a test of a separate animal species, that its members do not normally, under natural conditions, interbreed outside their own circle. Many also go further in thinking that reproductive isolation is in itself the essential element in species formation and maintenance by keeping interbreeding populations apart by barriers to genetic exchange. Such barriers include inbuilt repugnancies to mating with those who look different; geographical isolation and also social separation due to social distinctions. Group consciousness and distinctiveness, defining the edge of a new gene pool within which interbreeding is confined, may thus have played some part in new subspecies formation and even account for the sudden creation of a new species. This is species formation due more to social distancing than to evolution by natural selection.

Class or racial consciousness may for instance have been instrumental in keeping the Anglo–Indians apart as a separate breeding group or incipient subspecies due to social distancing enforced upon them by the Indians on the one side and the British on the other. Likewise the Spanish-Indians of modern Mexico. Also the former Russian aristocracy who kept socially to themselves and were entirely different in height and other features from ordinary Russians of their time, and were referred to in the 1914 Baedeker Guide to St Petersburg as a separate race. Perhaps this ruling class had indeed begun to turn into a breeding group and separate genotype before being exterminated as 'enemies of the people' at the time of the Russian Revolution.

We are not, however, here so concerned with speciation or race formation as with racial group consciousness using racial distinctions as the hallmark of *us* and *them*. In any event any basic animal tendencies responsible for such social distancing must be more muted in human subsidiary species and thus be more amenable to being culturally overridden.

It is only recently that the occasion has arisen for human beings to identify on the basis of races or segments of races as opposed to tribes. When they do so, moreover, they never answer to the names somewhat arbitrarily ascribed to biological races by the taxonomists. This nomenclature is merely that of the first textbook writers on race (the original 'ethnologists') and anyway changes from time to time, like botanical names. No Nepalese would ever answer to the name of Mongolian; nor Black African to the name of Negroid, let alone Kaffrid, both racial names ascribed by early taxonomists and now regarded as indicative of White supremacy. On the contrary it is now as Blacks (in English rather than in Latin) that Africans proudly identify— though this is a comparatively recent phenomenon resulting from the growth of Black consciousness or Négritude. The name 'Africa' was given by the Romans to that continent having been taken from the Afarik tribe once inhabiting Nubia which was Berber and White. However, once collective identity takes over and people need a collective name to be known by, they will identify with any suitable one to hand. Indeed Black Africans now resent the purloining of 'their' African name by White Dutch Afrikans who in turn originally adopted it to show their distinctiveness from their own Dutch relations. The Afrikaners are thus extremely aware of themselves as Whites in contrast to Blacks and indeed try to emphasise their racial distinctiveness by a policy of apartheid which is, however, hardly conducive to inspiring identification with, and loyalty to the South African national state on the part of its Black majority.

It seems that people can only identify with the whole or part of a biological race or subrace when in juxtaposition to others of different race and so become collectively aware of their physical distinctiveness. Primitive man therefore throughout the African Continent cannot have been conscious of being Black when all other persons in proximity were also seen to be so. At that time it can only have been other differences of physique, such as those between Bushmen and Hottentot, which can have caused racial group consciousness.

Weber in his essay on Race in *Selections* (1922) says that the sense of being a member of a race depends upon a subjective feeling of common identity and he also emphasises the importance of aesthetically conspicuous differences in external experience. However, he adds: 'Generally speaking, racial characteristics are only important in the formation of their belief in ethnic identity as limiting factors, in cases where the external type is so different as to be aesthetically unacceptable: they do not play a positive part in forming a community.'

But since Weber's day new evidence has emerged with the growth of racial consciousness in Africa. This tends rather to support Tajfel's theory (1978) that 'in order for large numbers of individuals to be able to hate or discriminate against other individuals seen as belonging to a common social category, they must first have acquired a sense of belonging to groups or social categories which are clearly distinct from . . . those they hate, dislike or discriminate against'.

In the nineteenth century the whole of Africa was divided into some 50 colonial units by those White European nations which now comprise the European Economic Community. Each colony was then run as part of a mother country under that country's national flag and supposedly owed allegiance to that country's Sovereign or Head of State. No new national consciousness was at first intended to be created and most colonies were regarded as strategic trading locations. Expatriate colonials, settling in such colonial territories, still regarded themselves as British, French, German or Belgian as the case might be and hoped to create new national reflections of their mother country, at least among a Black élite. The artificial boundaries of these new colonies also paid scant regard to existing tribal identities or languages.

The native peoples then brought under colonial control did not at first identify either as Africans or Blacks. They simply identified by clan or tribe, under such names as Zulu, Shona or NdeBele and felt an attachment to Zululand, Shonaland or NdeBeleland. Some of these tribal groupings were already becoming transformed into tribal nations, for although their group consciousness was tribal it was becoming more widespread and territorialised.

The colonial powers subdued and civilised the tribal groups and even detribalised many natives attracted into the new towns and industrial cities. There they became more like their Afro–American cousins on the other side of the Atlantic.

Although the colonial nations, particularly France and Portugal, hoped to make new Blacks in their own metropolitan image with allegiances centred upon the mother country, nevertheless in every European colony the group attachment trait began to operate the other way, with a growing awareness among Blacks of being Black as opposed to white. In short, the natives everywhere became racially aware of their *we-ness* as Blacks in contrast to Whites with a new sense therefore of Black consciousness, stimulated by an awareness of their inferior class status within the colonial territory concerned. Many were nevertheless acquiring European culture and civilisation when educated upon European lines. It may also be remarked that a similar awareness of being Black and inferior, with a need to be more collectively assertive, arose about the same time in the United States.

A process of social identification, with Blackness as its hallmark, thus began to form within the confines of the 50 or so colonial administrative units, encouraged by some continental stimulation by Black politicians. As it took shape however it also began to suffer transformation from a racial into national consciousness within each colonial unit to form a new embryo nation-state, regarded as 'usurped' by the White Europeans from which the Blacks desired to be 'free' to assert their own identity.

Yet all these units in which they lived had really been designated by European governments with little reference to pre-existing identities. Many too had acquired the cultural civilisation of their colonial masters which was all they knew above the level of the tribe. Thus in French or British colonies they acquired French or British culture and became Francophones or Anglophones for supra-tribal communication. In the adjacent ex-colonies of Gambia and Senegal there was thus prevented the junction of Francophone and Anglophone Blacks of the same race and native language whose attraction to a French or British way of life so far inhibits their mutual identification within a single more viable economy. In the Anglophone sector there are even some Black Orange Lodges who march to celebrate the anniversary of the Battle of the Boyne wearing orange sashes and bowler hats.

The new racial group consciousness which was the main catalyst of this freedom movement was shared by the children and everywhere derived from the confrontation of peoples in a state of superiority and inferiority. Each colonial administration in Africa in the 1950s and 1960s became a new independent nation-state. National consciousness, however, still had to be created to support them once alien rule was removed.

For ease of identification, most of the ex-colonial countries thus chose to change their names on independence to new African ones to signify that they had now become Black and free. At the same time they also adopted new national flags and emblems instead of the old European national ones; and each chose a new national anthem instead of that of its European mother country. New national airlines bearing the new national insignia were also introduced. The Gold Coast then became Ghana, Northern Rhodesia became Zambia, Nyasaland became Malawi, Tanganyika became Tanzania and Rhodesia became Zimbabwe. While these new African names were appropriate for Blacks to identify with, they were less so for the remaining Whites many of whom, when still a White ruling class, had even been prepared to answer to the former colonial names in preference to British.

Kenya is often cited as one of the most successful new Black African nation-states with a strong national self-consciousness of its own. But it started with the unusual drawbacks, first, of having a large population of white settlers, whose national loyalties were initially in doubt; secondly, of having considerable numbers of Asian traders whose presence the Black Africans resented; and lastly, in having in addition to some Somalis, at least 12 major tribes, the most powerful of which was the Kikuyu, Kenyatta's own, among whom the Mau-Mau rebellion originated. Nevertheless, Kenyatta, as first President, managed to stimulate a degree of supra-tribal loyalty and to rise above tribalism, even above racial consciousness, by setting himself up as Father of the Nation and in his own words as 'President of all the Kenyans'. He declared 'There is only one tribe now which is Kenya', and further proclaimed as the new national motto 'Harimbee', being Swahili for 'Altogether'. Swahili was also chosen as the national language alongside English in preference to the predominant Kikuyu. The rival Kenyan political leader, Mr Odele, endeavouring to start a class struggle according to the precepts of Lenin, now that Kenya was 'liberated', found that the only 'class' prepared to follow him to electoral defeat were members of his own Luo tribe.

The richest and largest new African nation is Nigeria with five main tribal groupings recognised as nationalities within a new federal nation-state. It remains to be seen whether sufficient national loyalty and probity can be stimulated to hold it together. Zimbabwe, on the other hand, is a unitary state still endeavouring to hold together the rival tribal 'nations' of the majority Shona and the minority NdeBele, the latter having once been the ruling class. The state of Uganda has still to find its supporting nation.

Pan-African consciousness denotes a continental Black identity supposed to extend over the whole continent, among all those inhabitants prepared to answer to the African name. The founders of the Organisation of African Unity were mostly detribalised urban Blacks, resident in America or the West Indies where the greater majority of the world's Blacks now live. These would-be leaders of a new Pan-African racial identity, dreamed of a new tribeless Africa in which returning Blacks, like themselves, could at last find a genuine home. A tribeless Africa of course means one where identities have disappeared at the tribal level and have been substituted by a new Continental African one. It was in this hope that many returned to Africa from the other side of the Atlantic only to find, outwith the cities, predominantly tribal societies with old rivalries and feuds they could not comprehend.

Racial identity focused upon a whole continent is thus not all that easy to achieve and still less to maintain. Group recognition and attachment by biological race tends, therefore, to occur more frequently and easily in smaller *us* and *them* situations where fragments of a race can readily become aware of themselves as a distinct people in contrast to others.

Racial feelings and a sense of racial pride can of course occur in all races, regardless of skin colour. Blacks in East Africa regard themselves as socially distinct from Brown resident Indians whom they tend to regard as inferior. In Africanised countries, White is also now regarded as the 'wrong' colour and hence not truly African. The abortive Central African Federation foundered on such White and Black racial distinctions. The Caribbean

Federation was intended to be based on the concept of a new multiracial West Indian nation. But this disintegrated at birth due to racial distinctions between Black and Brown which the previous White government had held together. The Malayan Federation likewise collapsed owing to racial distinctions between indigenous Malayans and immigrant Chinese, each with their different cultures and physical appearances. All that these different racial peoples shared was the English language and some acquired British culture.

But mixed Black and White societies can work and a multiracial nation-state can survive provided its Blacks and Whites share a sufficient degree of national consciousness and allegiance, as now in most of the United States or Bermuda where most identify as Americans or Bermudans.

The red 'Indians' of North America have recently become aware of their Indian identity and now answer, for the first time, to Columbus' great misnomer. In their heyday however they answered to tribal names like Sioux or Iroquois. In Middle America, where the Aztecs were subdued by the Spanish, the Indian race have recently reasserted themselves as co-equal with their former conquerors and so almost as to form a new mixed racial identity. Likewise, the Eskimo, known as Inuit or 'people' in their own language now see themselves, not as tribesmen, but as a single distinctive race most of whom now inhabit the new independent nation of Greenland.

So all these varieties of racial consciousness, whether at a higher or a lower level, still represent the group consciousness of individuals. This is confirmed by the presence of the so-called 'social' races which are not proper biological variants so much as the social identities of people who simply call themselves a race or are regarded as such by others. At best they may be small segments of a biological race who are regarded as sufficiently distinctive. For example, the Armenid or western variety of Jews are part of the Jewish religious people. But the latter includes a different biological variant now known as Sephardic or Eastern Jews. The latter if displaying group antagonism towards western Jews in Israel could rightly be said to be displaying racial group consciousness as would western Jews towards Arab Palestinians.

Other 'races' are simply so-called because they are expatriots temporarily or permanently removed from their homeland. Even the Americans or British sometimes refer to themselves as a 'race' when living abroad.

The Japanese caste of three million untouchables or Burakumin is also loosely referred to as 'the Hidden Race'. There is equal ambiguity concerning castes and races in India. All, however, are really reflections of group distinction. Indeed, to the social psychologist, there is no fundamental difference between the group consciousness of biological or social races.

It now seems that social identity can be stimulated by racial differences into a sense of racial group consciousness such as has occurred throughout the African Continent but which in the process transformed into separate nations defined by new artificial boundaries.

SOCIAL ATTACHMENTS AMONG THE HIGHER SOCIAL ANIMALS

Most sociobiological works proceed directly by extrapolation from the animal to the human. The following indirect animal evidence is in contrast now only put forward as an indirect indicator of possible animal origins for group consciousness. Direct evidence of human behaviour is obviously to be preferred. Yet humans are still members of the Animal Kingdom and are, in particular, mammals sharing with the latter many biological features and developmental phasings including a long maturation period within a relatively long life span. They also belong to the order of *Primates* and share with other primates within the superfamily of *Hominoids* the characteristic of having evolved to live in relatively stable groups.

From field observations it now appears that those social animals which live in such stable family groups, nurturing their young and succouring their old, are in differing degrees all collectively aware of own kind comprising those which, under natural conditions, would be their biological relations. This, however, is not just confined to the order of *Primates*. Evidence of group formation and recognition is to be found, for instance, among the hunter carnivores, including wolves, from which our own domestic dogs are descended.

The Lawick-Goodalls (1970) have observed in Africa the behaviour of wild hunting dogs and hyenas. In Kenya the latter occupy distinctive clan territories, the borders of which they scent mark. Hyena group war-fare, like human tribal forays, revolves around these borders which they defend to the death against interlopers from other clans of their own subspecies. This behaviour appears in part, however, to be cultural for the hyena cubs have been observed being led by their mothers around the bounds of their territories scent marking them. But the basic group recognition trait nevertheless appears to be inborn for it involves the use of a special group recognition scent gland beneath the tail which is distinct from the sexual one.

Every dog owner is aware how his household pet adapts itself and copies human ways and how territorially loyal and defensive it can become on his behalf. He is also aware of other canine traits, including socialisation by smell, which under natural circumstances would be displayed towards co-members of a pack. Even more so, every sportsman who keeps a hunting dog to enable him to flush or retrieve game (in exercise of his own primeval hunting impulse) realises how much stronger is the hunting trait in hunting dogs, specially selected for keenness and, in particular, with a good nose for game. Whilst such dogs are trained for sporting purposes, the best hunting strains are those with a genetic propensity in this direction.

Among other genera of *Primates*, sociability also appears to be a dominant characteristic and all live in related family groups whose cohesion is particularly strong. Thus families of howling monkeys guard their territories against other families of their own species. Likewise lemurs. None of these animals are carnivores but some are mildly predatory of other animals, whereas our proto-human ancestors were strongly so and possibly the most strongly cooperative of all. Other primates also have in common with man the intermittent breeding of mainly single offspring with a prolonged maturation period during which they have to be nurtured in family groups for protection. Most are, in consequence, long-lived. The basic social unit among the chimpanzees, baboons, rhesus monkeys and macaques is a matriarchal one of a mother and her descendants. Primate males do not breed within their immediate but within a wider family circle. Nonhuman primates indeed do not know who their fathers are—any more than once did the Australian Aboriginals.

There is also a human parallel with other primates in our elaborate systems of endogamy and exogamy which appear to be reinforced biologically by the initial 'imprinting' against later mate selection between siblings who have been nurtured together. This has been claimed by Shepher (1971) to show itself among human infants nurtured together in crèches in the Israel kibbutzin. It also applies to adoptive infants brought up together (although not among stepchildren introduced at a later stage)—all of which seems to challenge Freud's theory of an Oedipus complex.

So a sense of group consciousness, involving attachment, and what, in human terms, would be described as group loyalty may not be unique to humankind and may even be shared with other social animals, including primates. Solitary animals, in contrast, do not need group recognition or attachment for their survivance.

Any consideration of animal evidence in the order of *Primates* turns inevitably to man's nearest relation the chimpanzee, now possibly more closely related than originally supposed by the Paleontologists still searching in vain for an earlier 'missing link' that may not, in fact, exist. It was an eighteenth-century Scottish judge, Lord Monboddo, who first proclaimed man's relationship to the chimpanzee.

Microbiology now reveals these charming and intelligent creatures to have a basic physiognomy and genetic composition which is nearly identical to our own. They even share with man certain basic gestures of nonverbal communication like grimacing and crying. When reared in captivity they can also be taught elements of human sign language which enables them to communicate with us at a simple level. Their separate evolution, however, probably places them nearer in the zoological tree to the now extinct hominid species called *Australopithecus* or Southern Ape which inhabited South Africa until about a million years ago alongside the emerging *Homo erectus*, our more immediate ancestor. The chimpanzees only differ from the Southern Apes in their adaptation to a forest habitat. The latter lived in the open African savannah whereas the free-swinging chimpanzees have always lived in, or perhaps have taken to, the forests. Skeletally they are about the same height and have about the same brain size as had the Southern Apes, and are also mildly predatory of other animals. *Homo erectus*, however, our direct ancestor, was so strongly predatory that he might have developed the features of carnivores proper, had it not been for his existing manual dexterity and use of hunting weapons which made this unnecessary.

Chimpanzees are also tool users and manufacturers; and even use branches and stones as weapons against other animals. They exist in Africa in two separate races—a pygmy and an ordinary one. When reared in captivity they behave differently from in the wild where they form more or less stable groups of 30–40 members centred upon a core of females, with some interchange for breeding between groups. Unlike humans, however, there is no persistent pair-bonding.

De Waal (1982) confined a number of chimpanzees in an artificial forest habitat on an island at Arnhem Zoo where their social behaviour could be observed from outside. These are dangerous animals and the striving and fighting for status within the group was a constant preoccupation giving some indication of a need for group hierarchy. But there could be no indication of any group identity as such in relation to other chimpanzees, for there were no other groups to be distinguished from.

Field observations in the wild, do now seem to indicate some degree of group identification and cooperativeness, particularly when chimpanzees are involved in hunting or meat-sharing as noted by Goodall in *The Shadow of Man* (1971). Japanese observers in denser forest habitats have also observed the advanced signalling systems of chimpanzees for telling own kind from other kind. They also noted that chimpanzees can be territorially distinctive— although this was not so easy to observe in the denser forests.

In Goodall's contribution to *The Quest for Man* (1980) examples are given of occasional hostility towards 'outsider' chimpanzees from different groups who are sometimes killed and even eaten. Such behaviour (except for one female aberrant) did not occur within the chimpanzee's own family group although the latter could be quite fierce in their frequent battles for status.

During Goodall's observations in 1972 at the Gombe Stream Reserve, one chimpanzee group, grown overlarge, suddenly subdivided led by a rival group of males, so leaving the original group occupying the northern and the new group the southern section of the territory. Thereupon running battles of great ferocity ensued between the male warriors on either side. As a result seven males and two females disappeared, presumed killed.

Goodall was forced to the conclusion that chimpanzees are even more like humans than she had first imagined.

So the animal evidence may be summarised as indicating that those animals which live in stable groups, in contrast to solitary species which only join together for mating, display group attachment behaviour based on lineage, with a developed sense of group solidarity and distinction. They appear to identify by small nurture groups which live and hunt together and within which all cooperativeness and gregariousness, including hunting, appears to be confined. But they have no possible means whereby they can identify by whole species or subspecies so they are never racially conscious.

Darwin wrote in *The Descent of Man* (1891): 'In order that primeval man, or the ape-like progenitors of man, should become social, they must have acquired the distinctive feelings which impel other animals to live in a body.' Presumably these could also have been inherited from earlier primate ancestors.

The survival functions of a close-clinging reciprocal attachment between a human infant and its mother are self-evident. Indeed such first attachments are also shared by all mammals of every kind, whether solitary or social. Wider social attachments, however, to a stable nurture group, importing a continuing ability for group recognition and distinction, would also have served a survival function not only for our human progenitors but even for proto-human ones, enabling them to assist each other in the struggle for survival. If human infants and the young of other social animals requiring protection during their long maturation period had possessed no such inbuilt tendencies and hence had viewed all others as own kind—regardless of whom they were— they could hardly have survived. This would indeed have been maladaptive.

Whatever the provenance, however, of a group attachment trait the latter appears to exist as an inborn faculty for social attachment involving feelings of loyalty and allegiance with corresponding feelings of *us* and *them*. Whatever its origins, such a trait no longer, in practice, operates only in favour of biological relations but is extended in favour of wider communities conceived to be own kind in contrast to others seen to be different.

LOYALTY TO THE WHOLE HUMAN SPECIES?

If our analysis so far of group consciousness be correct, then a world loyalty requires a sense of attachment to the whole living race of *Homo sapiens* as well as identification with the whole territory of the Earth we inhabit. Here at once the difficulty is seen. For there is no other people or territory to be distinguished from at a world level nor a situation capable of inducing a sense of world-wide loyalty *as humans* in contrast to others.

This is not to decry worldwide humanitarian and religious movements but, if directed to creating a loyalty to the whole human race, this particular aim seems unlikely to succeed. For it is not how the group attachment trait appears to have evolved either among humans or other primates.

It is difficult indeed for individuals to regard the whole world as their mother country or their own to which they feel they belong, when the essence of 'home' or 'belonging' is somewhere familiar as opposed to somewhere foreign or strange.

It must be emphasised too that loyalty to the whole human race literally means a *racial* allegiance or identity with *Homo sapiens* just as much as does Black consciousness signify a sense of loyalty to the whole African Black race. It would involve the group consciousness of individuals taking human racial identity on a world scale as its hallmark and regarding the whole of humankind as *we* or *us*. Yet it has proved difficult enough for Black racial consciousness to embrace the whole of Africa. The tendency has rather been for such racial identification to split into smaller national identities where group consciousness is easier to foster.

It seems therefore that the group attachment trait did not originally evolve to cope with worldwide groups in the absence of perceived or supposed differences.

While it may not be essential to group consciousness that all individuals should look or speak alike, and while contrary perceptions may be over-ridden by the cultural stimulation of a sense of identity among heterogeneous peoples, this can normally only be induced in small distinctive groups. Then indeed can be inspired some sense of national or even regimental distinction. But such smaller distinctive groups are no reliable model or guide for a world loyalty or group consciousness based upon the whole of humankind. They only demonstrate the feasibility of creating smaller so-called international organisations, with some sense of loyalty within the organisations them-selves.

An all-human racial consciousness or world loyalty does not therefore seem feasible. Perhaps there may, at one time, have been some sense of racial identity centred on groups of *Homo sapiens* when the *erectus* type he replaced still lived in large numbers. But in Australia, before a more civilised and humanitarian outlook was enforced by law upon white Australians, they used to engage in Abo shooting. Even now they have difficulty in identifying with their Black compatriots most of whom are also reluctant to answer to the Latin name for 'Southerners'.

So human racial consciousness focused on the *sapiens* type, if it ever existed, may not have been all that attractive. The enlargement and enhance-ment too of group consciousness regardless of consequences, is not always to be preferred. For group consciousness and loyalty are not the same as humanity; and can even lead to inhumanity and widespread brutality.

This very difficulty of stimulating world consciousness tends to confirm that it is but a wider level of identification trying vainly to use racial con-sciousness as its hallmark. While difficult if not impossible to achieve, group consciousness at a world level need be no more humanitarian than at any other.

The problem is rather, by cultural means, to make group attitudes more humanitarian.

4

Mother Tongues

The prevalence of racial group consciousness, overriding tribal identities, has been observed changing into national consciousness. It is now proposed to consider other identity types, still depending upon the social identification of individuals. Again the presence of the consequential loyalties and allegiances will be taken to indicate where social identifications lie. The phenomenon of disloyalty will also be used to provide evidence of identification in other directions.

In every case, however, the underlying substratum will be seen to be psychological rather than economic involving a sense of group consciousness shared by a majority of individuals.

The strand of identity now to be considered is that of language, so vital to intercommunication between *us* but also to excommunication from *them*. It has just been observed how certain language groups are coincidental with biological races or segments of races thus indicating not only their ancient origin but also the prevalence of social distancing from other kind.

The attitudes described are not therefore new. Indeed they are very old and were even noticed by the first historian Herodotus (480–492 BC), who might also be called the first anthropologist. For he had observations to make on nation formation out of groups or confederations of tribes, particularly where a 'royal tribe' or house predominated to provide a national name. Herodotus reported this reply to the King of Macedon when he suggested to the Athenians that they might desert the Greek cause against the Persians:

> 'It is not well that the Athenians should be traitors to the Greek nation which is of like blood and like speech and has common buildings to the gods and common sacrifices and manners of the same kind.' (Herodotus VIII. 144-2)

This contemporary observation reveals the degree of identification with an all-Greek nation above the level of the city states, but with some suspect loyalty (and therefore identification) on the part of the Macedonians. Herodotus's assessment of the different strands making up a Greek sense of identity were, first, racial; second, linguistic; and, third, religious. These remain today the principal strands combining to form the core of most national identities.

A major strand in this all-Greek sense of identity was thus in having their own Greek language distinct from that of other races. Language enables distinctive cultures to occur in which people are brought up, and through which they are induced to look upon the world as if through a separate window. Even by the age of three, infants can perceive own kind by language, giving them a distinctive outlook. As they grow older it becomes increasingly difficult for them to socialise with those who do not speak the same tongue. This also imports a social signalling system. Most of the early languages seem to coincide with races or supposed races like the Celts, Slavs or Turkids each with a general language structure and local derivatives indicating subsidiary groups whose socialisation was confined to own kind. Were these language communities or sub-races? Herodotus was acquainted with the Celts or Keltoi of his day, spread throughout central and southern Europe. When later observed by the Romans they had an entirely different language, culture and distinctive appearance, having by then spread into southern France and the British Isles. On the western fringes of Europe the Celtic tongue still provides a cross-current of culture as well as a sense of Gaeldom.

Other minority languages have been large enough to threaten or actually to disrupt whole nations through the disloyalties they engender. This indicates that for their speakers, the language is, or is contrived to be, the hallmark of a new group consciousness which became the strongest identity strand of all.

In the Belgian nation-state formed in 1832 out of the Kingdom of the Netherlands the different language identities of French and Flemish soon rose to the surface with the French-speaking Walloons in the south looking over their shoulders to France; and some Flemings looking over their shoulders to Germany. These split identities have from time to time placed the Belgian state in jeopardy through demands for separation of the two language communities, or even the Union of Wallonia with France, leaving Flanders on its own. Now there is a Federation. But today the country is largely divided into language 'islands'. Motorists driving on the new motorways leading into this embryo capital of the European Community find themselves confronted by road signs in one language or the other depending upon which language territory they happen to be driving through.

Such then is the force of group consciousness based upon language, even within a developed European nation, overriding all questions of economic advantage.

The French-speaking province of Quebec has the strongest separate identity of any of the Canadian provinces and in 1978 forced a referendum threatening secession from the Canadian union which would thus have been split in two. The separate identity of the Quebecois is a linguistic and cultural one augmented by a Roman Catholic strand, all of which would have been sufficient to combine to form almost a separate nation had there not been a strong federal structure to hold them together. So here again, in no way caused by economic factors, a highly developed country remains partially divided by separate language and culture.

Spain has likewise been beset throughout its history by separate language and cultural identities that once caused the King of Spain to be styled 'King of all the Spains', including Portugal. A failure to identify as Spaniards has been endemic among many Catalans and Basques, as well as many (formerly Moorish) Andalusians who are all separate language-peoples with their own independent cultures to match. The Spanish national state in contrast grew out of the separate kingdoms of Old and New Castile with its capital first at Toledo and then at Madrid. Its language was therefore Castilian. The Spanish Empire of South America, now represented by 13 separate South American nations, was essentially Castilian and the expression *Hablar Castilano* still means to speak 'Spanish'. The Castilian language, however, is not what the Basques or Catalans speak among themselves. Their primary loyalty is not therefore as Spaniards to Spain but as Basques to Euskadi or Catalans to Catalonia and with Basque or Catalonian as their mother tongues. Hence while Spain is now a nation-state or Kingdom it has as yet to gain a full sense of national consciousness.

Portugal, once one of the separate Crowns of the Spanish monarchy, has long since defected from Spain. It was eventually allowed by the Spanish monarchs to go its own way as a separate nation even with its own overseas Empire of Portuguese-speaking Brazil. Originally a Spanish dialect, Portuguese has now become an entirely separate language.

Social distancing by separate identification can therefore aid dialect formation or even the evolution of separate languages.

All the examples so far given of language identities occurred 'naturally' in the sense that they were not consciously fabricated; but this does not mean that the ability to speak a particular language is itself inborn. Indeed if infants are switched soon after birth they will simply grow up speaking the language of their adoptive family.

In contrast we now consider conscious language fabrication, including the standardisation of existing languages or dialects, with the deliberate intention of stimulating national homogeneity. Leaders of national movements in the nineteenth century who went in for such language standardisation or fabrication were well aware that there is nothing like a shared but distinctive language, for causing individuals to perceive that they are indeed a separate people in charge of their own destiny. For it provides an aural as opposed to a visual awareness of being distinctive. Weinstein (1979) says: 'The reinforcement or the creation of a cultural network around language transforms an unconscious language group into a self-conscious identity group.'

The strongest identity strand within modern Turkey is its separate Turkid language, so different from Persian or Arabic. The language of the modern Turks however is a new standardised form specially introduced in 1922 by Ataturk (Father of the Turks) using the Latin script so as to make a complete break with the former Ottoman Empire. Ataturk thus foiled a wider pan-Turkish movement for a new Turkish-speaking Turkistan incorporating Turkey and parts of Central Asia.

The Dutch colonists in South Africa when they found themselves ousted from their original Cape colony by the British, discerned that to maintain their distinctive identity among so many Anglophones, they needed to contrive a modern language of their own out of their Dutch patois. So they invented a new written language called Afrikaans with its own new standard grammar and syntax, and even erected a monument to the occasion in Pretoria inscribed with the words 'for us this is serious'. There has thus resulted a distinctive Dutch-African or Afrikaner culture, quite different from that of the Netherlands, which has also successfully maintained its social distance from the British.

There are other European examples, of the manufacture of new homo-geneous languages distinct from that of neighbours and designed to provide a basis for a new or stronger national consciousness. A linguistic identity was thus encouraged among peoples of a particular territory to become a new national motherland where people speak the same mother tongue.

By the sixteenth century there existed distinct Swedish and Danish national states and identities, each with different languages which were however, mutually comprehensible so indicating a common Scandinavian (or Nordic) racial origin. The identity of the Norwegians, then ruled by Denmark, was less distinct. Danish was the language of the Norwegian upper class and of the Norwegian scriptures. At the beginning of the nineteenth century, Norway ceased to be ruled by Denmark and became joined to Sweden under a joint monarchy as a result of which, however, Norwegian loyalties and identities remained blurred. As Khlief has written (1979): 'If boundaries define belonging, if identity itself is defined by boundaries, a decreasing emphasis of, or blurring of boundaries, would be regarded as a threat to group existence, that is to allegiance, social coherence and conformity.' So the Norwegian patriotic movement got to work on the basic language question by creating the modern written language of Norway, christened 'Nynorsk'. Aasen and his followers then consciously fabricated this new written language out of the locally spoken Landsmal with a new grammar and dictionary intended to be used by Norwegians of every class. This did not however appeal to the upper class of Oslo anymore than has Erse to most Dubliners. Nevertheless it has contributed to the creation of a more classless Norwegian society which looks to the boundaries of Norway rather than to those of Sweden or Denmark.

In 1904 complete independence from Sweden was eventually achieved. Through basic affinity of language structure, however, and common Nordic appearance, there still remains an overall Scandinavian identity with both racial and linguistic strands shared by Norwegians, Swedes, Danes— and, to some extent, Finns.

Finnish is the original language of the tribal Finns, but under Swedish rule it became the language of a lower class whose rulers spoke Swedish. For a long time it remained the official language of government. During the early nineteenth century, however, a new Finnish national movement emerged among intellectuals of the lower middle class coupled with a demand for the use of Finnish side by side with Swedish in public life. A new national sense of awareness thus grew out of the Finnish language question and hence was directed principally not against the Russian government (by then the Czar was the Grande Duke of Finland), but against Finland's own Swedish-speaking upper class. A language ordinance of 1863 placed Finnish on an equal footing with Swedish and thereafter Finland officially became a bilingual country. But it took an internal civil war before Finland became an entirely independent nation in 1918. Now Finnish-speaking 'true' Finns and the other Swedish-speaking inhabitants can for the first time identify together as Finlanders—whereas formerly the upper class tended to regard themselves as Swedes. There is still, however, one small Swedish-speaking area near to Sweden where all classes have always spoken Swedish and for whom Swedish is still their mother tongue. Finland, however, has now become their mother country.

In such a national and imperial situation may also be seen the changing importance of social class.

The formation of the modern German identity—indeed the very concept of a single Deutschland—was also due to the deliberate standardisation of local dialects of Deutsch spoken in 39 different German principalities. Deutsch, as already mentioned, means 'the people' in old High German. This standardisation occurred at the end of the eighteenth century and was the deliberate work of linguists like Herder and Humboldt who even invented the science of linguistics. The former proclaimed that national character is imprinted on language and reciprocally bears its stamp. Humboldt considered that the making of a unified German nation out of many principalities depended upon the creation of a standardised language and a major new German literature. This was then deliberately brought about and Germans like Goethe, Schiller, Holderlin and others were not only great authors and poets but also the creators of a distinctive German culture which could not have occurred without the prior standardisation of the German language. Once so standardised, it grew to vie with French and English and even to become for a time one of the co-languages of inter-national science.

Through using the now standardised German language and sharing a common culture, the hitherto divided principalities and the two larger German-speaking states of Prussia and Austria, became more consciously aware, even arrogantly so, of themselves as Germans, in contrast to others and with a sense of Historic Mission.

There now arose a dispute between the supporters of greater Germany and lesser Germany—Gross and Klein Deutschland—and in particular whether the German-speaking peoples of the Austrian Empire should or should not be included. Behind Gross Deutschland lay the idea that Germany should be wherever German is spoken.

The second Prussian-dominated Reich, excluding Austria, represented Klein Deutschland. Hitler's Third Reich sought to encapsulate all German speakers apart from the remoter dialects. Under Hitler too the new national consciousness of the Germans, once aroused, was also induced to assume a bogus racial guise with the idea of a Herrenvolk or superior Aryan race, based upon supposed Darwinian precepts. Such however need not change the labelling of this identity as originally linguistic, turning later into a national one. As that great German, Max Weber (1922), once wrote:

Correspondingly unclear are all those concepts which appear to imply some purely ethnic basis for communal action in the sense of a belief in blood relationships. I have in mind such concepts as those of the 'nation', the 'race', or 'the people' each of which is normally used as a subdivision of the concept following.

Under Hitler and with a re-aroused German identity of a most aggressive and intolerant type, those pointed out by State propaganda as Peoples' Enemies or Untermenschen came to fear for their lives. Traditional German antagonism as Christians now turned not only against Jews but also against their own loyal German Jews who were sent to the gas chambers along with the rest of the six million murdered. It was not enough for them to protest that they had chosen to solve their own acute identification problem by seeking to become German and Christian rather than followers of Zion. It sufficed for them to be shown to have Jewish 'blood' and with the acquiescence of their compatriots, for them to be 'smelled out' and sent for extermination.

Thus was the conscience of a sophisticated and supposedly cultivated European people occluded towards those they were all too readily induced to regard as nonpersons or other kind. It is difficult to think this was entirely due to German culture rather than to inherited traits dangerously aroused and stimulated by stereotyping. In German-occupied parts of Western or Eastern Europe, it was only occasional people, who humanely and bravely felt able to lift a finger to protect their own Jewish compatriots. The Danish King told Hitler that he himself would wear a Jewish yellow star if his Jewish Danes were forced to do so; and was party to their smuggling overnight into the safety of Sweden. Many Dutch also behaved heroically in defence of their own Jewish people.

When group consciousness is inflamed into active social antagonism under state direction—whether on a racial, national or class basis then *Homo sapiens* can become a dangerous species indeed. Even Jews in Israel or Dutch in South Africa are capable of racial discrimination and if sufficiently aroused or provoked, of genocide.

Since the Second World War the German national identity, now subdued, appears to have reverted to a predominantly language and cultural one divided, however, between the two new nation-states of the Federal German Republic and the German Democratic Republic both composed of German-speaking Germans. The 1968 constitution of the GDR described East Germany as 'a socialist state of the German nation'. This was changed in 1974, along Soviet lines to 'a socialist state of workers and farmers'. So now there is the concept of a separate socialist German nation with a new national consciousness to support it. Yet in 1983 the West German Chancellor proclaimed to the Bundestag:

There are now two states in Germany but there is only one German nation. Its existence is not contingent upon governmental or majority decisions. It is a product of history, part of the Christian and European cultures and shaped by its location at the heart of the continent. The German nation's existence preceded the formation of a national state and has outlived it.

At the end of the First World War when the Austro–Hungarian Empire collapsed, the League of Nations created Czechoslovakia and Yugoslavia out of the local Slav populations whose common language stem again indicates racial affinity.

The Slav racial/language group appears, at one time, to have split into three: the Western Slavs who became Poles, Czechs and Slovaks, each with their own language dialects turning eventually into separate languages. The Southern Slavs of the Balkans comprising Serbs, Croats and Slovenes, each again with their own mother tongues, but now forged into the new South Slav Union of Yugoslavia. Finally the Eastern Slavs, comprising various peoples known generally as Russians (from the Norse nickname given to Kiev Rus) which include Russians proper (or white Russians), Lithuanians and Ukrainians.

In that part of the Austro–Hungarian Empire represented by the former Kingdom of Bohemia, a Slav lower class spoke Czech while the upper class not only spoke German but looked to Vienna as their capital. They regarded *Kaisertreu* (loyalty to the Emperor) as their main allegiance. A more widespread Czech awareness based on local language was then deliberately stimulated through the standardisation and use of Czech in official circles to become the badge of a new Czech national consciousness. There was also introduced a systematic Czech grammar and history of the Czech language which gave rise to a lively new Czech culture entirely due to the language fabricators. A popular song of the day 'where is my home?' was later to be adopted as the Czech national anthem. Bohemians, who spoke German, in contrast, preferred to regard themselves as Germans and, by the same token, tended not to be regarded as 'true' Czechs even when sharing the same Protestant religion. This was still the situation when the new Czechoslovak Republic was created by the League of Nations in 1919. In 1945 3½ million Sudetan Germans were expelled. In 1968 Czechoslovakia was turned into a federation, like Belgium, to accommodate, on a bi-national basis, the separate Czech and Slovak language and cultural identities.

A new Yugoslavia was formed by the League of Nations at the same time as Czechoslovakia, based this time on an enlargement of the Slav Kingdom of Serbia with its capital at Belgrade. There existed however religious distinctions between Orthodox Serbs and Catholic Croats, the one spelling their Slovak language in Cyrillic and the other in the Roman alphabet.

This exercise in new nation formation in Eastern Europe by the League of Nations was conducted on so-called 'ethnic' grounds, meaning the creation of suitably sized new nation-states corresponding as nearly as possible to existing racial language groups. But in most cases a new national consciousness had still to be fostered.

The Russian language was also standardised at the end of the eighteenth century to form the basis of a new Russian national culture, vying with German, to be spread throughout the dominions of the Czar in a deliberate policy of Russification. An attempt was even made to introduce Russian culture into Poland, in the same way as the Poles had once attempted to Polonise the Lithuanians. This Russification of the 'little Russias' of the

Empire had only proceeded some way—but hardly at all in the Muslim colonies—by the time of the Russian Revolution in 1917. When the Bolsheviks assumed power Lenin and Stalin simply had to develop their own ideas for running the first Workers' International State, supposedly divorced from all concepts of national identity. Some of the Russian colonies, like Georgia and Armenia which had once been ancient Christian kingdoms, even managed to obtain their temporary independence before being brought to heel.

In the Russian colonial empire, now recaptured by the Red Army on behalf of the Workers, they also had to face up to the language and so-called ethnic question.

Stalin was appointed first Commissar of the Nationalities and was thus directly involved not only in the designation of peoples by language group, but even in language fabrication.

Five new Muslim national republics were then set up on the basis of language identities. Kazakhstan was carved out of the steppes of Central Asia with another republic called Kirghizia to its south. There had been no distinct Russian colonies of these names or precise boundaries before. The local languages had to be standardised and reduced to writing, with that of Kirkhgis achieved in 1924. The different Turkid-speaking peoples living within the USSR were also formed into three new language peoples and national republics, namely, the Turkmans of a new Turkmenia; the Uzbeks of a new Uzbekistan and the Tajiks of a new Tadjikistan. Again these various languages and dialects required to be standardised in order to be written in Latin script to differentiate them from the rest of the Muslim world. When the nearby Turkish Republic, however, also adopted the Latin script, Stalin, to be different, simply ordered all Soviet Muslims to switch to the Russian Cyrillic alphabet that was invented by St Cyril in the tenth century and is still in use throughout the Soviet Union to the present day.

These separate new languages used in the five Muslim Soviet republics have now grown further apart as the inhabitants of each have acquired a sense of identity and nationhood.

Use of language as an aid to nation formation is not, however, confined only to Western and Eastern Europe or the Soviet Union. It has also occurred throughout the Middle East, Asia and the Far East.

Under the new Indian constitution of 1950, the official language of India was stated to be Hindi in the Devanagari script but with English intended to be used for a further 55 years. However, in 1963 this was amended to provide for the continuance of English for official purposes and for parliamentary business. English is only spoken by a minority of Indians, among a multitude of other languages and dialects. India has therefore now been divided into 21 provincial states, each designated on language lines according to the Soviet model. One of these, Tamil Nadu attracts a cross-national language and cultural identity with the Tamils of the northern part of nearby Sri Lanka with a consequent split of loyalties and identities within that island.

In Indonesia, towards the end of Dutch rule and in response to a new sense of Indonesian national awareness, it was realised that the continuance

of Dutch as the new national language would not be acceptable. So the neighbouring Malayan was chosen as the only written language suitable—although
then only spoken by about 10 per cent of Indonesians. This was facilitated,
however, by calling the new adopted language, 'Indonesian'.

As a result of a conference in China in 1955 on P'u-T'ung-Hua or Common speech (PTH for short) a new standardised form of Chinese came to be
introduced throughout all the 30 provinces of China. In the official version
of Chinese thereafter promoted it was described as 'The speech form based
phonologically on the dialect of Peking, grammatically on the structure of
the North Chinese dialect group and lexically and stylistically on the works of
certain representative modern Chinese writers' including Mao Tse-tung.

A standardised national language is of course essential for the application
of modern technology including appropriate words to describe various
modern techniques. Small confined national languages or dialects are thus
inappropriate and purely oral ones impossible unless combined with another
written language in general use.

We leave to the next chapter the group consciousness, as Arabs, of those
who speak Arabic. For the Arab identity is so closely linked with the spread
of Islam, which acted as its vehicle, that it is best considered under the
heading of religious group consciousness in the next chapter. Here it need
only be observed that the Arab language identity is often expressed as an
Arab national one with a sense of belonging to a Greater Arab nation. The
similarity to a pan-German identity is obvious with Germany being wherever
German is spoken. So too all Arab speakers are now regarded as Arabs.

To summarise, it appears that separate and distinct languages, have often
been used as a basis for nation formation whether consciously or uncon-
sciously. They provide a means of identification as well as of intercommunication among distinctly recognisable peoples. Provided, however, there is a
sufficient sense of national distinctiveness by other means, as represented by
other identity strands, there is no need to contrive a separate language one.
Indeed, a distinctive accent may suffice like that of lowland Scots compared
with ordinary English; or English spoken with Welsh or Gaelic intonations;
or English as spoken by Irish or Americans using their own distinctive accents
or phrases.

In the Irish case was it thought necessary to try to impose a native language
different from English to maintain or recreate a separate Irish sense of
distinctiveness. As De Valera once remarked a nation without its own
language is only half a nation. The trouble, however, was that most
Dubliners and many others did not speak Erse. Also, the attempt to elevate
Erse to the level of the primary language of the country was hardly likely to
attract Ulstermen. This endeavour has now largely failed, despite the
enforced use of Erse in schools as well as in the public service. Although Irish
has been a compulsory school subject for over 40 years, the 1961 Irish Census
revealed that 73 per cent of the population then declared itself to be non-Irish
speaking. An Irish sense of identity separate from the British (and thereby
unintentionally also from the north) has rather been preserved by the
Catholic religious strand. Indeed a linguistic strand is usually only one among

many. But it is the vital one for the continuing presence of Gaelic identity and culture.

While identities can exist without separate languages some small ones would indeed disappear in their absence. But small language-communities, if their children are not to be disadvantaged in the wider world, are all the better for having their children also instructed bilingually in one or other of the major international languages of intercommunication and science.

5

Faith and Nation

Religious identities will now be discerned by seeing where the religious loyalties lie; by observing how group consciousness engendered by distinctive religious beliefs or practices can turn into national consciousness; and how national consciousness can become split by rival religious identities as in India, Cyprus and Northern Ireland.

In such a confined type of scrutiny, the truth or untruth of particular religious beliefs is not of course involved; only the unintended consequences of social attachment in action in the religious field from which it is difficult, except by special effort, to exclude it. In short, one is concerned only with the sense of *us* and *them* resulting from upbringing within different religious faiths causing even children to become conscious of religious own kind as opposed to other kind seen to behave differently.

As with linguistic groups, economic factors again play little part in the formation of religious group consciousness although different classes within a nation may prefer their own blend of religion, just as of language or dialect. Furthermore, different religious sects within a faith, in trying to maintain their distinctiveness, may prove even more antagonistic towards each other than to members of a completely different faith. For it is the element of distinctiveness which is all-important to the maintenance even of religious identification.

One hastens to add that no founders of any great religious faith, least of all the Christian, ever intended to inspire group antagonism. That such consequences may, however, unintentionally result among the faithful indicates an underlying proneness to form such attachments and be conscious of religious *us* and *them*. The observed differences too of the latter may be exaggerated by the stereotyping of disconformities in the religious field as in any other. While the aim of saints may be to tame the darker side of human nature, their humane aims are apt to be frustrated by the faithful in their treatment of the infidel or heretic.

Loyalty and allegiance to the Faith thus indicate social identification by religion. While contrary to the concept of brotherly love, cruelty too often occurs when religious outsiders (the original 'ethnics') come to be regarded as opponents. Both the Crescent and the Cross were originally popularised as battle emblems. Cruelties then perpetrated against religious other kind are as bad as any committed in the name of class, race or nation. Indeed, due to religious fanaticism, they are frequently worse. A fanatical religious Shiite sect, encouraged by religious leaders, may be guilty of the greatest atrocities in the name of God the All-merciful. But then the Scottish Cameronian sect once marched into battle behind a banner bearing the strange device of *Jesus and No Quarter*.

It is these malign tendencies which need better understanding and taming in the furtherance of humanity.

There were no economic factors to account for the three great monotheistic religions of mankind which arose in similar economic circumstances in the Middle East. First, Judaism, and a thousand years later the Christianity of the New Testament replacing the Old; and 600 years later again, Islam, incorporating much of the teachings of both. The changes wrought by these three great religious cultures upon mankind have been profound and now account for widespread social identities.

It is intended here to consider first the Islamic one and then some Christian identities to show the force of group consciousness when centred on or affected by religious distinctions. It must be repeated that group consciousness itself has little to do with religion. Yet it cannot be entirely disassociated if a particular identity would not have existed in its absence. Nevertheless, the ensuing descriptions of religious group consciousness are admittedly superficial in the sense of not fully describing the beliefs or motivations of devout Muslims, Orthodox Greeks or Irish Christians. It is only their basic loyalties and allegiances to which attention will now be directed, to try to ascertain how a sense of *us* and *them* comes to arise from these different religious beliefs and practices.

ISLAMIC IDENTITIES

Islam started with the revelations of Muhammad regarded by Muslims as the mouthpiece of God and the last and greatest of His prophets. Muslims identify with that nickname but not as Muhammadans which would be regarded as blasphemous. They also follow a new dating system from the Hegira of AD 622 when the Prophet set up the first Islamic community or *Ummah*. Islam now claims some 800 million adherents.

Within a century of the Prophet's death, Islam had spread over the central area of the civilised world, partly by force but also by attracting pagans of the Middle East and also many Christians confused by the dogmas of Byzantium. Many Christian Egyptians turned Muslim and adopted Arabic as their language leaving only a residue of Egyptian-speaking Copts. Muhammad, as the new prophet of God, first flirted with the Jewish and Christian communities around Mecca and Medina. But he then cast them aside to base his new *Ummah* on the loyalties of his own Bedouin tribesmen to be forged into a new community of Believers, ultimately intended to embrace the whole of mankind. At first he used the Sheikhs in a holy war to this end, leading them into battle under his green war banner. His appeal was thus to tribal and family values in the service of God. Uplifted from the Old Testament was the book of Genesis, the belief in a single God as well as Paradise and Hell, to one or other of which everyone would be assigned at the Last Day of Judgement. However, a person was assured of Paradise if killed in the Holy War or Jihad against the infidel.

Islam signifies the Holy Way of God and it is as Muslims that followers identify. The *Ummah* are those people who follow that way, whatever their tribe or race or class. Islam is thus a great social leveller. There is also no formal church to stand between the Believer and his God. Even Muslim nation-states must observe the Way of Islam. A Muslim nation-state is thus, in theory, only tolerated in so far as its rulers follow the dictates laid down in the Koran and its subsequent interpretations. Indeed, those fundamentalist Muslim states of today, Iran and Saudi Arabia, one a Shiite republic and the other a Sunni Kingdom, do not strictly regard themselves as nations at all, but rather as sections of the international religious *Ummah* happening to be excluded by surrounding national borders from the world at large. They are the religious counterpart of the original Soviet nation-state, conceived not strictly as a nation, but as an enclosed segment of the international working class.

The basic religious practices required of every Muslim are also comparatively simple to follow and hence their wide appeal, particularly in Africa. They nevertheless appear peculiar when practised daily in the face of others. These practices include dietary prohibitions, the ritual slaughter of all meat, ablution and purification requirements and the saying of prayers five times a day facing Mecca. Such distinctive observances and disciplines seem strange even to young children brought up to observe other practices—or none at all. Islam, above all involved the use of Muhammad's own Arabic language, 'the tongue of the Angels' whereby God appears almost as a different person when addressed as Allah.

These are of course only the external trappings of Islam as opposed to its basic theology and beliefs, but they are nevertheless those factors which count above all in forming a sense of identity and distinctiveness. Even more alien is the Koranic penal code requiring flogging for drinking alcohol; dismemberment for stealing; and stoning to death for adultery.

So the *Ummah* started with an inescapable Middle Eastern flavour which was hardly worldwide and indeed, in some practices, owed much to eighth century Arabia. It also started, like Judaism, with tribal distinctions of 'blood', still perpetuated in certain Muslim sects. The main scism even today within Islam derives from the disputed succession to the Prophet and as to whether the subsequent Cailiphs should or should not have been chosen in the blood line of his own Quraish tribe through his cousin and son-in-law Ali. The Shiites, as followers of Ali, regard the first three Cailiphs as usurpers and even now await a new hidden Imam. The Sunnis, in contrast, represent the more orthodox and wider philosophical tradition of teaching. Iranians (or Persians as they used to be called) have always been Shiites to maintain their national distinctiveness. Elsewhere Shiites tend to belong to subservient or uneducated classes among whom the most fanatical and merciless religious sects are still to be found.

The tribal Arabs were down-to-earth people and could not contemplate Allah sireing a son through the Virgin Mary. This, as the Koran states would be quite unbecoming: (19:28) 'Allah forbids that He himself should beget a Son! When he decrees a thing he need only say "be and it is".' To Muslims, Jesus of Nazareth was, therefore, not the actual Son of God and so they deny the incarnation. They also refer to Christians in Arabic as *Nazraun* or followers of the man of Nazareth who is nevertheless venerated as a great prophet, second only to the Prophet Himself.

The spread of Islam, as far as Spain, in the century after the Prophet's death soon, however, began to cause territorial identifications inconsistent with an international Ummah. Islam now began to be identified with particular areas as the Abodes of Belief in which Christians and Jews were only tolerated as second-class citizens. But as Children of the Book they were better treated than Kaffirs or infidels who, under Islamic law, were allowed to be enslaved. It was Muslims who thus started the African slave trade.

The capital of Islam, now conceived as a territorial area where the Caliphs ruled, was first at Mecca, then Damascus and later at Baghdad. Most of existing Islam was later taken over by the Ottoman Turks, recent converts to Islam, who under their House of Othman, formed the Ottoman Empire. The Sultan of the House of Othman then assumed the title of Caliph as both spiritual and temporal leader. The ruling class under him, however, answered to the name of Osmanlis. They ruled first from Bursa in Asia Minor then, following its capture in 1453, moved over the Hellespont to Constantinople so as better to control their new European provinces.

The international religious Ummah had now become an Islamic Empire with many peoples subject to its imperial rulers. Gone was the community of tribesmen or the international Ummah.

The rule of the Ottoman Turks was one of great magnificence with the building of huge mosques and beautiful palaces. They were the Normans of the Middle East. Their infantry corps (called the Hearth) of Janissaries was recruited originally from tributary Christians thereafter brought up more Muslim than the Muslims. But later the Sultans became so effete and over-protected in upbringing as to prevent any future Sultan ever acquiring any worthwhile knowledge of the outside world. Numerous peoples throughout the Islamic Empire then began to suffer under Ottoman sloth, corruption and indifference and could hardly experience any loyalty to the Sultan or Caliph, let alone identify with the Ottoman Empire.

Islam itself, however, as a religion and religious identity, was able to survive the collapse of the Ottoman Imperial State, which, in any event had never included African Muslims or those of India and the Far East. Being such a personal religion too, without the intervention of a church, made it easier to survive the collapse of an imperial state from which it could more readily be disconnected. Muslims were even able to carry on as such in the confined new secular Turkey.

Reference has already been made to the Arab identity of Arab speakers coinciding with the spread of Islam throughout the Middle East and beyond.

It did so for the very practical reason that Arabic was a developed and standardised written language with its own calligraphy which could then be learnt by tribal peoples having only an oral language, like the Berbers of North Africa. So Arabic became the almost universal language of Islam, except where it came up against other established written languages such as Persian or Turkish.

The Arab name itself derives from Aribi, the nickname given to the wandering Bedouin of the desert who also gave their name to the territory of Arabia. Muhammad came from their Quraish tribe and spoke Arabic. It was therefore in His own language that the Prophet handed down those revelations now contained in the Holy Koran. Since Muslim scriptures, commentaries and inscriptions were all written in Arabic, this naturally became the mother tongue of Islam with language and religious identities combined.

The original tribal identities, however, of the Aribi of Arabia no longer represent all Arabs. Arabs are where, due to the spread of Islam, Arabic has come to be spoken. An Arab nowadays simply means an Arab-speaker. This definition includes Egyptians who never were Arabs but now call themselves *Misri* (countrymen) in Arabic. The constitution of the Muslim Ba'athist Party confirms that the Arab identity is linguistic. Islam, however, is no longer entirely coincidental with the Arabic language, for it includes Turkish-speaking Turks, Persian-speaking Iranians, Soviet Muslims, Pakistanis, and also Indonesians and others of the Far East none of whom speak Arabic or consequently answer to the Arab name.

However, the heartland of Islam is still Arabic. An Arab identity originally confined to a tribal one has thus been transformed, through the spread of Islam, into a wider sense of community with millions of persons now answering to the Arab name as Arab speakers.

That this Arab identity is linguistic is also demonstrated by the fact that peoples of other religions such as Christian Arabs of the Lebanon and Jordan and some Jewish Arabs still identify as such by virtue of being Arab-speakers. Thus Islam and Arabdom are no longer coincidental and the latter identity signifies a level of identification shared by millions now living in different nation-states.

Unlike other languages, Arabic conveniently provides different words for all these different levels of identification. First there is the *Watan* or nation now represented by several nation-states in the Middle East—all of them modern creations. Then there is the *Quam* or community of all Arab-speaking peoples apt, from time to time, to conceive of themselves as a Greater Nation depending on a degree of group consciousness or awareness. At a still wider level comes the *Ummah* or whole religious community of Islam as originally conceived by the Prophet but which would surely begin to evaporate if it ever really began to embrace the whole of humankind.

A single nation or *Quam* of all Arab-speaking peoples might indeed have been created if Britain and France, under secret treaty, had not opposed the setting up in 1919 of a Greater Arab Nation. This was to have had its capital at Damascus and stretch from the Turkish border to the Red Sea—as the leaders of the Arab revolt against the Turks had been led to expect by Lawrence of Arabia. In retrospect its formation might have led to a more peaceful Middle East. Fearing, however, a revival of the Islamic Empire, the Allies divided the Arab-speaking peoples of this area into several new artificial states under express mandate from the League of Nations to bring each to national self-government and independence. So here, for the first time, was the open recognition of new nation-creation with a national consciousness in each case to match. At the inception of these new Muslim states, however, (at the same time as the new Soviet Muslim states were being created) most of the inhabitants regarded themselves as Muslims and Arabs at long last freed, due to their own efforts, from Turkish rule.

This was then identity formation in earnest with the arbitrary designation of Arabs into new states, each with artificial boundaries within which the inhabitants were then expected to identify. Beforehand there was no Iraq, Palestine, Lebanon, or Jordan nor any Arabs at that time answering to these now familiar national names.

Despite the adverse circumstances, the process of collective identification in most cases has succeeded, thereby indicating a human propensity in this direction.

Iraq with new artificial boundaries was carved out of the Mesopotamian region with its capital at Baghdad and placed by the British under a Hashemite King of the Prophet's bloodline. Most of the resident Arabs have now identified as Iraqis. In recent fighting against the neighbouring Iranians (whom most Iraqis still refer to as Persians), it might have been expected that the southern portion of Iran, once settled by Arabs, might have defected. But those inhabitants of the area known as Arabistan have no more defected than the Iraqi Shiites in favour of the Shiite Iranians. All Iraquis are prepared to fight the Persians so that national identity now appears to have taken over as their strongest identity strand.

At the same time as Iraq was formed, Syria was carved out of the former Ottoman Province of Greater Syria as a small nation-state under mandate to the French. But in 1926, at the request of local Arab Christians to preserve their separate identity, Syria was further fragmented to form a new nation-state of Christians and Muslims called the Lebanon. A highly successful commercial city arose in Beirut supported by an uneasy alliance between Christian and Muslim Arab communities with a convention of power-sharing in a communal Lebanese Cabinet. But this was later upset by the Palestinian influx and Israeli invasion so that there no longer exists a sufficient all-Lebanese sense of identity to hold these two religious communities together. Indeed at present the Lebanon seems to have broken down into a state of political anarchy with insufficient national identity to support a nation-state and with the young bloods of the separate religious factions all fighting each other.

There was also carved out of the Ottoman Province of Greater Syria a new state of Palestine under mandate to the British from the League of Nations to give effect to the contradictory terms of the Balfour Declaration. This was to allow the setting up of a Jewish National Home without prejudice to the 'the civil and religious rights of the existing non-Jewish communities in Palestine'. A Hebrew University was then instituted at Jerusalem to revive the Hebrew language, as 'native' tongue of all the new Jewish settlers. The Jews were not at first opposed by the local Arabs. For, after all, Jews too are Children of the Book and had long lived throughout Islam with Sephardic Jews even becoming the friends and advisers of the Sultans. The Hebrew language too is of the same stem as Arabic. In Arab mythology Eastern Jews are supposedly descended, like themselves, from Abraham.

But that was to overlook the influx of Western Jews from Russia and Poland of different race and outlook. They did not speak Arabic or biblical Hebrew.

The Jewish Agency was formed to encourage illegal immigration in the face of the British and was directly supported by Jewish voters in the United States. It became virtually a foreign organisation within the state of Palestine and formed its own militia. It saw to it that no incoming Jews were allowed to regard themselves as Jewish–Palestinians or as compatriots of the local Arabs. Illegal immigration on a massive scale was on the contrary encouraged as the solution to the *European* Jewish problem, a problem of identification which hardly existed in the Middle East. Under crossfire the British remained only long enough for a contrary Arab identification to emerge and for the local Arabs, for the first time, to become strongly aware of themselves as Palestinians under that name and of the land of Palestine as being exclusively theirs. The Holocaust magnified Jewish identification with Israel by causing surviving European Jews no longer to identify as Europeans. When the British withdrew in 1947, a new Jewish nation-state came into being with its first borders happening to be where the British-trained Arab Legion brought the Jewish freedom fighters to a halt.

Transjordan, the home of the Arab Legion, had also been carved out of the Ottoman Empire and handed over to British tutelage under yet another Hashemite King of the Prophet's bloodline. It was renamed Jordan (an easier name to answer to) when the Jordanian army in 1967 succeeded in annexing the West Bank only to lose it again in the next Israeli–Arab conflict. Orthodox Jews identify with this area as the Biblical Judea and Samaria ordained by God to be part of the Promised Land. Such is the force of religious identification in relation to territory.

To the south east of Israel lies the Hejaz, or Arabian heartland where Mecca and Medina lie and also the Kaaba—religious symbol of the centre of the earth. Here the Arab inhabitants are now ruled by the Royal House of Ibn (Son of) Saud which ousted the local Hashemite Dynasty in 1932 with the help of the fierce Wahabi religious sect. Saudi Arabia is still a medieval kingdom, the richest in the world, rather than a modern nation-state. Its inhabitants do not call themselves Arabians, but Saudis, so assuming the name of the new royal house or tribe—there are only some 4,000 in the direct bloodline. Perhaps, one day, the inhabitants will come to call themselves Arabians.

The Islamic religious identity of the *Ummah* remains in places a strong one which not only unites but also splits embryo nation-states.

The movement between the two World Wars for Indian independence from British colonial rule assumed the familiar form of reaction against an alien ruling class or race. A sense of Hindu religious distinction, however, had once been the force behind the Indian Mutiny and of incipient Mahratta national consciousness. It was also the inspiration of the Hindu Sikhs directed against the Muslims who had for centuries been their over-lords. The opposition to the British was centred in the Indian National Congress from which however Indian Muslims later withdrew to maintain their distinctiveness. In 1940 a separate Muslim Congress at Lahore declared for a Muslim National Home within the Indian continent based on the western and eastern Indian provinces where Muslims predominated—the first letters of their names being joined together to form the new name of Pakistan. These Muslims numbered about 100 millions out of a total population of 400 millions. Thenceforth the growing identification with the Indian name, rather than with that of Imperial Britain, and a corresponding sense of disloyalty to the Crown was more widespread among Hindus. Muslims, in contrast, tended to prefer the British presence. While some British-educated Indians tended to regard themselves as secular in outlook and looked forward to an 'India for all the Indians', most Congress members—and practically all its supporters—were nevertheless practising Hindus. Yet the Hindu religion with its many incarnations of God, its belief in human reincarnation, its hereditary religious castes and above all its idolatry, were anathema to Muslims. For they were brought up from infancy to believe that there is only one God; that Muhammad is His Prophet and also to have nothing to do with the uncircumcised. Nor did they believe in sacred Mother India..

An *us* and *them* situation of Muslims versus Hindus now began to polarise which even Mahatma Gandhi could not prevent, despite his saintly protesta-tions. It was a direct product of religious beliefs and distinctions. Indeed the Islamic poet, Iqbal, outlining his plan for a separate Indian muslim state in 1930 went so far as to observe: 'It is no exaggeration to say that India is perhaps the only country in the world where Islam, as a people-binding force, has worked at its best.'

As the move towards Indian independence gathered strength, the Muslim minority began to grow fearful of the impending British withdrawal. In their own interest they supported the British war effort in the Second World War, contributing about one-third of the British Indian Army. Try as Gandhi and others could, Indian leaders were quite unable to persuade Muslims to join in a national opposition as 'United Indians'. Muslims feared they would simply be submerged, if not slaughtered, when the British departed. Such by now, however, were the anti-British feelings, that the political partition of India on religious lines had to be conceded. While the All-Indian Army stood firm the largely Hindu Indian Navy mutinied. So, to bring matters to a head, and to avoid the wholesale breakdown of law and order, the British Viceroy intimated in advance that the British would withdraw on 16 August 1947.

The resultant clash of religious identities found its sparking point in the Punjab. This province contained a Muslim majority over the fierce religious sect of Hindu Sikhs who had once ruled the entire province. It was also the home of the famous Sikh regiment.

On the night of 15 August 1947, the day before partition, the Punjab simply exploded. Its Muslims moved west and Hindus and Sikhs moved east. It was religious *us* and *them* with a vengeance and the spontaneous massacre of religious opponents saw sectarianism or communalism at its very worst. A million persons are believed to have been slaughtered regardless of age or sex, including whole convoys and train loads of terrified displaced people trying to move over to the safety of their own religious kith and kin.

The British boundary force of military regiments tried in vain to hold the ring and prevent this indiscriminate killing, but could do little more than try to maintain law and order within their respective fields of fire. Indeed, their own regimental spirit was strained to the limit, since many regiments comprised both Hindu and Muslim squadrons or companies which, hitherto had been serving happily side by side. In some units, soldiers' wives and families had to be ferried to safety through the murderous religious picket lines in lorries driven by drivers of the opposing religious faction. But regimental loyalty in these small face-to-face societies proved stronger than religious antagonism.

The Continent of India was then partitioned between a new Pakistan and a new India to the latter of which all Indians now feel they belong. Although the Indians now answer to that name, paradoxically it derives from the river Indus which is situated in Pakistan. The latter nation-state was divided into West and East Pakistan. East Pakistan was the Muslim portion of the former British province of Bengal; but people cannot readily identify with such detached portions and so East Pakistan has become the independent nation of Bangladesh. It still retains, however, a Bengali sense of identity and Indian immigrants into Britain who originate from this region call themselves Bengalis. Likewise, Sikh immigrants into Britain prefer to answer to that name rather than to that of Indians. They too maintain their distinctive attire as hallmarks of that fierce and separate religious identity which gave rise to the case of *Mandla v Dowell Lee*—and the assassination of the Indian prime minister.

So India became divided on British withdrawal by rival religious identities which had nothing to do with economic factors such as uneven economic development between the two portions of the Continent. Indeed it was to the economic disadvantage of Indian Muslims to be so separated; but they felt it necessary to preserve their religious identity as Muslims in a sea of Hindus.

The subsequent national disaster of losing East Pakistan containing so many Muslims has since provoked a crisis of identity in the rest of Pakistan. It led to the setting up of a Congress at the University of Islamabad entitled *The Quest for Identity*. A Note to the official proceedings quoted by Mortimer (1982) asks:

> What is the soul and personality of Pakistan? What is our national identity and our peculiar oneness which makes us a nation apart from other nations? ... If we let go the ideology of Islam, we cannot hold together as a nation by any other means ... If the Arabs, the Turks, the Iranians, God forbid, give up Islam, the Arabs yet remain Arabs, the Turks remain Turks, the Iranians remain Iranians, but what do we remain if we give up Islam?

Mortimer also reports the reply given at the Supreme Court trial of Wali Khan, a Pushtun leader tried as a national traitor who was asked to confirm his Pakistani loyalty. His reply was: 'I am a 6000 year old Pushtun, a 1000 year old Musselman, and a 27 year old Pakistani. After all what makes us think that a Pushtun cannot become a Musselman, or a Musselman a Pakistani, these are historical facts and we cannot just shut our eyes to them'.

There is some recognition here that the new nation-state of Pakistan now needs something more than a mere Islamic identity to create a proper territorial national consciousness. Hence the need also to promote Urdu as the new national language. Apart from a Muslim identity distinct from Indian Hindus, which gave it rise, the new Muslim Homeland within the Indian Continent has otherwise no traditional boundaries or marks of identification to encourage a distinctive sense of *us* and *them*. In point of fact, there are today more Muslims living in India than in Pakistan. Many Pakistanis thus remain more aware of being Muslims with an allegiance to a supposed Islamic nation as a whole rather than to their nation-state.

It remains to be seen whether this new nation-state can create a sufficient sense of national rather than of purely religious group consciousness to hold it together, distinct from other nations. Even an Islamic identity cannot therefore escape the influence of the group attachment trait or the tendency of humans to feel they belong to certain peoples or territories as being their own in distinction from others. This is even so in the Far East where the largest Muslim country of Indonesia contains some 157 million persons situated in 27 provinces of which two (East Timor and Molucca) are distinctive as being Christian and Catholic. The nation-state is, however, secular like Turkey and its universal language is imported Malayan. Yet practically the entire population are devout and practising Muslims.

THE ORTHODOX OF CYPRUS

On a smaller scale, and in greater detail two contemporary Christian identities in Cyprus and Northern Ireland will now be observed with religious loyalties or disloyalties again signifying the dividing lines of religious identification. Such small-scale examples can be more instructive than larger ones because the loyalty alignments are easier to discern; and, moreover, being contemporary, individual's own expressions can be used as indicating who *they* think they are. This indeed was no more than the sociopsychologists were asking of their students on whom they experimented, but under laboratory conditions.

Small scale does not mean, however, that they are any less important than international examples like those of Islam and the Arabs. These small examples constitute major international nuisances out of all proportion to geographical size or population, for they can involve other nations with which the rival communities identify and look for assistance. In short they involve bi-national situations inspired by religious group consciousness.

The Cyprus Question is one which has dogged the Middle East throughout this century and is out of all proportion to the size of the island itself with only 650,000 inhabitants. But, like Israel, it nevertheless qualifies as a major international nuisance due to its strategic position and the involvement of neighbouring nations forced to identify with a portion of its inhabitants.

This sideways tug of loyalties in a bi-national situation is of particular importance to our present thesis, as also to the workability of bi-national constitutions without a sufficient overall national consciousness to support them.

It may be questioned, however, what the Cyprus question has to do with religious group consciousness and indeed why it should figure in this particular chapter at all. The matter is examined here because the strongest identity strand now contributing to the modern sense of Greekness or Greek national consciousness appears to be Orthodox Greek Christianity within the great Byzantine tradition which was its foundation. In contrast, in Herodotus's day, the main identity strands were the local ones of being an Athenian, a Theban or a Spartan and with only an embryo all-Greek sense of identity due to shared race, language and religious practices. In those days an Athenian was predominantly just that and only vaguely a Hellene, whereas under Byzantium Athens was not even a Christian bishopric and the pagan Parthenon was allowed to collapse into ruin.

The Orthodox Christian Church arose under the Roman Empire when the Emperor Constantine made Christianity its official religion with himself its head. The Empire was, however, soon divided between West and East with the latter surviving the former, in considerable splendour, by 1000 years. The Eastern church became the greatest of all the Christian churches under the Emperor Justinian, lawgiver and theologian, who built the largest existing building in the world, Hagia Sophia, in Constantinople. It was under the Eastern church and its various councils of bishops sitting in Asia Minor and Constantinople that the basic Church doctrines were promulgated, including that of the Holy Trinity. The Eastern Empire was at first Roman with Latin as its court language but increasingly, after its severance from the West, the language became Greek. They referred to the Western Christians as Latins, from the Italian language spoken by the See of Rome. In 1204 a Latin crusade against the Muslim infidels was deflected into capturing and sacking

Constantinople which never really recovered after the withdrawal of these Frankish or Latin crusaders. Afterwards there was a complete division between Western and Eastern Christendom.

The Greek Byzantine tradition nevertheless still remained one of great ecclesiastical splendour and was adopted in the tenth century into Russia. There the Russians sought to perpetuate Byzantium after Tsargrad had fallen to the Ottomans. The Russian Czars thereafter maintained a close interest in all Orthodox living under the Ottomans as well as the maintenance of the Christian holy places. This was later to lead to the Crimean War and to cause widespread Greek rioting in Crete, Cyprus and other places against the Allies in favour of the Orthodox Russians.

After the Fall of the weakened Eastern Empire to the Ottoman Turks in 1453, the Orthodox Church was allowed to continue with its religious leaders still remaining as leaders of all Greeks in their domestic affairs. Hence the Orthodox Church existed as the main focus of Greek national identity being essentially Byzantine and distinct from the Latin and European.

It may be protested that it is not the Orthodox or Byzantine tradition which underlies the modern Greek identity so much as the classic Hellenic one nowadays also taught in Greek schools. But this is a recent innovation and had all but died out under the Ottomans.

The layout of an Orthodox Church, whether in Greece or Russia, its decoration, the vestments of the priests, the Easter vigil, even the timbre of the church bells are all distinctive from those of Western Christendom and even appear oriental to most Europeans. Western Christians are still known as Latins by many Greeks. The name the Greeks of the Eastern Roman Empire answered to and by which they still call themselves in country places is 'Romaioi', being Greek for Romans. Not only did these Greek–Romans regard themselves as such, but they were also so called by the Ottomans who referred to Constantinople as Rum (Rome) and Greeks as Rumi. These separate identities and names are indicative of a surviving all-Greek identity throughout the entire Ottoman period.

The Ottomans had organised their subject peoples under the *millett* system of subservient nations designated by religion whether as Orthodox, Jewish, Armenian or Maronite. All were regarded as Children of the Book, subject to imperial taxation but otherwise left to regulate their own internal affairs under their own religious leaders. Thus the orthodox of Albania were treated as Greeks, by virtue of being Orthodox. From the earliest days of the Ottoman occupation of Cyprus in 1571, its Greek inhabitants also had their own religious Ethnarch or Leader to control their own affairs. Cyprus was also settled by Ottoman officials and Turkish immigrants, who, by the present century, had come to comprise about 20 per cent of the Cypriot population.

In 1821, the Greek revolt against the Ottomans commenced in the Pelopponese with the new national flag first raised by the local Orthodox Church. There were fearful massacres of entire Turkish populations by Greeks and vice versa with, for instance, in retaliation, the Turkish extermination of the entire Greek population of the island of Chios. With the help of the Western Allies, and numerous Philhellenes there was created for the first time in history a small Greek nation-state comprising about one-third of the land area of Modern Greece. This did not, however, include the Mediterranean Islands or the numerous Greek settlements of Asia Minor.

That the religious strand of Greek identity was now stronger than the linguistic one, is indicated by the fact that this identity was thought to enclose Albanian speakers in Northern Epirus (to which Greece has only recently dropped its territorial claim) and also some Orthodox of Asia Minor, probably Anatolians, who spoke Turkish and had their own Turkish Bible. It did not, however, include Greek converts to Islam.

A growing sense of Greek national pride now demanded the recovery of all Greek territory in all those places where the Greek Orthodox Church existed and Greek was mostly spoken. The territory of the new Greek State thus came to include Athens, as the new capital and the idea took root of a Greater Greece extending over Asia Minor and even including Constantinople where the Sultans still ruled. The Aegean Sea, where the Argonauts had once sailed, was even regarded as entirely Greek, including all its islands. The 'Great Idea' of a greater Greek identity even led to a Greek Army in 1921 crossing the Aegean and reaching the very walls of Ankara until repulsed by Ataturk.

After the ensuing massacre of Greeks in Smyrna about 1½ million Greeks were hurriedly evacuated under League of Nations auspices out of Asia Minor and one million Turks moved to safety the other way. The latter included the whole Muslim population of Crete, but not of the Dodecanese islands then placed under Italian rule; nor of Cyprus itself, by then under British administration. Had the British not then controlled Cyprus, the Turkish Cypriots numbering about 100,000 might have been safely moved, like others, into Thrace with a suitable adjustment there of Greek and Turkish Borders.

With hindsight, these massive evacuations can now be seen as a relatively successful operation.

When in 1946 the Dodecanese were removed from Italian control and 'returned' to Greece, the entire Turkish population promptly fled to the Turkish mainland. Greeks in Cyprus now regarded it as their turn to be freed from colonial rule and 'returned' to the Greek Motherland of the Orthodox Church. Greek identification demanded nothing less, and wherever the Greek Orthodox church existed, there was Greece.

The ensuing Greek movement in Cyprus for independence from the British was therefore synonymous with Enosis or Union with Greece. There was no Greek support for setting up a new independent nation-state of Cyprus within the British Commonwealth.

In the Greek National Census of 1951, out of a total population of 7½ million, all but 100,000 described themselves as Orthodox and members of the official church. Church membership as the test of being a 'true' Greek is also confirmed by a Greek Cypriot anthropologist, Peristiany:

The Greek language and the Orthodox faith are so interconnected that the Greek Cypriots find it difficult to differentiate between them. A Greek is a Greek in so far as he is an Orthodox. The Priest is therefore always a firm believer in the Enosis movement as Enosis to him means the reunion of the temporal and spiritual which have been artificially disjoined.

In contrast the local Turkish Muslim Cypriots, protected on Cyprus under British rule, saw no reason why *their* Cypriot territory should now form part of the Greek National State run from Athens to which Cyprus had never been historically connected and which, above all, was likely to be hostile.

In defiance of the British administration, the Greek Church now led the movement for Enosis or Union with Greece, entirely disregarding the position of the Turkish minority whom they regarded as not entitled to be in Cyprus at all, and only there on sufferance.

The Turkish–Cypriots identified primarily as Cypriots, Muslims and Turkish speakers but not wholeheartedly with Turkish mainlanders across 40 miles of sea. Most regarded themselves as Turkish–Cypriots rather than Cypriot–Turks or Turks happening to live in Cyprus. To most Greeks, however, the emphasis was the other way, regarding themselves as Cypriot–Greeks, rather than as Greek–Cypriots. They thought of themselves as Orthodox Greeks who happened to be living on the Island and with no fundamental sense of attachment to it or its inhabitants.

One of the few who did identify as a Greek–Cypriot, Stavinides, wrote a book entitled *The Cyprus Conflict: National Identity and Statehood* (1975) deploring the Island's later partition and urging a new Cypriotness or all-Cypriot sense of identity from which the present analysis of Cypriot loyalties (or lack of them) is largely drawn.

To create such a new sense of Cypriotness the British would have been better to have insisted upon English being taught in all the schools as the primary language of both Greeks and Turks, instead of allowing the Greek Church to control Greek education under nationalist Greek teachers in separate Greek schools flying the Greek flag. For such intensive Greek education was not only anti-British but above all anti-Turkish and yielded no common language through which both communities could speak to each other.

The rival identities and the coming clash with the British now came to resemble the situation in India with the minority community coming to dread the pending British withdrawal.

The Greek national flag was now flown on all churches and schools and anti-British propaganda was preached from every Orthodox pulpit. In 1948, the future Archbishop Makarios organised a plebiscite for 'Enosis and only Enosis' required to be signed—for or against—in every Parish church. To sign against was heresy. In 1950 he was elected Ethnarch. In 1951, by now Archbishop Makarios III of Cyprus, he met with General George Grivas and together they planned the War of Liberation through the National Organisation of Cypriot Fighters (EOKA). It started in 1955 and for four years was waged with great savagery and with vengeance against those Greeks who continued to work for or support the administration. Many were assassinated.

The Monastery of Kykkos where Archbishop Makarios had been educated as a Novice, was a centre for the armed struggle providing a refuge for the Freedom Fighters. The Official Guide to the Monastery written by its Abbot and with a foreword by Makarios states:

> During the Rising of 1955–1959, the monastery hid, either in its own precincts or in hiding places in its own gardens at Vasilika and Paradhisi, men of EOKA and General Grivas himself, supplying them with food, and helping them in every way. Some of the men of the Monastery were also initiated into EOKA.

With the growing success of the Greek freedom fighters, the Turkish minority began to retaliate as freedom for Cyprus loomed nearer and the British civil administration began to breakdown and give way to military government. Finally, in 1960 a new Greco–Turkish constitution for an independent Cypriot nation-state within the Commonwealth was promulgated. But this was still regarded by most Greeks, including originally Makarios himself, as merely a stepping stone towards Enosis. Indeed, some Greeks even regarded the very founding of an independent Cyprus State as a betrayal, particularly when a new Cypriot flag was seen to fly on public buildings instead of the Greek one. As Stavinides points out there was henceforth no reason why the Turkish–Cypriot minority should continue to try to identify as Cypriots when the Greek majority chose not to do so. So a typical *us* and *them* situation arose with the Turks becoming more conscious of their Turkishness and the Greeks more conscious of their Greekness, one reacting against the other and with each indicative of rival group consciousness.

The details of the new Greco–Turkish or bi-national constitution of Cyprus are of more than just Cypriot interest. For, in microcosm, the constitution shows the difficulties which face any new state organisation which tries to encapsulate rival identities sharing wider horizontal as opposed to vertical allegiancies. The new nation-state involved a president as head of government who was to be Greek with a vice-president who was to be Turkish and with three Turkish minority members in a governing council of 10. The Turks were also to have 15 representatives in a Parliament of 50 elected members. The Turks thus had a slightly greater representation than their population (about 20 per cent) warranted which was to be a continuing cause of complaint on the part of the Greeks.

In the light of these new constitutional arrangements, it was unfortunate to have Makarios as first President rather than, as a temporary measure, a British Governor General. As Archbishop and elected Ethnarch of the Greek Orthodox, Makarios could only represent and answer to his own religious constituents. He thus found himself unable to speak for 'all the Cypriots'. Nor was he able to encourage Muslim Turks to think they were also 'his people' with a sense of belonging not only to the island of Cyprus and its nation-state but also to its inhabitants as fellow countrymen. On the contrary, in a widely reported speech in his home village on 4th September 1962, President Makarios said: 'Until the small Turkish community that forms part of the Turkish Race and has been the terrible enemy of Hellenism is expelled, the duties of the heroes of EOKA cannot be considered as terminated.'

His Turkish vice-president wrote protesting and asking for a withdrawal of these remarks but Makarios never did so.

Makarios also appointed to his Greek posts of government, former EOKA fighters who were explicit about their attitude towards the Turks and the eventual future of Cyprus. By 1963, the Greco–Turkish constitution, unsupported by a sense of all-Cypriot identity, had broken down and become, in effect, a constitution for the Cypriot–Greeks. The embattled Turks, overruled at most points by the Greek majority then withdrew to form their own separate armed enclaves or 'no go' areas as in Northern Ireland. They also began to look more to Turkey as their motherland for support and to maintain their rightful place in Cyprus under the bi-national constitution for which Greece, Turkey and Britain were the international guarantors. Turkey now sent in military advisors. Makarios then formed the Greek National Guard under Greek Army Officers from the Greek mainland. These moves directly involved the Greek and Turkish governments in the Cyprus issue. Perhaps by this time Makarios had doubts for law and order was completely breaking down and even he was having second thoughts about the virtues of surrendering power to Athens under its then ruling army junta. When General Grivas died, the junta took up his fight for Enosis and, on 15 July 1974, the Greek National Guard temporarily overthrew President Makarios whom they now regarded as beginning to prevaricate on the Enosis issue. With Athens approval, they installed an EOKA leader as new president in his place.

Turkish Cypriots were now in mortal peril, and a Turkish reaction to their call for urgent help became irresistible. The Turkish Army moved in to occupy the Northern half of the island, to force out 200,000 resident Greeks and to make way for 60,000 Turks from the southern part of the island and also some mainland Turks from Anatolia. This action caused the Greek junta, who found themselves unable to intervene, to fall.

Cyprus is now partitioned geographically with 40 per cent of the Island occupied by the Turkish Army and with the two national and religious communities now forcibly segregated. The North is now 'Turkified' with the Turkish Crescent flying everywhere and statues of Ataturk in every market place. The United Nations Forces also now police the dividing line.

This dividing line where the fighting ended is also a boundary of identities which failed to take second place to a higher Cypriot one. The northern inhabitants of Cyprus now look over their shoulders to Turkey while the southern look over their shoulders to Greece but are effectively blocked, for the time being, from union with Greece. These identifications are therefore as Greeks or Turks with less local identity as islanders or Cypriots. Yet a lingering Cypriotness in some Turks might have been developed with more foresight by both British and Greeks, for they do not regard themselves as totally Turkish. Many have indeed chosen to emigrate to Britain. In identity terms, however, there is no self-contained Cyprus but only two separate communities regarding themselves as integral parts of two different larger nations. As Stavinides writes:

The point remains, however, that Greekness and Turkishness, even when these characterise people born and bred in Cyprus, constitute different national identities. National consciousness among Cypriots has traditionally either been Greek or Turkish, and the assertion of national consciousness and pride, in other words nationalism, has traditionally either been Greek-oriented or Turkey-oriented.

IRISH PROTESTANTS AND CATHOLICS

A similar *us* and *them* situation involving rival horizontal identities caused largely by religion is also to be found in Northern Ireland. There two-thirds of the inhabitants, being Protestant, regard themselves as British, and the other one-third, being Catholic, mostly regard themselves as Irish.

How these distinctive religious identities came to arise with corresponding allegiances to the Union Jack or the Irish Tricolour is again important to the present thesis, for it illustrates not only the transformation which religious group consciousness can undergo, but again the vital part it can play in the disruption as well as the formation of nation-states or provinces.

Statehood and nationhood are thus seen as not always synonymous although one indeed is usually dependent upon the other. Statehood however can only create a sense of nationhood insofar as it manages to arouse national consciousness and a sufficient degree of loyalty and allegiance to support it. In all-Ireland the Protestants lacked such loyalty at an Irish level, while Catholics in Northern Ireland lacked a sufficient British one to support a separate British province.

How such intense disloyalties as well as loyalties came to arise will now be scrutinised in the same way as were the rival religious identifications of Cyprus.

As in the Greek instance, so in the Irish, it is difficult to know where to begin for clear evidence of an Irish sense of identity. Of the earliest days it may merely be remarked that the Celtic Irish tribes were of the same racial-language stem as other inhabitants of the British Isles. They however spoke Celtic Q or Goidelic rather than Celtic P or Brythonic as spoken by those Britons inhabiting the Roman province of Britannia. The Romans never invaded the country they knew as Hibernia, and which was to become, along with the Scottish Highlands, the last refuge in Western Europe of that Celtic culture which had once included the Gauls.

The early Irish Christian Church, using Latin as its language, with minor differences of practice from the Roman Catholic was founded from Britain by a Romano-Briton called St Patrick. This church exercised a gentle and civilising influence, later introducing Christianity not only to Scotland and Northern England but even reintroducing it into parts of Western Europe. So the early Irish Church probably contributed some incipient sense of Irish identity and of Gaeldom. Holy Ireland indeed has remained staunchly loyal to the Catholic Faith despite a Pope conferring the lordship of Ireland on the English Sovereign. By the thirteenth century Ireland had its own

separate parliament on the English model. But when England turned
Protestant and the majority of Irish remained Catholic, the religious distinctions tended to become national ones. Irish disloyalty reflected in subsequent
rebellions was usually Catholic inspired. One might have expected the
Scottish Stuart dynasty, on becoming Kings of Ireland by mere succession to
the English throne, to be able to create a higher British level of identity
throughout the British Isles, in place of the vain enforcement of an English
one. For, after all, the name British was Celtic and the Stuarts were Catholic
sympathisers, if not actually Catholics, with a considerable Irish following.
King James II, however, although an open convert, was still titular head of
the Anglican church, and when, in disregard of Parliament, he tried to confer
equal legal rights on all his Catholic subjects he was as a result forced to flee
the country although temporarily he was still supported by most of his Irish
subjects.

The Protestant Stadholder of the Netherlands was now invited to replace
King James and elevated from Prince of Orange to the rank and title of King
William III. He was married to a Protestant Stuart and regarded himself as
the Protestant champion of all Europe. When James II tried to retrieve his
throne through Ireland at the head of an Irish Army he was defeated by
William at the Battle of the Boyne on 12 July 1690. To this day 'the Twelfth'
remains the principal date in the Irish Protestant Calendar with King 'Billy'
still toasted by Irish Protestants as 'of glorious pious and immortal memory'.
The English Parliament then in effect outlawed all Irish Catholics resident in
Ireland and put all power and prestige into the hands of the Protestant
minority or those Irish who chose to convert, as a matter of convenience, into
Anglicans. These new penal laws were directed not against a minority but
against nine-tenths of the Irish population. They sought to prevent Catholics
from legally inheriting any land or, in due course, owning any land in their
own country. On a Catholic's elder son declaring himself Protestant he
became the owner of his father's landed property, and the father sank to the
position of life-tenant. Catholics were also debarred from holding any public
office or (until 1794) from voting, and were even forbidden to worship in
their own churches. Unless converted to Anglican use, these simply fell down
as on the Rock of Cashel. The Irish Parliament now became entirely
Protestant with Catholics debarred from membership.

Such measures were hardly likely to convert other than a few place-seekers
to English loyalty or the Anglican faith. On the contrary, they were bound to
give rise to a growing sense of outrage and of *us* and *them* among all Irish
Catholics. It should be noted, however, that these religious discriminations
also applied to other non-Anglicans including Scottish Presbyterians, now
numerous as settlers in Ulster, who were likewise debarred from public
office, from standing for parliament or attending university. The Ulster
Presbyterians therefore also regarded themselves as maltreated by such
English and Anglican imperiousness.

The first sign of an incipient all-Irish awareness, therefore, based on
territory rather than on religion, was displayed by certain Protestant leaders
moved by a sense of 'Ireland for the Irish'. Inspired by the American

Revolution some talked of 'the Protestant Nation' and in 1782 even obtained legislative independence for the Irish Protestant parliament. The French Revolution in 1789 also aroused radical and egalitarian ideas among the Presbyterian Scots of Ulster, disgruntled by English and Anglican treatment. The 'Society of United Irishmen' was organised from Belfast and was directed to uniting both the Irish Catholic and Protestant 'nations' into a single new all-Irish Republic. The Dublin Protestant Wolfe Tone urged substitution of the common name of Irishman for that of Catholic or Protestant. But as no peaceful political progress could be made he misguidedly supported a French invasion with the aim of invoking a republican revolution. This invasion ended in fiasco. The subsequent uprising of 1798 was suppressed with the utmost brutality. Many of the Ulster Presbyterians now re-emigrated with their families to the United States where they came to be known as the 'Scotch–Irish' and to make a contribution there to public life out of all proportion to their numbers.

The Loyal Orange Order was now formed to ensure that never again would any Protestant (whether Anglican or Presbyterian) be disloyal to the British Crown or ally themselves with or even marry Catholics.

In 1800 the Irish Parliament, comprised by law entirely of Protestants, was abolished. This abolition was short-sightedly acquiesced in by Irish Catholics in favour of a single British Parliament and a new unitary nation-state under the new name of 'the United Kingdom of Great Britain and Ireland'. An attempt was then made to establish an Episcopal Church of England and Ireland. Catholic emancipation favoured by Pitt was strongly resisted by the Hanovarian monarch as Head of the Anglican church.

How were the Irish inhabitants of this new nation-state of 'Great Britain and Ireland' expected to identify, and, in particular, by what name were they expected to call themselves? 'Great Britain and Ireland' hardly yielded an appropriate name although the Union Flag now incorporated the Cross of St Patrick. The name British was not even used in England where the London Parliament was regarded simply as carrying on under English convention and usage without any written constitution at all. The Irish members were simply allowed to take their seats in the English Parliament as the Scots had done in 1707. If the Scots could not bring themselves to identify as English, how could Irishmen be expected to do so? Many Irish thus came to regard the new constitutional arrangements as an attempt to create a Greater England enshrined by the Church of England. To offset such criticism the Episcopal church in Ireland was re-christened the Church of Ireland but its membership tended to be confined to Anglo–Irish landowners and their supporters.

Only in the north where most of the population were of Scots descent was the legal name of 'Britain' and 'British' allowed to come into general use.

It is hardly surprising that following the union of 1801, the new Anglo-Irish state failed to create that supporting identity which all states require for their continuance; or that Irish Catholics failed to regard themselves as loyal British, let alone English. Within a few years of the union, new laws were being passed for the suppression of Irish Rebellion and 'the protection of His Majesty's faithful subjects in Ireland'.

The faithful, however, by this time were nearly all Protestants.

This is not to overlook, however, the occasional Protestant Irishmen whose Irish loyalties were still stronger than their English or British ones. But these were now a minority. Few Protestants, now thought of creating an all-Irish Nation of 'United Irishmen' or 'Young Irelanders'; and the Loyal Orange Order was always at hand to ensure that they did not do so but, on the contrary, engaged in public marches against Papists and Fenians. Catholics in consequence were coming, more and more, to be regarded by Protestants as rebels and nationalists which indeed they often were.

Inflamed by English inappropriate constitutional arrangements, there thus foundered upon the rock of rival religious identities the chance of creating an overall British identity coincidental with the whole of the British Isles and answering, at a higher level, to the British (originally Celtic) name.

O'Connel now gave leadership to the Catholic cause campaigning for repeal of the Act of Union as well as for Catholic emancipation. He, above all others, was thus responsible for linking Roman Catholicism and Irish national consciousness into the single identity strand so powerful at the present day. In reaction, most Irish Protestants, differing now from some of their forbears, came to accept that the best hope of maintaining their ascendancy lay in the preservation of the British union. They thus became Unionists or British Loyalists prepared to march in the ranks of the Loyal Orange Order of Protestants every 'Twelfth' wearing bowler hats and orange sashes. These were their marks of identity. In the south of Ireland, where they were fewer, their religious sect was fast becoming transformed for protection into a social class. It was said that in the south the Loyal Orange Order was like an army of officers with insufficient other ranks, while in the north, it was like an army of other ranks with insufficient officers.

The belated granting of Catholic emancipation with widespread land reform in the middle of the nineteenth century made for better understanding between the two communities: but without really altering their rival identities and loyalties. Step by step an inflexible *us* and *them* situation was being allowed to be created.

Following the union of Parliaments, there were by this time many Irish Catholic MPs at Westminster. Towards the end of the nineteenth century they even held the balance between the British Conservative and Liberal parties. The Irish MPs were now under the leadership of Parnell who declared in his maiden speech in 1875: 'Why should Ireland be treated as a geographical fragment of England as I heard an ex-Chancellor of the Exchequer call it some time ago? Ireland is not a geographical fragment, but a nation!'

Due to the efforts of Parnell and his fellow Catholic MPs, a Home Rule Bill for Ireland was eventually passed in 1913 under a Liberal Government, but in a British party political context where the Irish MPs held the balance. It did not therefore have the clear support of a majority of mainland British. The progress of this Bill had indeed been regarded by many British and most Irish Protestants with growing apprehension. When the Bill was eventually passed by both Houses of Parliament apprehension changed to alarm and, indeed, to an intention by some to prevent its implementation. In the face of such threatened insurrection the Liberal Government began to lose its nerve. Gladstone had declared: 'I cannot allow it to be said that a Protestant minority in Ulster, or elsewhere, is to rule the question at large for Ireland. I am aware of no such constitutional directive on which such a conclusion could be adopted or justified.' Parnell also said: 'We cannot give up a single Irishman . . . the class of Protestants will form a most valuable element in the Irish legislature of the future, constituting, as they will, a strong minority in exercising a moderating influence in making laws.'

But the religious identities and antagonisms, already formed, proved stronger than any would-be Irish identity now desperately needed to hold a devolved new Irish Parliament and government together within a higher British loyalty. Irish Protestants regarded and feared Home Rule as Rome Rule and the few Protestants who did not were branded as traitors. Indeed, the Irish Home Rule Bill was regarded by the Protestant majority as a betrayal and a threatened dismemberment of the United Kingdom.

Now led by Carson from Belfast, the Protestants took the initiative to prevent Home Rule, and, to use Carson's phrase, became 'rebels against rebels against the Queen'. They were also supported by the British Conservative Party whose leader proclaimed 'Ulster will fight and Ulster will be right'. With no interference from the Royal Irish Constabulary, a well-armed Ulster Volunteer Force of 100,000 men was hastily organised through the Orange Lodges, including bowler-hatted squadrons of armed cavalry allowed to ride about unmolested. An illegal Ulster provisional government was even formed. Churchill was for sending the British fleet into Belfast Lough, but was overruled by his Liberal Cabinet colleagues made more fearful by the threatened resignation of senior British generals.

In retaliation, the Irish Volunteers were now formed in the south to fight for implementation of the Home Rule Bill and the Sinn Fein organisation ('Ourselves Alone') acquired new support. Even the moderate Irish leader Redmond declared: 'Irish nationalists can never be assenting parties to the mutilation of the Irish nation; Ireland is a unit . . . the two-nation theory is an abomination and a blasphemy.'

On the outbreak of the First World War, however, in 1914, it was promptly agreed on all sides that the Home Rule Act should be shelved for the duration of the war. And in the face of the German threat Redmond himself enthusiastically engaged in recruiting campaigns on behalf of Britain. The 10th and 16th (Irish) Divisions composed entirely of southern Irish volunteers were formed with famous southern regiments like the Royal Irish Rifles, the Dublin Fusiliers and the Connaught Rangers. Also fighting alongside them—and practically annihilated on the Somme—was the 36th (Ulster) Division representing the same level of identity on the other side and composed largely of Carson's Irregulars. So here indeed was displayed a higher level of British identity which, if better played upon, could still have held all-Ireland together within the Union.

But the Easter Rising of 1916 put an end to all that when Pearce with his Irish rebels declared from the footsteps of the General Post Office in Dublin:

'Ireland unfree shall never be at peace.' Yet few Dubliners were then behind him and most educated opinion still supported the Union. Many still flew the Union Flag regarding the Easter Rising as a stab in the back while the fate of the nation hung in the balance on the Western Front. Dublin still had its royal (i.e. loyal) institutions.

The British Army having quashed the Dublin rebellion was then misguidedly allowed by the government to try the leading rebels by court martial and to execute them on successive days by firing squad as traitors to the Crown. The Irish Home Rule Party, which most Catholic Irish still supported, then drafted a resolution condemning the rising, but also condemning the executions and stressing that any more would have the most disastrous effect on the future loyalty of the Irish people. A day or two later the military were stopped short of executing De Valera himself. But by then, a higher British sense of identity among the Irish had simply evaporated, for in the eyes of most Irish the executed rebels were not terrorists or traitors but misguided patriots who had sacrificed their lives for Ireland. An outraged sense of Irishness was aroused and, in Yates' memorable words, 'a terrible new beauty was born'. It was the complete parting of the loyalty ways.

As the First World War drew to its close, civil war broke out throughout Ireland between the two sides in favour of or against Irish Home Rule. Sinn Fein now acquired wide popular support. Independence was eventually granted to an Irish Free State in 1922, with Dominion status within the British Commonwealth but still requiring loyalty to the Crown and a corresponding British oath of allegiance among all public servants. This was followed by an even more bitter civil war among the Southern Irish—between those who supported and those who were against the Treaty. Northern and Southern Ireland had been intended by the British Government to form the lower levels of an eventual all-Irish Federation, but this was promptly abrogated by the new Free State. A devolved Stormont Parliament was now brought into being initially against the wishes of northern Protestants and as part of the renamed 'United Kingdom of Great Britain and Northern Ireland'.

There was no doubt where the Ulster loyalties thereafter lay and what their attitude was towards Catholics. The Stormont Parliament was even found to be useful for keeping Protestant control. The first Ulster Prime Minister, Sir Edward Craig (later Lord Craigavon), who was to remain Premier for 20 years, said in the Northern Ireland Parliament that he prized the office of Grandmaster of the Orange Order of County Down 'far more than I do being Prime Minister . . . I have always said I am an Orangeman first and a politician and a member of this Parliament afterwards . . . All I boast is that we are a Protestant Parliament and a Protestant state.'

Correspondingly in the south, and step by step, the Ireland of the Irish Free State was now systematically Catholicised and all ties with the British Crown and Commonwealth severed. Again this was hardly conducive to attracting the loyalties of the North. President Eamonn De Valera who came to power in 1937 was quite incapable of speaking for 'all the Irish'. Under his Irish Constitution Act of 1937 he severed all remaining bonds of British attachment and all symbols of allegiance by turning Ireland into a Republic, removing even nominal allegiance to the Crown and causing Ireland to leave the Commonwealth. A Catholic republic with Erse as its primary language and with a special Vatican relationship was now instituted purporting to extend over the whole of Ireland including the northern 'six counties'.

Rather than be designed to give Protestant Northerners something to identify with as being their own, or to attract them at a higher level to the Irish name and flag, the 1937 Constitution was thus a sectarian one, as reactive and sectarian as the northern province itself; and was almost tailor-made to repel the one million Northerners who were simply regarded as Non-Irish or not entitled to be there. It turned Ireland into a bi-national territory and Northern Ireland into a bi-national enclave whose Protestant majority now had their backs to the sea.

As the Irish Prime Minister Dr Fitzgerald stated on Irish television (27th September 1981):

> The former President Eamon De Valera had instituted a constitution which had alienated the people of Northern Ireland. If I were a Northern Protestant I cannot see that I could be attracted to getting involved in a State which is also sectarian.

In answer to their own sectarian identity, it was now the Catholics and De Valera in particular, who deliberately removed every chance of accommodation between the two communities. Henceforth they went out of their way to cut themselves off from all British cultural influences and contacts, to which they had formerly contributed. This mutual antagonism between Irish Protestants and Catholics was also carried by emigrant Irish into Canada, Australia and New Zealand where Orange Lodges sprang up as loyal British institutions.

It is an unfortunate feature of all varieties of group consciousness, when so inflamed, to suppose that outsiders can be bludgeoned into abandoning their own identities in favour of those sought to be promoted. King William had vainly tried to do so against the Catholic majority of Ireland, and now it was De Valera's turn. There was as little understanding among Irish politicians of how to create an all-Irish identity as there had been previously among British politicians of how to create an extended (perhaps federal) British state incorporating the whole of the British Isles with a sufficient wider British identity, above the level of an Irish one, to support it. But any such settlement would have required to be on a constitutional basis.

The Irish Government now adopted a policy of neutrality in foreign affairs. So in the Second World War, Allied bases in the Republic were denied even to United States forces and conscription could not be enforced in Northern Ireland, due to the potential disloyalty there of so many Catholics. Nevertheless, some Catholics did join up voluntarily together with the overwhelming majority of Protestants to fight for Britain in such famous Ulster Regiments as The Royal Inniskilling Fusiliers, The North Irish Horse and The Royal Ulster (formerly Irish) Rifles. That they did so is still keenly felt by Ulstermen today. A preference for neutrality is not part of their temperament.

The Catholic minority in Northern Ireland, comprising about one-third of the inhabitants of the Province, is thus unable to identify as Ulstermen or with the Province as a whole because theirs is, in essence, a Catholic and Irish identity. Little, if any, British identity is now felt by them at a higher level. No form of devolution to Northern Ireland is possible therefore, other than to a Protestant-dominated local government and parliament, for there is no other existing loyalty to support it. Even the name Ulstermen or Ulster with which Protestants identify is resented by most Catholics. They also resent the use of the name Londonderry for the second city which, however, has recently been changed back to its original Irish name of Derry to placate them. Suitable names, as always, are vital aids to social identification.

In contrast the remaining two-thirds of the population of Northern Ireland (numbering one million) who still persist in calling themselves British represent an entirely Protestant identity. They regard themselves as British because they are unable to identify with all-Ireland and really answer to the British name because they are Protestants. They do not do so for the same reasons as other British do. For, unlike the latter, there is still an Irishness about them. They do not refer to Britain as the homeland but as the mainland; and they protest to a more genuine Britishness than the mother country.

When the population of the island of Ireland is viewed as a whole, then the rival identities can be seen to operate exactly the other way round with two-thirds of the all-Ireland population identifying with the island as a whole, because they are Catholics, and the remaining one-third identifying with Britain because they are Protestants. What is lacking, as in Cyprus, is a higher vertical sense of identity.

These religious allegiances have thus become territorial ones incorporating rival allegiances to different national symbols of identification. When the Queen officially visits Ulster, where she is greeted with great loyalty and affection, she is nevertheless regarded by most Catholics as Queen only of the Protestants. When the Pope, on the other hand, recently visited the Republic, the Holy Father was regarded with equal affection and loyalty, but was not allowed to visit Northern Ireland although the Catholic Primate of All-Ireland has his Seat there.

When the present bout of civil disorder broke out in 1968 with rioting so severe that British troops had to be called in to help the Royal Ulster Constabulary, they were at first welcomed by the Catholic community as providing much needed protection and better discipline than the local sectarian police. Many of the Civil Rights campaigners, as well as some political observers at the time, thought that the rioting was entirely due to socio-economic factors which, if removed, would dispel all social antagonisms which really reflected economic class differences. Yet changed economic conditions would hardly remove the barriers of *us* and *them* between the two communities of Northern Ireland any more than they could affect the border between Ulster itself and the Republic.

Ulster Trade Unions are affiliated to the Irish Trade Union Congress. Yet when in 1974 a power-sharing agreement was sought to be introduced upon the Cyprus model, it was promptly undermined by a general strike organised by the Ulster Workers Council and led by the shipyard workers of Harland Wolff. So this was not so much a class as a religious conflict directed against Catholics. Their impulse was rather a sense of distinctiveness which even workers can be readily induced to feel; but with disastrous effects if expressed against other people living within the same territory.

Such rival identities are, of course, all man-made in the sense that, apart from the basic ability to identify, no person is ever born with Catholic or Protestant feelings of *us* and *them*. These are only later acquired by upbringing. Indeed the Polish shipyard workers at Gdansk express their sense of Solidarity exactly the other way round with a strong sense of Catholic feeling against their Polish government. That such particular identities are not inborn is also plain from the example of identical twins mentioned in an earlier chapter and nurtured separately in Belfast and Dublin, but also from what is seen to happen to emigrant Irish now resident in Britain where they are allowed to carry both British and Irish passports as well as to exercise a British vote. If they, or their children, are brought up in Britain they come to regard themselves as British *and* Irish and were fully prepared to fight on the British side in the Second World War which their Irish compatriots refused to do. In fact there are more Catholic Irish now living in mainland Britain than there are in Northern Ireland. But then, of course, they are treated on equal terms and their children are not brought up on a diet of social antagonism.

That at one time the Irish could have been induced to experience a higher level of Britishness to keep Ireland and the British Isles together is thus apparent from the Irish in Britain.

In his 1982 Dimbleby Lecture, however, Dr Fitzgerald said:

> For such a problem there can be no simple geographical solution—no line drawn on a map, whether through the channel between our two islands or across the countryside of Ireland—that will of itself resolve the identity conflict. Attempts to find solutions of this kind in the past have in fact only intensified the problem. The problem which we face is thus one of senses of identity, largely formed by where people are born and how they are brought up. The sense of identity with a particular community may be given by chance but it cannot easily be transcended by design. . . . It is when more than one focus of identity is to be found within a single geographical area—whether it is the identity of white or black in South Africa or the southern States of America (or in Brixton), or of Greek or Turk in Cyprus, or of Christian or Arab in the Lebanon—then an explosive situation may be created. This is the nature of the problem in Northern Ireland.

6
Esprit de Corps

The previous chapters have so far been concerned with group consciousness as seen among young children and with the tribal, racial, linguistic or religious identification of adults. All involve collective feelings or attitudes of *us* and *them* and each of these forms of group awareness is capable of transformation into another, depending upon its particular focus at any given point of time. This evidence is universal and common to all races and hence combines to point to the inherent probability of a group attachment trait that is shared by all humankind. But no actual identities are ever inborn. They are culturally induced.

Thus 'ethnicity' which really means just people regarding themselves, and being recognised by others, as distinctive, can assume a class or religious form or later give rise to national identity. Group consciousness is not therefore constant. Its changing forms are really manifestations of a group attachment trait in man taking tribal, racial, linguistic or religious form in response to feelings of own kind and other kind. Whatever the classification system, it must be borne in mind that the basic consciousness of *us* and *them* can change its hallmark. As already indicated racial identity, as in Africa, when it becomes attached to a particular territory should be reclassified as national.

If these examples of human gregariousness indicate an inborn aptitude for group attachment, then it should be possible to test for its presence in adults. The small-scale Oklahoma experiment on school boys has already been described as indicating the likely presence of such a faculty and of how a sense of *we-ness* can be aroused in a matter of days. In this chapter small-scale examples of identity formation in adults will now be considered, achieved in a matter of months rather than days, but also resulting in the deliberate manufacture of group consciousness centred around the names or numbers of military units, most of which the recruits had never heard of before. Esprit de corps is, of course, none other than military group consciousness. In this type too, economic factors can play no part. Nor, in the British examples about to be given were prior linguistic, racial, class or religious loyalties usually involved. However in some of the Indian examples, prior identities of class or race certainly existed in the shape of loyalty strands thought likely to contribute to a sense of regimental pride and distinctiveness.

This book may seem already to have contained enough about civil and national warfare without now proceeding to consider the esprit de corps of fighting units. But the latter goes beyond mere military interest. Indeed the very facility with which it can be induced is perhaps the most revealing of all examples of this underlying human characteristic. It was moreover the origin of the book itself, whose purpose, it must be repeated, is directed towards the riddance or curtailment of warfare rather than its promotion.

Recent experiments by sociopsychologists on the social identification of individuals have mostly involved small groups of students used as dummies to display social identity, but with no opportunity for observing wider loyalties and allegiances. The Oklahoma experiment could not show the latter. It is difficult too under confined laboratory conditions to observe the different levels and strengths of identification of which human beings are capable. It is even hard to find groups of adults prepared to be brigaded into lasting groups for no other purpose than to observe their group identification and resultant loyalties. The human 'guinea pigs' involved would anyway be likely to act up to their outside observers. But, in the military sphere, their group consciousness is readily induced for national reasons and thus provides the very evidence now needed.

These small-scale examples now proferred of the group attachment trait in operation are as valuable as wider manifestations and are also easier to observe contemporaneously rather than historically. Above all, they show the capacity of the single individual to experience esprit de corps at more than one level and at different levels of intensity at the same time. It is thus a multilevel capacity being observed which will, in a later chapter, be used as evidence in connection with multinational states.

The units to which soldiers are induced to feel they belong may be said to have a good esprit de corps, or, in contrast, to suffer from a lack of it. It is the same with national identity and its resultant changes in morale. But the study of military identities goes further in enabling one readily to see how and why it is that human beings, once closely identified with a regiment, are prepared to die for it as selflessly as any tribal warrior for his tribe or patriot for his country. This therefore provides an insight into human warfare and its causes and again confirms the presence of a group attachment trait causing individuals to sink their self-conscious selves in that of a collectively conscious group to which they feel they belong.

The motive is not just individualistic reciprocity, but aroused feelings of group consciousness and attachment.

It must be emphasised, however, that viewing these military examples is not to suggest that regimentation is generally to be commended in peace time. Very much the reverse, for this would be to commend the totalitarian State. Nevertheless, it is important to observe the initial purposes of military training and in particular the deliberate inducement of young recruits to identify artificially with those units to which they have been designated. The very speed with which their subsequent identification is aroused provides strong evidence of a human proneness in this direction, already noted among young children. It also reveals a ready tendency to identify not only with the names of military units, but even with their random numbers and initials.

Esprit de corps can thus be artificially aroused and used to override other existing identities of race, class, language or religion simply by appeal to human collective feelings. Even distinctions of colour, that most telling of all hallmarks, can thus be overridden by requiring recruits of different races to wear the same distinctive uniform and answer proudly to the regimental name or number as being their own.

Group consciousness does not need therefore to be always of a national or racial variety but can focus upon any human grouping if its members are induced to feel a sense of pride or *we-ness*.

THE GURKHA BRIGADE

The human facility for group attachment is best illustrated by taking the most extreme example possible. This is the inducement of a sense of group consciousness between Nepalese hill tribesmen of Mongol race and Hindu lower caste on the one hand; and, on the other, of white English-speaking officers of European race and Christian religion. It is indeed difficult to think of two more diverse groups of individuals among whom to try to induce collective identification. For this involves individuals with separate identity strands who normally, and on a larger scale, would regard themselves as belonging to entirely different nations.

That it is possible to manufacture the combined esprit de corps of the Gurkha Brigade amongst such diverse peoples proudly answering to the Gurkha name is an important 'test' of the basic nature of group consciousness proving indeed, that it is probably a basic aptitude shared by all human races.

The process itself and the new loyalties thereby engendered is described in the British Army Manual for the Brigade of Gurkhas, four battalions of which still serve in the British Army today, and more numerous battalions of which once served in the former British Army of India.

The name Gurkha derives from that of an eighteenth century Hindu king who extended his kingdom to become what is now Nepal, and whose inhabitants answer to the name of Nepalese and speak the Nepali language, an offshoot of Sanskrit. The Gurkha name however is now only a military one answered to by mercenaries trained to fight on behalf of other nations. The Nepalese army are not called Gurkhas.

The loyalties of ordinary Nepalese are to tribe and to the kingdom of Nepal. By treaty the British have long been allowed to recruit in Nepal for their Gurkha regiments. When once part of the British Indian army, the officers of the Gurkha Brigade proudly knew themselves as Gurkha and not Indian officers to maintain their distinction.

In two world wars these hill tribesmen sustained 45,000 killed out of 450,000 recruited, fighting not for Nepal but for Britain. They manned 42 infantry battalions in the Second World War. As such they might be regarded as true mercenaries prepared to kill others, or to be killed themselves merely for money. Certainly the money is the main initial attraction to recruiting although only 25 per cent of what a British recruit receives. Hiring out the best of its manpower to Britain and India also provides the Kingdom of Nepal with about one-third of its foreign currency. But that is to overlook their esprit de corps, uncomplicated by patriotism, and geared to the honour and glory of the Gurkha Brigade and the several regimental battalions of which it is composed.

On the partition of India in 1947, by tripartite agreement between the governments of Nepal, Britain and India, six Gurkha regiments went to India and the rest to Britain. Britain was allowed to continue to recruit and train Gurkhas in Nepal, with their passage guaranteed through India to a training centre, since moved to Hong Kong. So the training process still continues for awhile and its results may be seen today in the smart turnout and fighting ability of the British Gurkhas. Now reduced in number, they comprise the Sirmoor Rifles, Queen Elizabeth's Own Gurkha Rifles, the Duke of Edinburgh's Own Gurkha Rifles and Princess Mary's Own Gurkha Rifles.

The recruits to these regiments all come from the Gurung, Magar, Limbus and Rais hill tribes near Mount Everest and are selected from the lower Hindu caste of peasants. The higher warrior caste is reserved for the Nepalese army. The recruits to Gurkha regiments are all 18-year-old youths recruited annually according to regimental requirements from the areas mentioned. Some bring with them their father's pride in the Regiment; others do not. The chosen recruits are then flown via an Indian transit camp to the training centre in Hong Kong. Here they are transformed from bewildered youths—few of whom have been beyond their hill valleys, let alone in a jet aircraft—into men proud of every inch of their new-found selves and above all conscious of being members of the famous Gurkha Brigade.

This transformation is achieved at the Hong Kong training centre as described by the Army Manual:

> For a period of half a year upwards (depending on circumstances) the hill man, raw, unco-ordinated, unorientated, is worked on by kindness, discipline and repetition until that great, great day when he is inspected by a very senior officer and marches past the saluting base; a new recruit at the start of the parade, a trained soldier at the end. Cynics will say that during the first five months of a Gurkha soldier's life all the initiative is slammed out of him and it takes five years (the normal time it takes to be recommended for lance corporal) to put it all back again. As in every half truth, a glib assertion is easy but inaccurate. Human nature being what it is, we have produced what is reckoned on balance to be as fine an end of product for that stage in a young man's life as anywhere else. The insistence on a very high standard is the capital outlay which pays such high dividends throughout a man's service . . . it is not the place here to give a weary catalogue of syllabi and training programmes. Suffice it to say that within a year of starting his long journey, the hill man arrives at his parent unit, battalion of infantry or regiment of signals or engineers, keen, smart, bursting to show his prowess and to prove himself, and very much aware that only now is he on the threshold of it all, man's service in the Brigade of Gurkhas.

At the end of his training period each recruit is required to take a solemn Oath of Allegiance to the British Sovereign.

The Manual does not go into the purpose of initial drill parades with their accent on smartness, uniformity of appearance and bearing. These mechanical aids to inspiring group pride will be considered later in this chapter. The success, however, of the end-product is plain to see in an esprit de corps shared both by officers and men which begets its own sense of loyalty and allegiance quite independent of pre-existing loyalties.

It was expressed by a British officer, Sir Richard Turner, writing of his old comrades in his dictionary of the Nepali language whose use is compulsory within the Regiment:

> As I write these words, my thoughts return to you who were my comrades, the stubborn and indomitable peasants of Nepal. Once more I hear the laughter with which you greeted every hardship. Once more I see you in your bivouacs or about your camp fires, on forced marches or in trenches, now shivering with wet and cold, now scorched by a pitiless sun. Uncomplaining you endure hunger and thirst and wounds; and at last your unwavering lines disappear into the smoke and din of battle. Bravest of the Brave, most generous of the generous, never had a country more faithful friends than you!

It will be noted that the higher national loyalties of British and Nepalese never took second place to this smaller loyalty. While a British Gurkha officer might think that he was prepared to die only on behalf of his country this could hardly be said of the Nepalese other ranks. In battle it was always the Regiment which counted most.

BRITISH INDIAN REGIMENTS

The esprit de corps of Indian regiments under the British Raj proved equally capable of overriding the rival identities of Hindu and Muslim Indians within their ranks in a way incapable of being achieved among the inhabitants of the continent as a whole. It even managed to survive the fierce animosities and clash of loyalties at the time of Indian partition.

The Indian Army was, and indeed still is, organised on British regimental lines. That is to say regimental training depots trained soldiers for the infantry battalions of each regiment in the regimental tradition giving each one a sense of identity focused primarily on his own regiment with corresponding loyalties and allegiances. These regimental loyalties were such that both Muslim and Hindus could be included in the same battalions, so happily indeed that the penultimate British Viceroy thought that using his all-Indian Army he might have been able to hold the whole of the Indian Continent together.

The regimental loyalties still linger on in the separate new armies of India and Pakistan. It is important to see how such trans-sectarian identities were created in order to understand how, on a larger scale, disparate or bi-national nations can be held together within an overall sense of identity. For the British managed to recruit and contain within the same regiments companies or squadrons each separately composed of Hindus or Muslims. Reasons of ritual and diet nevertheless decreed that these companies or squadrons could not in themselves be religiously mixed. Nor could Hindus of different religious class or caste be made to live together.

The words class and caste are used interchangeably in India, for a caste is only a religiously induced class into which one happens to be born and from which religion forbids escape. It is not a socio-economic one.

Unlike the other presidential armies of the earlier days of British rule, the original Bombay Army prided itself in taking no account of class or caste. Later all the presidential armies and finally the all-Indian Army came to use Hindu hereditary classes in the furtherance of esprit de corps. Indeed by the end of the nineteenth century, about two-fifths of the Army was comprised of class regiments. In the remainder, the caste system was also becoming established even in southern regiments from Madras and Bombay. The recruiting system was reorganised in 1897 and again in 1922 with the merger of many regiments into larger ones with joint training facilities and with recruiting offices in different centres for particular classes also referred to as the 'martial races', like Pathans or Sikhs. Hindus from the Rajput warrior caste were preferred and they even had separate regiments to themselves.

Originally all regiments had white British officers who firmly identified with names like Rajput or Sikh—even describing themselves as such and, where appropriate, wearing turbans although not really Rajputs or Sikhs at all. They nevertheless regarded themselves as being through identification with their comrades-in-arms.

According to the military year book of 1970, the Indian Army still continues to recruit soldiers upon a class basis. The year book states: 'The Indian Army is drawn from nearly every stratum of Indian life in every part of the country, and is composed of more than twenty "classes" each of which is virtually a fighting class on its own.'

This system of class recruitment, however, meant that in 1947 those regiments which contained subunits of different classes also comprised individuals of different religious faith, whether Hindu, Sikh or Muslim. Hence such regiments could not survive as complete units upon Partition, however happily their Hindu and Muslim companies of infantry or squadrons of cavalry had previously lived together. In the month of Ramadan, when from dawn to dusk devout Muslims must abstain from food and water, Hindus had in the past freely volunteered to do all their Muslim comrades' regimental duties. Now with Partition all this was ended. Complete regiments of Muslims, like the Frontier Force and Baluch regiments, were transferred to Pakistan; but their Sikh and Dogra companies had to be detached and transferred to the Sikh and Dogra regiments of the now separate Army of India. The Punjab regiment managed to survive the massacres on its own home ground and has since re-emerged as the separate Punjab regiments of Pakistan and India which have even fought against each other.

The pipes and drums of the Punjab Regiment of Pakistan, clad in Scottish tartan still beat retreat in the Shalimar Gardens of Lahore while the regimental depot remains at Mardan. Many Pakistan regiments remain affiliated to old British counterparts, and old regimental reunions still occur between British and Pakistani officers of the Frontier Force Rifles. In Pakistan the officers keep up the old mess traditions although the loyal toasts are no longer drunk to the King–Emperor but to the President of Pakistan. Many Pakistani regiments still have regimental shrines in British churches.

In 1947, Hindu regiments like the Central India Horse, also had to say farewell to their Muslim squadrons to become entirely Hindu regiments in the new army of India. As in Pakistan, however, the old British regimental traditions and the esprit de corps of these regiments still live on. The modern Indian Army still contains regiments like the Gurkhas, the Punjab regiment, the Mahratta Light Infantry, the Rajputana Rifles and the Rajput regiment, each with its own sense of tradition stretching back into the British years. It also contains many of the old British cavalry regiments still carrying the proud names of their founding colonels, like Skinner's Horse and Hodson's Horse. The horses have of course long been substituted by tanks or armoured cars, but the troopers still wear their spurs on ceremonial occasions as well as resplendent full dress uniforms like turbanned Life Guards.

Some of these Indian regiments used to bear royal British suffixes such as Duke of Connaught's Own, King George V's Own Light Infantry or Duke of Cambridge's Own—all dating from earlier days when Indian cavalrymen still felt a degree of loyalty to the King–Emperor.

In 1950 when India finally became a Republic, those regiments with the title of Royal had to discard it along with their insignia of King's colours or standards which then had to be replaced by national ones. Each Indian regiment then staged an impressive presentation ceremony at which the old colours were trooped with full military honours and the President of India awarded new colours for infantry and standards for cavalry. These ceremonies were attended by large numbers of old British officers who commented favourably on the high standard of drill, smart turn-out and the excellence of the regimental bands.

As described in the British Army review for 1971, two plane loads of old British members of Skinner's Horse, including the great-great-grandson of its founder, Colonel *James Skinner*, were flown out to India for the presentation of a new regimental standard by the Indian President.

The British contingent found their officers' mess, now at Jhansi, still watched over, as it always had been, by their old Muslim mess waiter, remaining from the days when the regiment used to have a Muslim squadron, now lost to Pakistan. In the mess, all the old regimental silver and trophies were kept polished to perfection. Even the old photograph albums of former days were treasured. The First of Cavalry or *A wul Risula*—as Skinner's horsemen proudly call themselves—now had Sikh, Jat and Rajput class squadrons— but of course no Muslim ones. At the ceremony the different religious priests each said separate blessings over the new standard to be presented. The silk for it had been donated by the visiting British contingent who were publicly

thanked for creating and upholding the great traditions of the Regiment—
sentiments of thanks that would hardly be expressed by India as a whole.
Then followed the march past by all the regimental tanks with their guns
dipped in salute and their crews superbly turned out standing up in the
turrets. Away out in front was the Commanding Officers' tank and painted
on its side in enormous letters the single word JAMES!

BRITISH REGIMENTS AND HIGHER FORMATIONS

To see how military loyalties of such strength and persistence can be forged
—and once forged so endure—we now turn to the British regimental system
itself on which the Gurkha and Indian regiments were modelled.

The British regimental system differs from that of the Soviet, German or
American armies in its creation of small regimental families in which most
soldiers get to know each other and in which they can usually expect,
throughout their military service, to remain. But it is less appropriate for
total warfare on a continental scale with huge casualties requiring instant
replacement and a consequent need for extra-regimental cross-postings. It is,
however, better suited to the professional role of peace-keeping than a largely
changing army of conscripts.

In peacetime, British regiments only contain one or two battalions. These
are collectively known as *the* Regiment to all members. Even soldier's wives
are induced to feel they have married into the regimental family whose
confines, however, can prove restrictive. But all are nevertheless made to feel
they really belong and that the regiment looks after its own.

The oldest existing regiment in the British Army is the Royal Scots or 'First
of Foot', raised originally in Scotland as mercenaries for the King of France.
They were later withdrawn into British service when there seemed some
danger of them being used to fight English regiments prior to the union of
Great Britain.

The Household Division is the British equivalent of the former French
Maison Du Roi. It contains two cavalry regiments, the Life Guards and the
Royal Horse Guards (the 'Blues'), the latter having originally been raised on
the revolutionary side during the Civil War to fight the King. The Household
Division also comprises five regiments of Foot Guards, the Grenadiers,
Coldstream, Scots, Welsh and Irish Guards. The Coldstream Guards were
again originally raised, as General Monk's regiment, as the infantry core of
the revolutionary army during the Civil War. The Irish and Welsh Guards
were raised during the present century. The Foot Guards have for over three
centuries guarded British sovereigns and fought British wars in the name of
Sovereign and Regiment. They have also done so, like the Gurkhas, quite
regardless of foe. During this period they have been required to fight both on
the side of as well as against the armies of France, Holland, Spain, Austria,
Prussia, Russia, the United States, Italy and Egypt.

The Irish Guards incidentally still manage to recruit from both parts of
Ireland, to include both Protestants and Catholics and have Catholic padres.

With such blinkered loyalties and identities centred on the Regiment and with soldiers even prepared to die for it and their comrades it is necessary to investigate how such group consciousness is achieved. The answer is not to be found in human male aggressivity or economic compulsion but rather in the factor of loyalty and allegiance to the Regiment to which, above all else, soldiers are induced to feel they belong.

On the outbreak of war in 1939 the 78 British infantry regiments then existing had hurriedly to be expanded to meet the national demand. This placed regimental training depots under extreme strain. Towards the end of the war, some regiments tended to run out of new recruits, no longer available from the general population, and so had to merge their battalions; or even take in men from other regiments. Nevertheless the small British regimental 'family' system did just manage, albeit with difficulty, to take the strain.

The initial expansion in 1939 involved the rapid expansion of all existing regiments by several battalions—rather than the creation of new ones with no tradition or esprit de corps behind them. All regiments, therefore, now found themselves having to expand to several battalions with the new recruits and the new satellite battalions to be trained in the old regimental tradition and mould. This meant imbuing the new recruits, in a matter of months rather than years, with a sense of pride and of belonging to a regiment into which they were drafted, and the name of which most had never heard before.

Some regiments had to expand by only one or two battalions, but others by many more. The Argyll and Sutherland Highlanders had to expand to nine battalions, the Black Watch to ten, the Queen's Own Cameron Highlanders to seven, the Royal East Kents (the Buffs) to nine, the Royal Welsh Fusiliers to ten, the Cameronians to seven, the Coldstream Guards to six and the Scots Guards to four.

In order to man these extra wartime battalions, each regimental training depot had therefore to train conscript recruits to share the old identities. The regimental fighting formation was the infantry battalion comprising about 800 soldiers, all trained at the same regimental training depot to regard themselves as belonging to the same regimental family. The Regiment was thus their first and main focus of identity. It was to a regiment's name and uniform that the recruit's loyalties were first attracted. 'Once an Argyll, always an Argyll.'

It is the tribal tendency to form loyalties and to stick to them upon which the British regimental system so effectively plays. In short it makes deliberate use of the group attachment trait so vital to human relations, particularly in the military field. It is strange that the British have never applied the same methods to industrial relations, as their wartime opponents, the Japanese, have so successfully done. The harnessing of the loyalty trait in the military sphere was able to produce lethal tight-knit units of tribal males with the most intense sense of mutual aid in the service of country—or, like, the Gurkhas, any country which cared to train them.

It is difficult to appreciate the strain which active service in the front line places upon the individual soldier, and the harsh demands, including the supreme sacrifice, which are required of him. It needs the soldier's selfless devotion and loyalty rather than any mere display of individual aggressiveness. These demands a soldier cannot meet as an isolated individual without the protective support of a regiment which looks after its own and which is also sufficiently small for him to feel he really belongs. To describe the soldier's selfless behaviour in action as solely the pleasurable expression of fixed aggressive instincts is to miss the point. It is also wrong to describe his motives as 'reciprocal altruism'.

Many regimental battalions during the 1939–45 war lost their frontline personnel several times over. The men knew this and the odds against them, which could hardly be surmounted by thoughts of aggression. A soldier, however, can still endure when he has a group to identify with. For he can then sink his individual self in the wider self and it becomes more a question of comradeship or of fighting for one another. Hence the need to stimulate a sense of esprit de corps centred on the regiment in whose name and on whose behalf soldiers are prepared to die.

The American combat analyst S. L. A. Marshall has written:

> I hold it to be one of the simplest truths of war that the thing which enables an infantry soldier to keep going with his weapons is the near presence or presumed presence of a comrade.

In the smoke of battle the nation is hardly seen and patriotism plays a lesser part than is usually supposed. it is more the confined patriotism of the regiment which wins battles. For wider patriotism can hardly inspire the Gurkhas or indeed those other mercenaries, the French Foreign Legion, few of whose legionaires are actually French; but whose new recruits, after only a few months initial and rigorous indoctrination, acquire an exceptionally strong sense of identity centred on the Legion in the service of France.

The purpose of initial military training to this end is well described by the social anthropologist and psychiatrist W H Rivers in a report (1918) for the Medical Research Council entitled *War-Neurosis and Military Training*. In this report Rivers described the chief aims of initial training to be to fit each individual soldier to act in harmony with his fellows, and to enable him to withstand the stresses and trials of warfare and so overcome his instinct of self-preservation. He wrote:

> In fulfilling the first aim of adapting the soldier to act as one of an aggregate in complete harmony with its other members, one agency is habituation. The elementary drill of a soldier consists of processes in which this agency plays a most important part. . . . One of the chief instruments by which this aim is met is that already considered, which makes the individual soldier act as a member of the aggregate to which he belongs in a closer sense than holds good in civil life. This does away with or diminishes greatly the tendency of any one individual in the group to react to fear or other emotional state in a way which would interfere with his military competence.

During the Second World War, British conscripts called up for military service were sometimes given a choice of regiment, particularly of any local one in which their fathers had served. Mostly, however, recruits brought no existing regimental identity with them to the regiment into whose ranks they now found themselves drafted. The transformation, however, of civilians into regimental soldiers able to withstand the stresses of war was not all that difficult. The methods used were at first purely physical. They were drilled to move physically in unison and to see themselves moving as a group in response to orders from their own NCOs and officers. There was thus instilled an abiding respect for discipline. Initially at least, there was no appeal to reason or training in weapons or tactics. That came later once the recruits had become aware of themselves as members of particular units, in contrast to others.

The Australian wartime journalist, Allan Moorehead, wrote of the Gazala battle in 1942:

> The drill, the saluting, the uniform, the very badges on your arm all tend to identify you with a solid machine and build up a feeling of security and order. In the moment of danger the soldier turns to his mechanical habits and draws strength from them.

This purely physical and irrational process leading to group identification is best seen by considering the formation of regimental identities in the worst of all possible circumstances, namely where there were pre-existing rival attachments which had to be overridden. The process was nevertheless the same as used on new recruits to British, Gurkha or Indian regiments.

Towards the end of the Second World War many units of the Foot Guards, like other regiments, began to run out of their own regimental recruits, but as Household troops were better placed than some for avoiding cross-postings. Both the Scots and Coldstream Guards were, however, forced, near the end of the war, to take transfers of men from the Royal Air Force Regiment set up initially to guard home aerodromes. They successfully insisted, however, before returning to battle, on being allowed a few months' grace to convert these RAF Regiment men into their own regimental soldiers with corresponding new loyalties. The 2nd Battalion Scots Guard was brought home in depleted form after the Italian campaign and was made up to strength again for the invasion of Germany by adding about 350 new RAF Regiment recruits to man all the frontline infantry companies. The identity of the RAF Regiment was anti-Army and anti-infantry in particular, because they were really Air Force. Indeed they arrived wearing blue as opposed to Khaki uniforms. Furthermore they did not at first care for the hauteur of the Guards. Their new host regiments also regarded them as if they were differently coloured immigrants which is indeed what they were.

The Scots and Coldstream Guards only had six months before going into action again in which to induce the newcomers to identify as *us* in contrast to *them*.

To digress, this was nevertheless a better situation than that faced by some shattered battalions in the Italian campaign which had to be quickly reformed in the front line with men from different regiments, including cavalry officers, rushed up from base. The result of this attempt to mix men from different social groups and expect them to integrate immediately in the front line was usually a disaster. There was even a mutiny on the Salerno beaches by individual soldiers who refused, on being landed as reinforcements, to be sent up the line to any other regiment than their own. It was their very regimental loyalties which were their undoing. The results were better in North Africa when there were a few weeks of training time available for the Cameron Highlanders to integrate as 'Camerons' a reinforcement draft of some 200 Leicesters and Sherwood Foresters. Yet, until the end of the war these were jocularly known as 'the Free British'. The occasional Englishman, however, recruited into the Camerons from the start of his military life was regarded as just as much as a 'Jock' as anyone else and therefore to have a new national, or indeed tribal identity, imposed upon him.

Such a loyalty transformation was now what had to be achieved with the new RAF Regiment recruits to the Scots and Coldstream Guards. That it could be done at all, however imperfectly, provides an interesting example of how existing human loyalties may exceptionally sometimes be changed. Few are therefore entirely irreversible.

When the new recruits arrived in camp their strange blue uniforms were whisked off them and replaced by khaki battledress. They were pounced upon by the regimental drill sergeants as a bunch of RAF riff-raff and for several weeks were paraded up and down in drill attachments by platoon and companies until they could hold themselves erect, take some pride in their new appearance and conduct basic drill movements in unison.

By drilling soldiers into a sense of uniformity, the members of each unit then come physically to act and, above all, perceive themselves on parade to act, as one man. The suggestive patter of the drill sergeants was incessant. The first ten minutes of each drill period was expended in 'warming up' or 'chasing' in double quick time—left turn, right turn, about turn, Halt!— and woe betide the man who ended up facing in the wrong direction. A growing sense of uniformity, however, began to outweigh the fear of, and indeed the necessity of, punishment which could then be moved into the background.

Every regiment has its own peculiarities of drill and when someone made a wrong movement he would be snarled at and told he was not in the 'bloody so and so's'—or some other outside unit. It was like the Bull Dogs and Red Devils writ large, but with the rival identities even more actively encouraged.

A great deal of this patter ('bullshit' in army parlance) was purposely humorous. During the panting intervals of 'stand easy', regimental questions (the equivalent of national or tribal mythology) were fired at the new recruits until they knew all the right answers. There was great emphasis on regimental tradition, history and battle honours and awards. Then there was the enforced saluting (symbolic of obedience) of all officers who had to salute back in return. Bullshit not only embraced the crude enforcement of homogeneity mentioned by Rivers, but also the crude recognition of distinctions and the contrived regimental prejudices which were the other side of the coin. Nicknames abounded and the Germans the recruits were about to fight were referred to as Jerries or Krauts.

Battalion parades were important group occasions. The parade ground itself was sacred territory across which every man had to march properly to attention. On battalion parade the new recruits were able to see exactly where they fitted into the various platoons and companies of their new battalion and to see its hierarchy of officers—to whom military obedience was owed—standing out in front. There was thus a great appeal to the visual senses. They could see who their leaders were and they thus became less remote. This was loyalty formation in a face-to-face situation and the unit was sufficiently small for each man to become properly conscious of 'his own'.

All platoons and companies had numbers and letters. It was not long before each recruit began naturally to identify himself with the particular number of his platoon or the letter of his company. Above all, he came to regard himself as belonging to a particular battalion of the Regiment which he came to regard as his own and superior to all others.

There is no better way of enforcing a sense of uniformity among a conglomeration of individuals than by making them wear the same distinctive uniform, that is, one that singles them out as belonging to the same group—but which also serves to distinguish them from others.

In the interlude between body armour and camouflage—and indeed up to the present century—soldiers dressed in splendid and distinctive uniforms in which they actually fought. These were specially designed by military tailors for each regiment, and men dressed themselves like peacocks in order to kill their fellows. The 11th Hussars led the Charge of the Light Brigade in the Crimea wearing pink tights, fur-trimmed jackets and shakoes. Some of these military uniforms—now worn only on ceremonial occasions—incorporate the furs of other animals such as bears, leopards, seals and even badgers. Headdresses of some of the Scottish Highland regiments were concocted out of ostrich plumes and the tails of blackcock. Other animals—including dogs, goats and ponies—are also still used as regimental mascots. Little has changed when it comes to tribal finery. In the American Civil War some of the Union regiments dressed up as North African Zouaves in embroidered waistcoats and billowing red trousers in order to fight their southern compatriots.

In the British army, the field, as opposed to ceremonial, uniform was now a dull khaki battledress into which, as already mentioned, the RAF Regiment recruits were transferred when they joined the Scots or Coldstream Guards. It could therefore only be the blue or red shoulder flashes, each bearing regimental name, and the distinctive peaked caps with separate cap-stars, which served as visible ensigns of regimental distinction.

As time went on, the RAF regiment recruits were subjected to fewer drill parades and increasingly trained in weapon and fighting techniques under actual fighting conditions. Over a period of six months, the process successfully overrode an alien identity in the shape of former loyalty to another regiment with a new loyalty to a new regiment which now became *we* or *us* to all the newcomers. At the end of six months, the new recruits were regarded as sufficiently integrated to be ready to take part in the invasion of Germany. Although not perhaps such committed Guardsmen as recruits received from the regimental depot, these RAF Regiment recruits had been sufficiently integrated. If anyone asked what they were, they would answer 'I am a Coldstreamer' or 'I am a Scots Guardsman'. For that is what they had now become.

Wider identities, however, above the level of regimental battalions, also existed in the British as in other continental Armies, centred on the higher formations of brigades, divisions, corps and even occasionally Field Armies. The British (and Indian) system was only peculiar in concentrating esprit de corps at the level of regimental battalions which was better suited to a small professional army.

The 7th, 11th and the Guards Armoured Divisions, however, all had strong esprit de corps of their own. Like other types of identity, esprit de corps does not need to be confined only to one level. Infantry divisions whose soldiers had fought side by side for most of the war also acquired a distinctive spirit and character. Such were the 15th (Scottish) with its Lion Rampant insignia and the 51st (Highland) Division with its blue HD on a red background. These two divisions also embodied a degree of Scottish national feeling—as did other national divisions like the New Zealand and Australian ones or the 4th Indian and 17th Indian Divisions. It was the same in the American and German armies with certain crack divisions like the American 82nd Airborne or the German 90th Light each proud of their individual names and emblems and sometimes even attracting the regard of military opponents. The Soviet Army too had its special crack Divisions including Guards Divisions.

Exceptionally, a whole Corps, like British 30 Corps, comprising three divisions, could attract some identity of its own under an outstanding commander; but, more usually, the component divisions of corps were so moved around for different military campaigns that there was insufficient permanency for individuals to develop a degree of distinction, at corps level. That a whole corps, however, can sometimes attract an esprit de corps of its own is demonstrated by the American Marine Corps with perhaps the finest fighting spirit of the US Army. It incorporates all arms. But on such a scale the initial time-honoured way of submerging the identity of the individual within his group—here a huge marine corps—is fairly brutal. All are shaven clean like monks at entry so as physically to change the individual's appearance. Their subsequent harrassment in the name of the group under extreme discipline backed by hard punishment is taken to the extreme. It is also coupled (as in the Soviet and German armies) with the taking of oaths of allegiance). The resultant esprit de corps created over a period of about four months is, however, impressive and, once aroused, the individual's harrassment can be dropped and his esprit de corps left to look after itself in conjunction with firmly united comrades.

The requirement of permanence, however, made it unlikely that a strong identity could attach to a whole Field Army which was usually too temporary and vast for most soldiers really to know what it was, in relation to others. The US Third Army under command of General George Patton however was a brilliant exception. They all knew their charismatic general. His army was kept together under his command all the way from North Africa through Sicily into North-West Europe. He brought to this army, who worshipped him, all the dashing appeal of a cavalry commander of the south wearing two pearl-handled revolvers and looking as if he should be wearing spurs.

The only complete British Armies in the Second World War to attract a strong identity were the 8th Army in North Africa, under Field Marshall Montgomery and the similarly isolated 'Forgotten' Fourteenth Army in Burma. Both were permanent formations whose components suffered little change. At the battle of El Alamein in 1942 under Montgomery's command, the 8th Army comprised two armoured and one infantry corps, the latter containing the 51st Highland, 4th Indian, 9th Australian, 2nd New Zealand and 1st South African Divisions. These were all national divisions from the British Commonwealth. Within each brigade of each division, however, were battalions of different regiments where the soldiers' strongest loyalties lay. The British 8th Army adapted their dull uniforms to include silk neck scarves, suede desert boots and white webbing equipment, the latter destroying their uniform's camouflage effect but which looked distinctive. Their speech even came to include a certain amount of 'Wog' lingo. An 8th Army man on leave could thus be readily distinguished from any other British soldier. If he had any cultural affinity with other units, it was more with his Afrika Korps opponents enjoying a similarity of desert lifestyle. Indeed post war annual reunions of 8th Army veterans have come to include some Afrika Korps veterans as well and in 1984 the salute at the march past was taken by the sons, standing side by side, of the late Field Marshalls Montgomery and Rommel.

When the 8th Army eventually defeated the Afrika Korps in North Africa and met the 1st British Army advancing eastwards, having just arrived from England, their meeting was less than enthusiastic. Each regarded the other, although British, as somewhat foreign. 8th Army regarded 1st Army men as different and felt they lacked the true 8th Army spirit, also that they did not yet really known how to fight. In contrast, these self-styled Desert Rats appeared to the men of the 1st Army to be unable to shake the sand from between their toes. The war ribbon granted to all participants for the North African Campaign was the Africa Star. But Montgomery insisted on his men being allowed to wear a number 8 in the middle of the ribbon to distinguish them. Possession of a number 8 thus became a proud hallmark of military distinction.

Except in North Africa and Burma, British Field Armies tended to be temporary amalgamations of different corps and divisions joined together for some major offensive. For example, at the Salerno landings in Italy in 1943, 201 Guards Brigade was taken out of the Eighth Army to which it felt it belonged and placed in a new division within a completely reconstituted corps. Its other British Divisions had been extracted from the 1st Army and then joined with an American corps to form the 'American' 5th Army commanded by an American general. Doubtless this made logistical sense. The result was, however, that there was no 5th Army spirit to compare with that of the 8th Army—nor was there at first even a divisional spirit shared by the men of 201 Guards Brigade who, despite orders to the contrary, resolutely refused to wear the divisional emblem of a black cat.

This tendency to refuse on amalgamation, or change of unit, to adopt another's insignia or uniform was also prevalent in the American Civil war. Kearney's famous battle-hardened 1st Division of 3rd Corps all used the red linings of their great coats to form a distinctive red band to their Kepis. When their depleted Corps was required to amalgamate with another the men themselves contrived a distinctive cap badge embodying the insignia of both corps rather than of the latter alone.

For the invasion of NW Europe in 1945 a 'Canadian' 1st Army was formed under command of a Canadian general, with British as well as Canadian Divisions. The former, however, could hardly be expected to identify as Canadians. Perhaps a simple number, comparable to that of the 8th Army, might have better enabled soldiers with different national identities to share a single military one.

This was indeed a binational situation akin to expecting the Irish to identify as British or English within a new 'United Kingdom of Great Britain and Ireland'. The comparison is not so far fetched when it is borne in mind that some of these Field Armies in which soldiers became collectively conscious were larger than many small nations. The Canadian regiments of the 1st Canadian Army, where the chief loyalties lay, comprised the 1st Canadian Scottish Regiment, the Cameron Highlanders of Ottawa, the Highland Light Infantry of Canada, the North Nova Scotia Highlanders, Le Regiment de la Chaudiere, the Regina Rifle Regiment, the Royal Rifles of Canada, the Royal Winnipeg Regiment, the Stormont Dundas and Glengarry Highlanders, the Winnipeg Grenadiers, the North Shore (New Brunswick) Regiment and the Queen's Own Rifles of Canada. These regiments were all trained on British regimental lines.

Unlike these close-knit regiments, the 'American' 5th and 1st 'Canadian' Armies, were large temporary formations, with no existing sense of pride or tradition to aid the individual's identification nor suitable names to answer to. It is easier for the individual to identify with smaller face-to-face societies whose principal members are actually known to him. Nevertheless a sense of we-ness can be artificially contrived if they are made to look alike while yet distinctive from others by wearing the same uniform or insignia. Group consciousness too can exist even in Field Armies if made to seem like segments of the nation on the march.

These then were some of the proud distinctions which soldiers of several nations shared at various levels in the Second World War, with the strongest loyalties in the British and Commonwealth Armies being with the Regiment. Some of these military loyalties still linger on among civilians long demobilised, as expressions of continuing identity or at least of nostalgia for lost comradeships by people now sadly deprived of anything with which to identify. Reunions are mostly of regiments, though there are also divisional and Army reunions, like those already mentioned.

With the persistence of regimental loyalties, once created, it is hardly surprising that postwar proposals to disband or amalgamate certain British regiments met with widespread opposition. Under this post-war reorganisation, to facilitate recruiting and joint training, 52 British infantry and cavalry regiments disappeared by absorption, amalgamation or disbandment. The preferred solution, where possible, was to try to combine two regimental identities, including the symbols of each regiment, in a new regimental badge and colours, and, above all, in a new combined regimental name.

The proposed amalgamation for instance, of the Seaforth and Cameron Highlanders caused much stress over such matters as a new regimental badge, new headgear, dress tartan and sporran. But the amalgamation emerged successfully under the new name of Queen's Own Highlanders. Some amalgamated names, however, like the Royal Scots Dragoon Guards (combining the Scots Greys and 3rd Carbiniers), were too complicated to use, and indeed the renaming of some of the amalgamated regiments presented as much of a problem as that of the United Kingdom itself.

The Argyll and Sutherland Highlanders refused to amalgamate with any other regiment and were thus ordered, like the Durham Light Infantry and other famous regiments, simply to disband. Only about 800 men were involved but they represented a Scottish tradition and the loyalties of thousands. A national petition was then launched by regimental veterans to 'Save the Argylls'. The petition collected no less than 1,086,590 separately checked signatures, many from overseas, before it was presented to Parliament in December 1968. In 1970, the single-battalion regiment was resurrected and continues in service to this day.

So the esprit de corps of regiments can be very persistent indeed. It is, however, human individuals, whether soldiers or civilians, who undergo the process of social identification. Their esprit de corps is merely the end-product which, once created, is not entirely irreversible.

7

Group Identity and Warfare

GROUP ANTAGONISM

Group identity in relation to warfare has two aspects. First, it can be used as an instrument of war by stimulating the esprit de corps of military units. Secondly, the group consciousness of peoples and their consequent sense of loyalty and allegiance provide the backing for a nation's capacity to wage war until the other side capitulates. However it must be remembered that warfare is not only international. There is also civil war, including its vicious sectarian variety, all of which are extensions of group antagonism.

So merely taming national antagonism need not eliminate belligerency.

By warfare, one does not of course mean fighting between individuals even when, like warfare, this happens to result in killing. Such can occur in a pub brawl when it will be charged as murder of a fellow citizen. Warfare, on the contrary, involves fighting between discernible groups and is usually conducted by armed forces against an enemy. It is carried on with selfless devotion to duty, but also with the entire occlusion of humanity towards the enemy who are stereotyped as evil. Far from the killing of an enemy being charged as murder, it is the occasion for public recognition of valour. The Fallen on one's own side are also buried with military honours.

In Iran, those now killed in the current war against Iraq, are even buried as martyrs who died from devotion to the Faith.

This moral dichotomy resulting from group identification is as old as history. In days gone by the treatment of defeated tribal enemies was to enslave or kill them. The fifth book of Moses called Deuteronomy contains the laws for the Children of Israel. One of the ten commandments in Chapter 5 Verse 17 is 'Thou shalt not kill.' Applying the ordinary canons of legal construction to the broader context, it is clear that this commandment meant only that one should not kill other Israelites. For in Chapter 7, verses 1 and 2, it is commanded: 'When the Lord thy God shall bring thee into the land whither thou goest to possess it, and has cast out many nations before thee, the Hittites and the Girgashites, and the Amorites, and the Canaanites, and the Perizzites, and the Hivites, and the Jebusites, seven nations greater and mightier than thou; and when the Lord thy God shall deliver them before thee, thou shalt smite them, and utterly destroy them; thou shalt make no covenant with them, nor show mercy unto them.'

It is later recounted how this was mercilessly done and how the enemies of the people can come to be viewed as the enemies of God.

A strong sense of group identity with feelings of *us* and *them* removes any sense of contradiction and has always tended to occlude humanitarian feelings towards an enemy, once group fear or anger is aroused. Then the foe are not regarded as being 'true' human beings at all.

This may indeed, like stereotyping, be part of a primitive defence mechanism.

Group identity as an instrument of war has just been described as well as its creation through individuals being taught to act like one man and regard the Regiment as family and home. Nepalese peasants were thus made capable of fighting for and dying for the Regiment rather than on behalf of Nepal where they originally belonged. A well-trained regiment is indeed the most lethal of military instruments for small scale fighting—being akin to the face-to-face tribal group or clan. Inwardly it may be seen to be composed of the nicest people; but outwardly it can be deadly.

The group identity of a whole nation, however, when mobilised for war, can be just as devastating in effect and just as persistent. During the Second World War the morale of the German population survived intact until virtually the end, despite appalling casualties and the flattening by aerial bombardment of most German cities. Their loyalty, to Germany, and to each other held them together. So with the Soviet people at Moscow, Stalingrad and Leningrad whose national morale prevailed despite 20 million killed.

In modern total warfare a sense of national identity and commitment is even more vital than in former days. Under Napoleon in the revolutionary armies of France, total warfare began to call for total popular involvement and not just formal battles fought between regular armies. The whole people are now engaged in warfare with the killing becoming more and more widespread. Indeed total warfare as now conducted with the modern weapons of mankind has become too dangerous to continue.

So one has to ask the question, why does widespread warfare need to continue and what are its causes?

MARX'S VIEWS ON WARFARE

It has already been observed how primitive tribesmen identified by clan or tribe and were apt to fight periodically with tribal opponents who interfered with or strayed into their food-gathering or hunting grounds. There is no evidence whatsoever to support Rousseau's notion of a primitive ideal world, prior to the introduction of agriculture, when no man's hand was ever raised against his neighbour and to which, if only we knew how, we could by some magic find the key and return. Even the apparently benign and now scattered Kalahari bushmen remain loyal only to clan and used to have their tribal forays against tribal opponents.

The problem of group identity and human warfare was one to which Marx and Engels gave much thought producing a theory of group consciousness based on class warfare. Their Communist Manifesto of 1847 describing the International Class Struggle was published just before Darwin's *Origin of Species* in relation to which Marx immediately wrote to Engels saying 'Darwin's book is very important and serves me as a basis in natural science for the class struggle in history'. The opening words of the Manifesto itself were: 'The history of all hitherto existing society is the history of class struggles'. In a later footnote to the English edition Engels explained that their theory was only intended to apply to all *written* history because, in 1847, the pre-history of society was all but unknown. He added that since then the American anthropologist Morgan (1877) had laid bare the organisation of the primitive *gens* and of its relation to the tribe in his studies of the now pacified Iroquois.

Marx was particularly excited with this antropological study and determined to publish as his greatest work a book on tribes and races dealing with the early stages of mankind and explaining the economic basis for each phase of human progressive development. But, despite a dozen years still to live and although making copious notes on Morgan's *Ancient Society* he was unable to fulfil his intentions. It was thus left to Engels, as he said in sacred trust, and using Marx's notes, to supply the economic sub-stratum to Morgan's anthropological study which Engels entitled *The origins of the family, private property and the State in the light of the researches of Lewis H Morgan* (1884).

It makes strange reading today.

Marx and Engels' theory of group consciousness was later adapted by Lenin and Stalin and later still by Mao Tse Tung. Nevertheless their main thesis remains, namely, that the level of development of the means of production in any given society determines the formation of classes and that, in turn, determines the relationship of individuals to each other. On that economic base rests what Marx calls the superstructure of ideologies, including religion, philosophy and art. As he wrote in his preface to the *Critique of Political Economy* (1859):

> In the social production of their life, men enter into definite relations that are indispensable and independent of their will. Relations of production which correspond to a definite stage of development of their material productive forces. The sum total of these relations of production constitutes the economic structure of society, the real foundation on which rises a legal and political superstructure and to which corresponds definite forms of social consciousness. The mode of production in material life determines the social, political and intellectual life process in general. It is not the consciousness of men that determines their being, but, on the contrary, their social being that determines their consciousness.

Economic substructure is thus seen as the cause of all group consciousness. Remove the economic inequalities beneath and all group antagonism will automatically cease and international peace prevail.

In positing this economic basis to all social antagonism Marx, however, suggested no social mechanism which could operate even on young children to make them class or nationally conscious. He indeed disregards national and tribal feelings and does not completely explain class consciousness itself. The last page he ever wrote (Capital Vol III p 862) stated, 'The first question to be answered is this: what constitutes a class?'. After naming various distinctive economic groups the text then peters out without suggesting why some were group conscious and some were not. Yet he did come near an explanation of class consciousness in *The German Ideology* (p 41) when he wrote:

> The class making a revolution appears from the very start, merely because it is opposed to a class, not as a class but as the representative of the whole of society; it appears as the whole mass of society confronting the one ruling class.

But for the abstract word 'society' needs to be substituted the word 'nation' so as to clarify the different levels of identification. Marx's failure to comprehend these different identity levels misled him as to the nature and causes of class and other group feelings. Above all he abstracted himself from the international scene appearing in some of his works almost to equate the word 'society' with the whole human race. Yet the essence of *societas* is the feeling of group consciousness with a consequent sense of loyalty and allegiance. Hence a class is only a *segment* of a wider national identity which it may, however, as in Marx's revolutionary example, sometimes supplant.

Nevertheless economic factors may indirectly cause class consciousness which is not, however, the only form of group consciousness and may even be transformed into national identity. But the means of production do not cause religious, linguistic or racial identities, let alone esprit de corps.

Hence Marx and Engels theory of social antagonism is certainly incomplete. Despite their pioneer interest in social antagonism, neither provided a sufficient explanation of why primitive tribes, let alone complete nations, tend to identify as such and to fight each other even doing so against their best economic interests. Nor do they explain why social ownership of all the means of production by a nation-state should make that state and its constituent people less belligerent.

Such 'economic' explanations of warfare, however, still persist. Chairman Mao Tse Tung (1936) maintained the same view when he wrote:

> War is the highest form of struggle for resolving contradictions, when they have developed to a certain stage, between classes, nations, states, or political groups and it has existed ever since the emergence of private property and of classes.

Views akin to these are also still expressed by some western social scientists. Thus Reynolds (1976):

Frequent hostility between groups is much more likely to be a recent cultural innovation, resulting from the settled economy from agriculture, from pastoralism, and from property ownership, which made defence of territory more necessary than ever before.

Also Leakey and Lewin (1977):

It is possible to argue that this urge for group identification is the root of much of the conflict we have seen in the world: war would not be possible if people were not inclined to rally round their flag and fight for the good of their country, whatever that 'good' may be. To say, however, that the biological heritage of group identification and cooperation is the cause of war, would be the same as claiming that guns are the cause of war. Both simply represent the means by which war is waged. War only became possible when there was something to fight about; and here we must look back to the agricultural revolution, the transition from hunting and gathering to farming.

It is difficult to see however why a change from food gathering and the chase to settled agriculture should make humans more belligerent. Indeed one might have supposed the reverse.

Few biologists, however, now share such views. Nearer to the point are the observations of the biologist Morris (1978): 'Ironically, the inborn factor which is most likely to be making the major contribution to the savagery of modern war is the powerful human inclination to cooperate. This is a legacy from our ancient hunting past, when we had to cooperate or starve. It was the only way we could hope to defeat large prey animals. All that a modern dictator has to do is to play on this inherent sense of group-loyalty and to expand and organise this group into a full scale army. By converting the naturally helpful into the excessively patriotic, he can easily persuade them to kill strangers, not as acts of inborn brutality, but as laudable acts of companion-protection. If our ancestors had not become so innately co-operative, it might be much more difficult today to raise an army and send it into battle as an organised force.'

FREUD'S VIEWS ON WARFARE

The theories of Sigmund Freud provide no better explanation of the human tendency towards group-fighting. Indeed, Freudian or neo-Freudian 'cures' could well act as stimulants to greater group antagonism. Unlike the economic theories of Marx and Engels, Freud's approach was biological with the emphasis on individual fixed instincts deriving from our primate past. These were said by him to be the primary drives of erotic energy, on the one hand, and destructive energy on the other, which opposites he chose to call Eros and Thanatos. The more intense the repression in civilised societies of these two basic instincts the greater the discontent of modern civilisation and the greater pent-up aggressiveness which somehow required to be 'released' or sublimated.

Freud, however, eventually came to realise that this abstract concept, unsupported by positive evidence, could hardly account for the slaughter of the First World War. He later sought for a better explanation than repressed libido for all the mass killings. So did Trotter in his *Instincts of the Herd in Peace and War* (1919) pointing a finger however at human gregariousness of different types, both benign and malign—the British being the former and the Germans the latter.

Freud's later views were expressed shortly before his death in *Why War?* (1933):

> Anything that encourages the growth of emotional ties between men must operate against war. These ties may be of two kinds. In the first place they may be relations resembling those towards a loved object, though without having a sexual aim. There is no need for pschoanalysis to be ashamed to speak of love in this connection, for religion itself uses the same words: thou shalt love thy neighbour as thyself. This, however, is more easily said than done. The second kind of emotional tie is by means of identification. Whatever leads men to share important interests produces this community of feeling, these identifications. And the structure of human society is largely based on them.

So Freud himself was by now alerted to questions of group attachment or identification as a main determinant of group behaviour. But he failed to observe that the emotional ties of identification can also be a cause of warfare as well as helping to prevent civil antagonism by higher identifications. In short he failed to notice the fundamental dichotomy present in group consciousness through feelings of *us* and *them*.

Present day followers of Freud, the so-called neo-Freudians, include animal ethologists like Lorenz. They blame warfare on the repression of an aggressive drive, shared with other animals which according to Freudian theory requires to be sublimated or released—or such feelings will explode in outright warfare.

Lorenz's views expressed in *On Aggression* (1963), however, are based not on human but on animal studies. He notes the distinction between predatory and aggressive animal behaviour. He also observes that, predation apart, those wild animals which do not die naturally are normally killed by members of their own species through males fighting for dominance or for females. This causes the strongest males, in accordance with natural selection, to survive.

Lorenz therefore concludes that man is not alone in his intra-specific killing.

But this is not strictly animal *warfare* that Lorenz was observing. Like human warfare, that only occurs when closely identified groups of social animals, like the clans of hunting dogs or spotted hyenas fight each other on a group basis with intense co-operation and loyalty within the group. Individual males fighting each other for dominance or for mates are not engaging in warfare.

Individual scrapping and group warfare are thus poles apart—although aggressivity can feature in both.

Jumping straight from animal aggressivity to man, Lorenz and other neo-Freudians now propose as a cure for such aggressivity and hence for warfare, that our pent-up instincts be 'released' in such harmless outlets as international competitive sports. The assumption is of the existence of a fixed instinct of aggressivity and the need to provide for its less lethal expression in war-substitutes. But the cure proposed in the form of international sports can be seen to act rather as a stimulant for group consciousness which is rarely in the forefront of most peoples minds; but can be quickly aroused so that sometimes they are conscious of little else. Competitive games stimulate rather than 'release' aggressivity against the other side. Indeed the whole fallacy of Freudian theory is to suppose the presence of fixed instincts rather than inherited aptitudes. Competitive games between rival groups of young boys in the Oklahoma experiment was seen to lead to fabricated antagonism between them and eventually to a 'civil war'. They did not need to 'release' or express their Red Devil or Bull Dog loyalties and rivalries for such did not exist five days before they were created by the experiment itself.

The human capacity for identification and distinction indeed remains malleable in expression and need not always be antagonistic. This is the ground for believing that warfare *as such* is not encoded in the human genes but is only an indirect and therefore avoidable result of group attachment. Tajfel (1973) in critising Lorenz's views wrote:

> There is no doubt that under *some* conditions all men can and do display hostility towards groups other than their own, be they social, national, racial, religious or any other. There is also no doubt, however, that under other conditions this hostility either does not appear or can be modified. The scientifically-minded biologist (as distinct from Lorenz's biologically-minded scientist) would have to specify for us in the case of human behaviour, as he does so often and so successfully for animal behaviour, the conditions under which social aggression in man does or does not appear; he would also have to provide criteria which would enable him to distinguish aggression from other forms of behaviour.

Groups of youthful fans, however, can be readily stimulated into group antagonism at football matches and frequently end up fighting fans on the other side. It is the very competitiveness of the game itself on a group basis which brings this about and the social identification with the two teams. This has become quite an international problem requiring special seating and screening arrangements to be made at international matches with the close police control of spectators. Many spectators in recent years have even been killed.

So international sports can act as national identity stimulants. While often relatively harmless they hardly indicate a cure for warfare.

Freudian theory on how warfare may be prevented also erroneously assumes that all warfare is between nations. But racial, religious and class warfare can be just as lethal. Competitive football matches between rival teams each composed of different races (as tried in South Africa) are hardly likely to clear the air. Even less do football matches between rival sectarian teams such as occur between Protestant Rangers and Catholic Celtic of Glasgow. Far from lowering the religious rivalries by their 'release' those group identities and rivalries are, on the contrary, stimulated by these football matches between the rival religious sides.

The International Olympic Games provide the highest arena of competition for athletes in their particular athletic fields. They also provide an innocent spectacle and entertainment for millions. But they hardly provide a war-substitute. Rather do they act as mild stimulants (or depressants) to national pride. Millions of spectators, not ordinarily so aware of their nationhood, suddenly come to identify with 'their own' athletes, although the Olympic Games are in theory supposed to be between individual competitors. Due to the group attachment trait, however, the international athletes come to be regarded as national representatives just as they did in the original Greek Olympiads where the athletes were applauded as Athenians, or Spartans as the case might be. Nowadays the medal winners evoke the national admiration of national viewers as the national flags are hoisted and the national anthems played. Winners of gold medals later return home to a heroes' welcome, whether in the Soviet Union or the United States.

Such reactions of ordinary people appear to be quite universal and regardless of the political systems in which they live.

But they go deeper and affect even the partisanship of the international judges. The judges are chosen from past exponents of their sports and have to judge, in a heightened national atmosphere and with the eyes of their own nationals upon them, those events like figure skating where style and execution count for marks rather than 'first past the finishing post'. The judges can prove so biased in favour of their own national competitors that their particular scores have been discounted by special methods adopted by the International Olympic Committee. They demonstrate publicly their national bias on their recording machines.

Freudian 'release' through competitive sports is not, therefore, a proper war-substitute; still less an outlet for an individual's repressed aggressive instincts. Perhaps there is latent aggressivity in young men as individuals which can be tapped when they are formed into military units. Probably young bloods do need some challenge to absorb such energies. But these traits, whether inborn or cultivated, need not take the form of warfare in each succeeding generation; nor need they be encouraged to operate in an aggressive or hateful way. Neither the Swiss nor the Swedes seem all the worse today for not having engaged in two World Wars, although at one time their young men provided the finest mercenary soldiers of Europe.

The flaw in Freudian psychology is to suppose fixed instincts to which vent must be given rather than to recognise a human capacity for group attachment which can be more beneficially contrived and controlled.

Koestler (1978) who had practical experience of fighting and of group antagonism in the Spanish Civil War, came to regard group identification as the cause of warfare itself transforming the individual from a relatively benign individual into a wholesale killer of his co-specifics. He wrote:

> The continuous disasters of man's history are mainly due to his excessive capacity and urge to become identified with a tribe, a nation, church or cause, or to espouse its credo uncritically and enthusiastically, even if its tenets are contrary to reason, devoid of self-interest and detrimental to the claims of self-preservation. We are thus driven to the unfashionable conclusion that the trouble with our species is not an excess of *aggression* but an excess capacity for *fanatical devotion*. Even a cursory glance at history should convince one that individual crimes committed for selfish motives play a quite insignificant part in the human tragedy, compared to the numbers massacred in unselfish loyalty to one's tribe, nation, dynasty, church, or political ideology *ad majorem gloriam Dei*.
>
> The emphasis is on the unselfish. Excepting a small minority of mercenary or sadistic disposition, wars are not fought for personal gains, but out of loyalty and devotion to king, country or cause. Homicide committed for personal reasons is a statistical rarity in all cultures, including our own. Homicide for *unselfish* reasons, at the risk of one's own life, is the dominant phenomenon in history.
>
> At this point I must insert two brief polemical remarks: First, when Freud proclaimed *ex cathedra* that wars were caused by pent-up aggressive instincts in search of an outlet, people tended to believe him because it made them feel guilty, although he did not produce a shred of historical or psychological evidence for his claim. Anybody who has served in the ranks of an army can testify that aggressive feelings towards the enemy hardly play a part in the dreary routines of waging war. Soldiers do not hate, they are frightened, bored, sex-starved, homesick; they fight with resignation, because they have no other choice, or with enthusiasm for king and country, for righteous cause—moved not by hatred but by *loyalty*. To say it once more, man's tragedy is not an excess of aggression, but an excess of devotion.
>
> A second polemical point concerns another theory purporting that the origin of war is to be found in the instinctive urge of some animal species to defend at all costs their own stretch of land or water—the so called 'territorial imperative'. It seems to me no more convincing than Freud's hypothesis. The wars of man, with rare exceptions, were not fought for individual ownership of bits of space. The man who goes to war actually *leaves* the home he is supposed to defend, and thus his shooting is far away from it; and what makes him do it is not the biological urge to defend his personal acreage or farmland or meadows, but his devotion to symbols derived from tribal lore, divine commandments and political slogans. Wars are not fought for territory, but for words.

In qualification of the last two paragraphs it must be observed first, that group consciousness and its derivative loyalties can sometimes be used to prevent warfare through overriding lesser loyalties by larger ones. Secondly, that humans do indeed sometimes identify with particular territories as being their own and hence this is a frequent (but not the only) cause of warfare itself. While there is no inborn territorial imperative nevertheless a sense of belonging to or owning a particular piece of territory is nevertheless a common feature of national consciousness. If a religious sect or class comes to do so it even acquires a sense of nationhood.

IDENTIFICATION WITH PEOPLE OR TERRITORY

There were only 21 years between the two great World Wars involving the larger nations of the world and each starting in the supposedly civilised portion of western Europe. Since then there have been some 150 conventional wars, but we have been fortunate so far in avoiding the total devastation of nuclear ones. The use of force to decide international disputes seems, however, if anything, to be on the increase. For instance, 1982 was a vintage year for wars with battles in Afghanistan, the Lebanon, the Persian Gulf, the Falklands and Central America—any one of which could have escalated into a wider international conflict. Hence the dangers of the present situation, now that the great powers are armed not with swords or rifles but a whole arsenal of nuclear weapons capable of destroying whole cities and populations.

The Falklands war of 1982 commenced with the Argentinian invasion and later British recapture of the Falkland Islands. This particular war was fought on the Argentinian side for the islands they called the Malvinas lying close to Argentina in the otherwise empty expanse of the southern Atlantic. Geographically they therefore looked as if they should be Argentinian rather than British. This indeed is what every Argentinian schoolboy is brought up to believe namely that the British had no right in 1836 to oust a small resident South American settlement run from Buenos Aires.

The British, on the other hand, identified not with this barren territory which most had hardly heard of before, but with its 1800 British inhabitants of whom they suddenly became aware when the Union Jack was seen on television to be ignominiously hauled down by the Argentinians. The Falklanders themselves identified primarily by that name and as British. None of them wished to answer to the name of Argentinians.

So the identification on one side was with territory and, on the other, with its current inhabitants.

The Falklands War was fortunately brief and confined. It nevertheless merits closer scrutiny as showing the strength of popular feeling on both sides *in favour of warfare* in particular circumstances: also the crucial part played by rival loyalties and allegiances, devoid of any contributing economic factors. The islands once provided a valuable coaling station for the Royal Navy but were now merely sheep and fishing stations.

Hardly economic grounds for sending a battle fleet to sea.

The War is also important to our present study as being the first in history able to be given film coverage in colour while still going on and as viewed from both sides at once. So the rival senses of *us* and *them* could each be seen as the counterpart of the other.

How this came about was partly due to the expert coverage by the BBC; but, even more, to the fact that neither side officially declared it to be a war at all. So BBC teams were allowed to remain filming throughout the War within the Argentine as well as in Britain and also aboard the task force itself. Viewers were thus able to obtain two-sided coverage of a war in action and to hear the contemporary viewpoints of both contestants. Television coverage, however, was largely excluded from the front line as bad for home morale in giving an unbalanced stretcher-bearer's viewpoint.

In April 1982 the Argentinian military junta, to universal acclaim, and perhaps to regain some popularity 'reoccupied the Malvinas'. As the Islands had been left virtually undefended there was no bloodshed and the Argentinians thought that they could simply get away with it. There is as yet no effective international deterrent to prevent such happenings and the Argentinians also supposed the British to be lukewarm about fighting to keep Islands 8000 miles distant and so near the Argentinian coast. The United Nations Assembly moreover had already been induced to pass a resolution that the Falklands be 'de-colonised' although the Falklanders could hardly be described as ruled by aliens.

The British reaction however was one of universal popular outrage against this unprovoked attack on British kith and kin living on British sovereign territory. A headline in the *Times* newspaper proclaimed 'We are all Falklanders now!' and went on to describe the event as 'an invasion of the national spirit'. A highly respected Foreign Secretary was forced to resign over his responsibility in failing to anticipate such an attack. Even the Prime Minister herself, if not the Government, might have fallen in the absence of a strong response—such was the sense of public outrage. The Prime Minister, however, articulated these gut reactions and a task force was quickly organised and put to sea, pending negotiations for an Argentine withdrawal.

The House of Commons voted almost overwhelmingly in favour of its despatch which also had the broad support of the British public. Those few members of parliament who opposed its sending even found working class audiences opposed to them.

The Argentinians could not now withdraw without the Argentinian President being likewise forced to resign in the face of Argentinian enthusiasm. Questions of National Face thus loomed large as also did the significance of the raising or lowering of National Flags. Indeed, among the obstacles to the negotiation of an attempted interregnum under the United Nations, loomed the question of whose flag would meanwhile fly.

Questions of National Face are, of course, those of national standing in the eyes of the world.

The task force was prepared with an urgency and efficiency not ordinarily matched nowadays by British industry. British shipyard workers, contrary to Union restrictive practices, worked night and day to see that naval vessels were hurriedly completed ahead of time. Trade Union leaders looked the other way. Civilian crews of commandeered Merchant ships also volunteered to a man to stay aboard when they went into action, including the whole staff of the luxury cruise liner Queen Elizabeth II—a sitting duck. There was a sudden surge of British national pride to the exclusion of self interest. Overnight national consciousness took pride of place. Little thought too was given to the expense and likely economic consequences of mounting a task force to recapture barren islands 8000 miles away or the cost of subsequently defending them, if retaken.

The 1800 Falklanders must by now be the most expensive islanders in the world.

When the task force sailed it had reporters aboard who never expected to be involved in battle. But as the task force drew nearer to the Falklands with no Argentinian agreement to withdraw, it became all too obvious that this was exactly what was going to happen—for empty resolutions of the United Nations Assembly could mean little in such circumstances.

When the landings started new missiles were tried out with deadly effect on naval vessels. The Argentinian conscript army outnumbered the British by about 3-1. The opposed landings themselves turned out to be a close run thing. The reporters then found themselves living with and identifying with units of the 2nd and 3rd Battalion Parachute Regiment and the Royal Marines who did the main fighting and whose sufferings and glory they shared all the way from Goose Green to Port Stanley. The Infantry which had to do the ground fighting in what was otherwise mainly a naval operation under naval command comprised only two Brigades against a greatly superior entrenched force. The Argentine Regular Marines put up a spirited defence towards the end but finally the Scots Guards and Gurkhas broke through the defences of Port Stanley to force the Argentinian surrender.

It had been a great feat of British arms and a classic amphibious operation.

When it was all over a service of thanksgiving was held in St Paul's Cathedral which some regarded as not patriotic enough in its sense of victory and national pride. But the bereaved, surrounded by fellow citizens, were able to experience a sense of pride together with sorrow shared. Awards for gallantry were made to soldiers and sailors of the various regiments and ships which had taken part. Posthumous awards were handed by the Sovereign personally to the bereaved widows. When afterwards interviewed by the media, their answers were always the same, namely that their husbands had died for the regiment or the ship in which they served; and that was where their medals really belonged. Those buried in the Falklands or re-buried at home, were always draped with the national flag and with a guard of honour to pay the nation's last tribute.

For the first time on television one could also see how things looked from the other side. As the British task force approached the Malvinas, one could see the Argentinian crowds, becoming more and more ecstatic packing the main squares of Buenos Aires and chanting 'Argentina, Argentina!' and everywhere waving national flags. One could watch the Catholic clergy proclaiming from their pulpits that a nation was reborn. Nothing quite like it had been seen since Argentina won the World Cup.

One could later watch the fury and the sense of betrayal when it was learned that Port Stanley had fallen and the fury directed at the Argentinian president, General Galtieri, who was promptly forced to resign.

Due to the absence of a formal declaration of war, all Argentinian and British wounded or prisoners were immediately arranged to be transferred home. So none languished in jails or prison camps. Another consequence was the ability to interview on television in Argentina some of the 18,000 local British residents. These Anglo-Argentinians form a business community with their own schools, Anglican cathedral and even a country club called Hurlingham. Theirs is not a bad life. During the television interviews some of those interviewed were even heard to use the word 'we' meaning fellow-Argentinians rather than British. This caused grave offence, particularly when some of the neutral BBC interviewers referred to 'the British' instead of 'us'.

These Anglo-Argentinians indeed showed that they now shared both British and Argentinian loyalties like Irish residents in Britain and if the war had continued they might have been placed in the difficult position of having to choose. From some of the interviews it appeared as if older Anglo-Argentinians brought up in Britain would in the last resort have given preference to being British. But their children, educated in the Argentine and brought up to believe the Malvinas were Argentinian, might have opted the other way.

It was group identification which therefore caused this war in the absence of any effective International Tribunal administering an accepted system of international law to which appeal could be made—and behind which leading politicians could be shielded *from their own domestic public opinion*. For leading politicians are not usually elected to give their own country's territories away.

Finally the nature of the two identifications, British and Argentinian needs to be repeated.

The British identification was not so much with a territory that few had heard of, but rather with a people regarded as own kith and kin forcibly placed under a foreign flag. In contrast, the Argentinian identification was with a specific territory, the Malvinas, rather than with its foreign inhabitants regarded as not being entitled to be there at all—and hence disregarded. All Argentinians are brought up in school to identify with the Malvinas as theirs; although no Argentinian nationals as such have ever lived there.

Finally, the loyalties and allegiances of the Falklanders themselves—all 1800 'kelpers'—were British, but perhaps in a similar way to Ulstermen to keep them distinctive from 'the Argies' their nearest neighbours. Indeed, in this regard, they are like the Gibraltarians who do not wish to be governed by the Spanish; except that the Falklanders are entirely of British stock whereas the Gibraltarians are mainly of the same Spanish stock as the majority of Argentinians.

It is curious what tricks, a sense of *we-ness* can play when particular peoples wish to maintain their social distance and distinctiveness from others.

Whatever one's views on the Falklands campaign it certainly demonstrates the connection between group identity, popular support, and human warfare. It also emphasises the need for a better system of International Law and, above all, enforcement. It is an illusion, moreover to suppose that the people of western democracies are any less bellicose, when occasion warrants, than those of more authoritarian regimes.

8

States and Nations

The main characteristics of group consciousness have now been described using recent and historic examples of how people identify, where their loyalties lie and by what names they are called. From these it appears that the human race is by nature extremely cooperative and gregarious, perhaps more so than other primates. Hence our ready capacity for making social attachments with shared feelings of loyalty and allegiance. This potential has been referred to throughout as a group attachment trait which due to its universality among all races seems likely to be inborn. Even so, it is only a faculty capable of arousal whose actual expressions in the form of particular identities are externally induced. How this potential is expressed depends upon each individual's capacity to identify, so involving both internal and external factors including, above all, the interaction of like-minded persons. While identity is, therefore, a social fact it is not a tangible one, whether in the form of national or any other type of group consciousness. That this capacity is probably inborn and so ready to hand means that it can also be focused where most needed and is therefore easier to employ than if it had to be entirely created by culture with no pre-existing potential to work on.

A knowledge of the emotional responses involved in social identification, therefore, enables one to see that there is nothing unique about national distinctiveness, whether at a higher or lower level, when compared with other forms of social distinction deriving from class, race, language or religion. Furthermore, it reveals the difference between the state and the group conscious nation which, in some cases, may not even have a state organisation at all or, which may be organised under a provincial state within a larger national one to which higher (but not always stronger) loyalties are owed.

A nation–state containing several national peoples or races is usually called socially plural or multiracial. So also however may a nation–state containing people separately identified by religion, language or social class. For these are all social identities making for a socially plural society without complete mixing. The only peculiar feature of racial group consciousness is the inborn distinctiveness of appearance which cannot be changed, but may still be overridden by cultural inducements in other directions. A peculiar feature of national identity, on the other hand, is that it is territorial, involving the attachment of peoples to a particular country and its inhabitants. It thus tends to be more stable and permanent than others and is moreover the only unit upon which international law can effectively operate.

Identities which are not territorially so attached are often miscalled ethnic. But again, if such ethnicity becomes territorial, it too simply changes into national identity, as do the identities of religious groups or even social classes.

The social identification of individuals on a national basis therefore really means their 'nationalisation' or, in a particular case, Anglicisation, Russification or Polonisation as the case may be. It is simply the individual's identification with a particular national territory and name.

In contrast the 'nationalisation' of an industry means the transfer of its ownership to a nation–state or a state board not necessarily carrying with it the social identification of its workers. Identification with the particular industry requires a sense of *we-ness* rather than a continuing confrontation between the *us* and *them* of workers and management which may indeed have caused the nationalisation of the industry in the first place. Mere change of ownership in favour of the state is not therefore the same as ownership by the workers, and although the nation–state is capable of generating national loyalty it is only in wartime that industrial workers will normally increase their output out of a sense of patriotism. In peacetime they need to be encouraged to identify with and feel they have a stake in the enterprise concerned and with a suitable name to recognise as their own.

Whatever the group activity, there is thus a positive side to group consciousness involving group attachments which cause individuals to cooperate in those activities which call for cohesion. This does not of course include every form of human activity, and certainly a sense of nationhood is not the same as one of humanity. It nevertheless helps individuals to recognise and cooperate with those various organisations needed in any developed and civilised country.

Total anarchy, on the other hand, tends to be uncontrolled group consciousness as presently seen in the Lebanon or, to a lesser extent, in Ireland or Cyprus; with the lack of an all-Irish identity embracing both Irish Protestants and Catholics; or of an all-Cypriot one including both Greek and Turkish–Cypriots. It is not group consciousness itself which is at fault so much as sufficient group identity at a higher level with no apparent means of now stimulating it. Other examples are to be seen in those new African nation–states which have still to find an overall sense of identity and of incorruptible public service rather than of loyalties (including nepotism) centred only at the lower levels of family and tribe. Or in the need to create an overall identification with and loyalty to the South African state encapsulating all races rather than just a ruling white minority, denying equal rights to all resident citizens. But a new Black African state with black majority rule, would likewise be confronted with the same problem of creating and maintaining an overall sense of identity capable of attracting a sufficient loyalty among Whites and Asians on whom much of the country's industry and commerce would still depend.

A sense of racial distinctiveness can be stimulated, however, all too readily, into violent social antagonism and disruption. But such disruptive tendencies do not necessarily condemn group consciousness itself. Nor, in any event, can group consciousness be removed if due to a hereditary trait. It simply has to be accepted and better efforts made to control it. Indeed, every one of the examples of major disruption given in previous chapters could, at one time or another, have been surmounted by attracting wider identifications embracing the inhabitants of all the territories concerned; or by taking care to avoid social confrontation in the first place.

Permanent immigration of persons of entirely different race or culture into a country so concentrated as to interfere with local identities poses serious social problems. For it is likely to cause local reaction. But social identification overriding racial distinctiveness can nevertheless, with difficulty, be achieved at least in the next generation if the children of immigrants are brought up to identify with their adoptive country, and to learn its language; provided that the host country allows them to do so and their parents do not try to prevent it. The White or Black majority must also avoid discrimination and learn to treat racial minorities for what it is hoped they may become, namely, fellow countrymen.

A considerable problem where separate racial 'homelands' are established in a foreign country is that of policing, with the danger of the local police coming to be regarded by coloured immigrants as *them* or even enemies, and the police tending to do the same in reverse. American experience shows the need in such localities to have a trusted multi-racial police force. Yet at the time of the recent London race riots the metropolitan police had only 300 black or Asian police officers out of a total of 26,000.

There is also now a Muslim identification problem, with over a million resident Muslims in both France and Britain needing to acquire a sense of Frenchness or Britishness instead of only a sense of allegiance to Algeria or Pakistan, which they continue to regard as home. In Germany and Switzerland such persons were only admitted temporarily as *gastarbeiten*. But in France and Britain they were at first freely entitled to enter as British or French citizens without, however, any national identifications to match. This was a relic of Empire.

Such problems are not, however, just confined to racial immigrants. They apply equally to resident social classes and different religious communities, as they once did to European Jews. In Northern Ireland the rival group identities there are not those of race but of religion, with a taboo against 'mixed' marriages—meaning in their case, those between Protestants and Catholics; and again with a tendency on the part of many Catholics to regard the largely Protestant Royal Ulster Constabulary as *them* or even enemies, and vice versa.

The crucial problem in controlling group consciousness is therefore to ensure that such feelings do not become too dangerously antagonistic or fanatical except in a genuinely defensive posture for which, by nature, they may possibly have been selected. Above all, it is necessary to avoid situations of confrontation where this is likely to occur.

On balance, therefore, the group attachment trait is far from maladaptive at the present day—provided that its hostile potential can be guarded against. This is particularly so in the national sphere. Everyone has to live with as well as within particular nations.

In trying, therefore, to encourage more benign group consciousness through wider identities national consciousness still has a significant part to play, most particularly in overcoming internal racial, religious or class distinctions and disloyalties. Due to its territorial attachment too it will generally make for greater stability and be more amenable to control by international law.

MULTINATIONAL STATES

The institution called a nation–state is not the same as the collectively conscious people who inhabit it and together comprise the nation. Statehood connotes a legal organisation controlling a territory within its own political framework. Halsey (1978) defines it thus:

> In modern societies by far the most important source of authoritative rules is the state. The definition of the state, at once most simple and most useful, is that it has a monopoly of ultimate force in the territory it claims. But societies are not identical with states, as the example of Scotland clearly shows. The integration of a society is based less on force and more on faith; that is, on cultural affinities and language, custom, belief and history which gives members a consciousness of kind and kin with each other and a sense of cultural boundary from other people. These bonds are more enduring, so that states and empires have risen and fallen more rapidly than have societies: a nation and people can live, politically or militarily-speaking, underground, through many generations of foreign rule.

National consciousness, therefore, involves collective feelings of own kind shared by a majority of the inhabitants which is not always coincidental with a nation–state and can exceptionally survive without one. Even subnations within nation–states are not all represented by their own separate federal states or provinces. However, without some legal structure or separate language to define them and generate a degree of national identity, such amorphous identities stand at risk; and should a majority of their individuals cease to identify as such or answer to the subnational name they will simply vanish. For all depends upon the group identification of a sufficient number of individuals. It is thus a central conclusion of this book—as it was of Seton-Watson's *Nations and States* (1977)—that statehood and nationhood are different. But he was unable to deduce a theory of nationhood or explain the causes of national consciousness. Our conclusion is that national consciousness is merely one among several types of group identification the causes of which are basically psychological.

The basic difference between states and nations now makes it easier to comprehend the difficulty facing the governments of large multinational states endeavouring to encapsulate several clearly defined and rival national identities within their borders. For, as at the lower level, so too at the higher, the social attachment of a majority of the inhabitants still needs to be attracted. Here one needs to bear in mind not only the possible presence of different identity strands which combine to form the national core but also the possibility of different levels of identification within a nation–state. Always, however, it is the identification of individuals which matters and their psychological sense of *us* and *them*—but at different levels.

Hence the possibility of subnations within larger state organisations. It is all a question of group identification.

A large nation like France, now appears to have a sufficient overall identity despite some rival peripheral ones on the part of Bretons (originally Britons), Basques, Alsations and others who, however, have now mainly been integrated and induced to identify as French, and look to Paris as their capital. But even the French could not absorb the German-speaking Saarlanders who ultimately insisted on being returned to Germany. The recent administrative regionalisation of France has now been carefully contrived to avoid any revival of contrary provincial identities. France, therefore, now seems to have little in the way of subnational territorial identities within its borders. In the process of such Frenchification, however, many local identities have simply been expunged.

Spain, in contrast, is a multinational state which is only now gaining a sufficient overall sense of Spanish national consciousness at a higher level, stronger than the local national identities of being Basques, Catalans or Andalusians. The state language of Spain is Castilian which is not, however, the primary language of the Catalans or Basques. The former Spanish Empire of South America was also essentially Castilian. The Spanish state, therefore, still needs to foster and encourage an overall *Espanolismo* or sense of Spanishness, being essentially that of *we-ness* or *Nosotros* in order to hold the multinational state together. In particular *Mi paisano*, or fellow countrymen, must come to mean fellow-Spaniards rather than just Catalans, Basques or Andalusians. Spain is thus, to some extent, still a nation–state without a complete sense of Spanish national consciousness to match. Its rival internal identities, maintained by geographical distinctions, now appear, however, to be moving closer towards a federal union. It is only Spanishness, however, that can maintain such a union.

Most of the older European nations, however, are composed of amalgamations of smaller ones whose peoples have since been induced to identify at a wider level.

Some modern nation–states even incorporate former kingdoms within their midst, like Great Britain, the German Federal Republic and Yugoslavia. These contain the former Kingdoms of Scotland, Bavaria, and Serbia, all now respectively submerged, some with and some without provincial status. To maintain the overall loyalties of these peoples within a larger nation, however, seems to require a durable legal framework at a higher level that cannot be too easily altered and, above all, a higher national loyalty or allegiance to hold them together.

Speaking to a newspaper reporter in 1978, President Assad of Syria observed:

> You ask whether we dream of rebuilding a great Arab empire. No, we do not, we are thinking of Arab unity. The Arabs are one nation, divided into various countries and states. The bonds which bind us are much stronger than those people who live within one state. Take Britain—you have the English, the Scots, the Welsh and Irish—four different nations living within one state.

President Assad was not of course quite accurate as the Irish now live in two states, one of which is no longer part of the British one. But he rightly remarks that not only may a nationally conscious people exist without a corresponding state by living within a larger one but, like Arab-speakers, they may also exist spread over several.

The German nation of German-speakers is at present divided between two nation-states, the German Federal Republic and the German Democratic Republic each using the German language and name. But there still continues an overall German sense of identity surmounting the two state frontiers only recently formed by the Allied armies confronting each other at the end of the Second World War. In 1952 Stalin offered reunification as an independent neutral state on the same lines as Austria but, by then, the rival confrontations of *us* and *them* between east and west had become too intense for him to be trusted. It would also have undermined the EEC.

So the boundaries of separate nation-states do not always coincide with a single national consciousness and many states are internally multinational. Nevertheless, for their survival, they too have to attract a sense of allegiance among a majority of their peoples and cannot confine national loyalty to a ruling élite which is unlikely to remain indefinitely in power on the basis of a fictitious nation.

Nationhood therefore ultimately depends upon an overall sense of group consciousness. For statehood to coincide with nationhood in a multinational state, requires not a multinational identity (for such is a contradiction in terms) but a greater *national* identity at the wider state level.

The Art of statecraft, therefore, largely consists in keeping the state organisation and its several identities together.

It is sometimes observed that the state is not the same as the community. A nation-state, however does not usually confront a single group conscious 'community' except in a situation of social revolution, which democracy is supposed to avoid. If, however, the state becomes synonymous with a ruling elite as it was allowed to do under the French Ancien Regime or in Czarist Russia, class revolutions are apt to result as people fight for their rights. It was, after all, Louis XIV who boasted 'l'etat c'est moi!' Usually, however, there is no single rival 'community' within a nation's boundaries, but many subsidiary ones. The sense of national consciousness too may be comprised of several strands not shared by all. Conversely, in the case of some new nation–states, like those of the Middle East, there were no pre-existing identities exactly coinciding and these had simply to be manufactured. In the Lebanon without a sufficient secular Lebanese sense of identity to support it, this small Arab nation–state has been undermined by the rival religious factions of Shi-ites, Druses and Christians whose loyalties are mainly to themselves.

The United States of America with its fifty states and China with its thirty provinces are not only the largest nation–states but manage to maintain the widest national identities with little in the way of subnational ones within their borders.

China is by far the oldest and largest continuous nation–state in the world having been created in 221 BC when the Emperor Qin Shihuang united six warring kingdom–states and forged them into a united Chinese Empire. He and his imperial successors then assimilated the laws and scripts within some 30 adminstrative provinces which continued under different dynasties until 1911, and thereafter as a national republic. It was at first, however, not so much shared national group consciousness, as the individual's cultivated deference to the state and its leaders through etiquette and recognition of status which was so successfully fostered. Only since 1949 in the new Chinese Peoples Republic has peasant class consciousness, changing into national consciousness, been brought into play.

The United States of America has had the advantage over other nations of being peopled by small boatloads of immigrants whose overall American identity, through enforced English-speaking and allegiance to the Flag, has been that much easier to induce. All American children in state schools are still daily required, hand on heart, to swear allegiance to the national flag in the following terms:

> I pledge allegiance
> To the Flag
> Of the United States of America
> And to the Republic for which it stands—
> One nation—indivisible—
> With liberty and justice for all.

By being so habituated American schoolchildren actually acquire an American identity to match their sworn allegiances. The USA is also the most flag conscious of nations. The Stars and Stripes appears on public buildings, private houses, in court rooms and behind all senior official desks. It is also a battle flag which American Troops still carry into action.

Nevertheless there still persist 'hyphenated Americans', like Jewish-Americans and also some with peripheral French and Spanish identities in Louisiana and New Mexico where French and Spanish are also spoken. But these former colonial territories have now been largely engulfed by the immigrant flood and all mainly induced by upbringing and English-speaking into a sense of loyalty and allegiance to the American Flag and Constitution. There is thus little in the way of multinational or territorial distinctiveness within the USA. The Blacks, however, with their slave background, have been more difficult to assimilate as Afro-Americans, being originally regarded as an inferior class or caste apart. Even in the Second World War American military units were still segregated (as they were in the civil war) into White and Coloured units, the latter under White officers. But this has now all changed by antidiscrimination laws causing desegregation, by shared *esprit de corps* in US military units and athletic teams in which Blacks excel, and, above all, by allowing Blacks to share political power. While some Blacks certainly remain resentfully self-aware by race, they have never felt they belonged to any distinctive region other than the USA. So America is not required, like Canada, to contend with the potential disloyalty of any national people strongly identified as such with a particular internal region.

It must not be forgotten, however, that the USA was in the last century split by the Black Question causing the rival loyalties of the northern and southern states—the former to the Union and the latter to themselves and the new flag of the Confederacy. The American Civil War of 1865 caused over a million casualties. In the south it was the loyalty to and sense of belonging to Virginia and other southern states which counted more strongly than loyalty to the Union. General Robert E Lee when asked to become Commander-in-Chief of the union army requested time for deliberation before sadly riding south to his own kith and kin in Virginia where he took over command of the Confederate army under a different flag.

Racial consciousness in the United States is now culturally overlaid by a stronger sense of loyalty to the Union shared by this otherwise most individualistic of peoples. This, however, involves no contradiction as it is individuals and not the state who experience group consciousness. While most Americans may not appear strongly nationalistic and, unlike Canadians, can take their identity for granted, when abroad they become more aware of their distinctiveness. At home their national awareness can also be suddenly aroused, as on the occasion of the Iranian or Lebanese seizure of American hostages regarded as a national insult.

In complete contrast to the USA with its individualistic democratic and consumer culture—including nevertheless a strong sense of national consciousness—the group identity of the USSR has in theory and practice been that of the international working class. Detailed consideration of the latter later transforming again into national consciousness will be postponed until the next chapter. Here it may merely be noted that the Soviet state encompasses several national republics some new and some old and even some ancient kingdoms. It is thus a multinational state.

Yugoslavia provides another multinational example. It was created as a unitary state under League of Nations auspices in 1918 on supposedly 'ethnographic' grounds of shared race and language, but under a Serbian royal dynasty with the former Serbian capital as capital of the new Serbo-Croat nation. A new Yugoslavian national identity was slow in coming due to the persistence of subnational rivalries so great that the Germans were able in 1941 to create a puppet Croatian state to fight on their side. The country was liberated in 1945 from the Germans by the Yugoslav Communist People's Army based on class, the leaders of which, under Tito, thus became the post-war Yugoslav government. The country then acquired a new federal constitution modelled directly upon the Soviet one with, in theory, the state not regarded as a nation at all but as an organisation of the working class run through local and central communist parties.

Under this new constitution Yugoslavia was declared to be a multinational state with six autonomous national republics and two autonomous provinces. These subnations, are called, as in the Soviet Union, 'nationalities'. The autonomous province of Kosovo, attached to the national republic of Serbia, is more Albanian and sometimes its people even fly the Albanian flag. They now seek their own national republic within the Yugoslav state in preference to being joined to the Serbian. The Serbs and Croats together make up about 60 per cent of the Yugoslav population and are of the same south Slav racial/language group. Under the Ottomans, however, the Serbs remained Orthodox and used the Cyrillic alphabet. The Croats, in contrast, were part of the Austro–Hungarian Empire, were staunch Catholics and wrote in the Latin script.

A Yugoslav sense of identity above the level of these subnational ones first really took shape under Tito within the *esprit de corps* of the People's Liberation Army. This spirit is still maintained in the ranks of the post-war Yugoslav army, kept at full strength to protect the country against 'liberation' by the USSR in the name of the International Workers. In the Yugoslav army all units are now racially and religiously mixed and nobody is allowed to serve in the national republic in which he was born—so helping to increase a sense of Yugoslav identity. As in the Soviet Union too, the central committee of the communist party in practice still retains overall control. But surveillance is more relaxed and new self-management schemes in industry now bear some resemblance to the industrial identities of the more progressive Western industrial firms—although still state financed and centrally supervised.

The continuance of the Yugoslav nation–state, however, must depend upon the degree to which a sense of Yugoslav national consciousness can be maintained at a higher level in the face of strong local identities which pull the other way. Hence the importance of the national Communist Party and of the pan-Yugoslav national army in holding the country together.

The Swiss confederation dates from 1291, and started with three cantons. By the sixteenth century it had enlarged into 13 with strong enough identities to survive the split between Catholics and Protestants at the time of the Reformation. Nevertheless, in Switzerland a Catholic–Protestant divide did exist, even incorporating class distinctions with the Swiss upper class tending to remain staunchly Catholic while the lower classes mainly converted to Protestantism. This division was later to erupt into the Swiss civil war of 1847 when seven of the then twenty-two cantons tried to secede, but were forcibly prevented.

The language distinctions of the Swiss are also considerable. Sixty-five per cent of the Swiss population speak a Swiss–German dialect which has kept them separate from other German-speakers; 20 per cent speak French; 10 per cent Italian and the remainder other languages which now include Anglo-American in banking and financial circles. The Swiss Federal capital is Berne, but the majority of German-speakers tend to look to Zurich and the French-speakers to Geneva. So there are strong local identities. A sense of distinction deriving from separate residence in separate valley cantons also favours such local distinctiveness and proud provincial identities.

But what then binds the whole Swiss people together in their separate cantons and causes them everywhere to fly the Swiss flag on their houses as well as on public buildings? An important factor must surely be the Swiss constitution guaranteeing the continuing culture of the separate Swiss cantons.

In an article entitled *What is 'Swiss'?*, Steiner (1938) lays stress on the physical distinctiveness and beauty of the country itself, in contrast to others; also the uniqueness of Swiss neutrality in two world wars and hence an independent attitude towards other European nation–states. He also remarks that the Swiss Federation appears stronger at its edges than at the centre and that it abounds in local cultures. There had been earlier struggles to be free not only from other European nations but also from their own feudal aristocracy which resulted in the Swiss becoming independent land holders with a system of democratic government running down to local levels. Hence their provincial outlook in the best sense of the word. Switzerland thus remains profoundly egalitarian without state ownership of the land or other means of production. It also abounds in small local industries, mostly employing under fifty people, which are highly adaptable, capable of providing almost full employment and avoiding any confrontation between the two sides of capitalist industry.

Steiner also surprisingly points to the Swiss army as providing the principal cement in the structure of the Swiss confederate identity—an army which this century has never fired a shot in anger. He writes:

> The great role of military service and annual reserve and territorial duties in Swiss life is undeniable. So, as well, is the importance in business and banking, indeed even within the academic establishment, of friendships formed and patronage cultivated during one's military training.

But this *esprit de corps* is apparently now weakening owing to opposition from many of the young to unnecessary military service. Others, in contrast, see this as 'the coming challenge to long-established convictions of Swissness'.

The Swiss example, however, shows that it is possible for separate language and religious communities to share local identities at canton level, but linked together at a higher national one, while yet maintaining their own strong individual cultures. Also, that it is possible to do so without strong central political control, as in the USSR. But this is obviously easier on the smaller Swiss scale and does appear to require a strong constitutional legal structure only alterable by general referendum.

What, in contrast then, ever happened to Belgium, not so dissimilar in size and population, to cause such internal social antagonism almost leading to the formation of two separation 'nations'?

Belgium came into being in 1832 principally as a result of Catholic revulsion against the rising Protestant Dutch national consciousness of the Netherlands. It was a kind of Ulster in reverse, aided, however, by identities acquired under the separate Empires of Austria and Spain. In this Catholic breakaway movement, two-thirds of the new Belgium's population were Dutch-speaking Flemings while the rest were French-speaking Walloons. There was also a class strand to the provocation on both sides, with an upper class in Brussels choosing always to speak French as opposed to Flemish. Far from cohering into a single nation to support the new Unitary Belgian state (the so-called Belgique de Papa), the tendency was towards the formation of the two separate language 'nations' of Flanders and Wallonia with Belgium thus becoming bi-national. The state has since been reformed in 1982 into a federation with the provinces of Wallonia and Flanders and a third province of Greater Brussels in the middle, the latter without a provincial legislature. So Belgium has recently become a federal state to accommodate its separate language communities.

This result demonstrates yet again that even where peoples enjoy similar geographic and economic conditions, they may still be at risk if their rival identities are allowed to be antagonistically aroused. Unlike Switzerland, there are no geographical distinctions in Belgium nor separate valleys in which people can live happily apart. Nor nowadays are there significant economic differences to account entirely for the social distancing of 'islands' of Flemings and Walloons. The hostile language communities with their 'No go' areas are indeed more akin to the religious communities of Northern Ireland which again are not so much due to economic differences as to rival distinctions of *us* and *them*.

Other such bi-national examples are Sri Lanka (the former British Ceylon) where a predominant Singhalese native population faces a smaller Tamil one which refuses to integrate and whose loyalties lie rather across the sea with other Tamils in the neighbouring Indian state of Tamil-Nadu, one of the twenty-two states of Federal India rearranged since British days on linguistic lines. Yet another example is the island of New Caledonia in the Pacific which has an equal number of native Tanaks and immigrant French, the latter still loyal to France. Another is the Jewish state of Israel recently extended on to the West Bank to enclose a large Arab population and so transform itself into a bi-national state composed of two-thirds Israelis and one-third Palestinian. The latter may soon outnumber the former. The nation–state of Israel is a unitary one, run by Jews, but no longer a state of the Jewish people. Indeed the Arab Palestinians are regarded as *Untermenschen* like the Jews themselves were once regarded in Western and Eastern Europe.

In the West Indies similar identity problems have arisen in Guyana, Tobago and Trinidad between Indians (original natives or imported labour) and Africans. There was thus no sense of being a West Indian nation to support the ill-fated Caribbean Federation which simply collapsed at birth. Rival national or racial identities and antagonisms between Malays, Indians and Chinese also brought the short-lived Malaysian Federation to an end. The same fate overtook the Central African Federation where a White ruling class based on Southern Rhodesia was supposed to provide initial guidance and a civilising influence. If the Blacks had been prepared to give it a longer trial it might indeed have evolved into a multiracial federation. However a reactive Black racial consciousness in the face of White racial and class domination killed it off at birth giving rise to the new black nations of Malawi, Tanzania and Zimbabwe.

These short-lived federal states all collapsed therefore before they had time or means to generate group consciousness at federal level. It seems that states comprising more than two subnations or nationalities, like the fifteen of the USSR, lend themselves more easily than bi-national ones to such federal arrangements. As just mentioned, however, the Belgian unitary state managed successfully to federalise in 1982 and Czechoslovakia, with only two provincial limbs, did so in 1968 after seventy years as a unitary state. However, their provincial limbs are not dissimilar in size or population. Yugoslavia has managed so far to hold together its six subnations and two autonomous national provinces. The Nigerian federation now has twelve provincial states, roughly based upon tribal groupings.

By independence in 1947 India had already acquired a sufficient all-Indian, but mainly Hindu sense of identity apart from the Muslim defection. Under the 1950 constitution it was reorganised into twenty-two federal provinces coincidental with language distinctions, but also in the Sikh case (the Punjab) with religion. The latter state is the most economically prosperous but has also caused the most trouble even threatening secession from the Union as an independent nation–state. It was granted a shared capital with a neighbouring state, now promised back as capital of the Punjab in return for some Hindu communities being moved the other way. This is to take better account of local Sikh loyalties.

Where there exist strong separate identities unlikely ever to be integrated, the tendency appears to be to favour either independent nation–states, if such are viable, or federal provinces still reflecting those identities but still hopefully with a sufficiently strong sense of wider national identity and loyalty to hold them together. There is presumably some point in size or distinctiveness which makes centralised government less competent or acceptable than the federal model. If unitary states have to pass separate laws for separate portions of their national territory this may indicate the need for a federation where such is feasible; but a full federation requires sufficient provincial limbs such as are to be found in Canada, Australia and the USA to justify equal representation at the higher federal level.

GREATER AND LESSER NATIONAL NAMES

The need for higher as well as lower levels of identification in multinational states has been seen to apply whether such states are unitary or federal. A major problem arises, however, where the wider loyalty, as in the case of the Greek and Turkish Cypriots or Protestants and Catholics in Northern Ireland, is not vertically to the Greater Nation but horizontally to other countries. A shared higher loyalty in a multi-national state requires a common name at the higher level for individuals to answer to that is not also that of a dominant national partner. This has not happened in the British Isles and has so helped to weaken an overall sense of identity at the British level.

Why this should have come about is of interest to any study of national identification. Perhaps the nearest parallel is the continued misuse of the name Russia to describe the Soviet Union—although such misuse rarely occurs within the Soviet Union itself.

The Union of England and Scotland into the new nation–state of Great Britain in 1707 had been preceded by a century of regnal union under a single monarch wearing both the English and Scottish crowns. In the context of European nomenclature and proposed European union it is hence of more than merely British interest to study the changing identification of individuals within the British Isles with the English, Scottish and Irish names. For until recently Britain has been called England by most of its inhabitants and also by most foreigners. An Anglo–French treaty for instance is never called a Franco–British one. In the 1970s, however, this all suddenly changed with the name of Britain coming to supersede England—although it took the national newspapers some time to decide whether their renamed readers should be called Britishers or Britons, finally opting for the latter.

The origins of the British name have already been explored in connection with Irish identity now reflected in an Irish state but not a province of a federal British Isles. Now it is necessary to consider the Anglo–Scottish dimension—bearing in mind that Scotland, unlike Ireland, had long been a separate Kingdom and nation.

The names British and Britain, like so many others, derive from the Romans who christened their westernmost province Britannia from the predominant racial/language group who spoke Brythonic or British, a variety of Celtic. To the north of the Firth of Forth was Caledonia inhabited by Picts or 'painted people'. These were later overlaid by immigrant Scots from Ireland, whose royal house or tribe, in the ninth century, created the Kingdom of Scotland. These Scoto–Irish spoke Gaelic (Celtic Q) in contrast to the Picts who spoke a variety of British (Celtic P). Their name Scotti, incidentally, appears to be yet another Roman nickname.

So the Britannia of the British was originally a Celtic language/racial identity held together by Roman rulers speaking Latin. After the Roman withdrawal leaving the Romano–British to themselves there occurred successive invasions of eastern Britain by Anglo–Saxons of yet another racial/language stem. The Angles settled mainly to the north and the Saxons to the south. The native British called these invaders Saxons or Sassunachs as Gaelic speakers still do to this day. But the invaders themselves took the Anglian or English name from their Anglian royal house and hence that of the English language, now spread throughout the world under the British Empire to become the most widely used of all languages today.

The last persons in the British Isles to answer to the original British–Celtic name were the Britons of the Kingdom of Strathclyde—although the name Britain or Great Britain still lingered on even in the Middle Ages to signify the whole country. It is doubtful, however, if there was then much of a British sense of identity. In those early days too, no-one ever thought of calling Ireland or Scotland, England. There was indeed then no love lost between the original British and the immigrant Angles or English, who were not even Christians and who were only later Christianised in the north by the Scoto-Irish church and in the south by St Augustine.

This England of the Anglo–Saxons, as later overlaid by a Norman aristocracy, became a homogeneous kingdom–state and nation in the fourteenth century when English, rather than Latin or Norman French, became the language of the Court. Meanwhile the kingdom of the Scots, having overrun the Anglo–Saxon lowlands, was extended to the River Tweed. It was thereafter hammered into a sense of Scottish nationhood shared by a majority of its Celtic, Anglo–Saxon and Norman inhabitants due to the repeated invasions of the English. The Scots were nearly subjugated and integrated into an English Empire but finally ensured their independence at the battle of Bannockburn followed in 1320 by the declaration of the Scottish Parliament at Arbroath addressed to the Pope:

> Yet Robert himself should he turn aside from the task that he has begun, and yield Scotland or us to the English King and people, we should cast out as the enemy of us all, as subverter of our rights and of his own, and should choose another King to defend our freedom: for so long as a hundred of us are left alive, we will yield in no least way to English dominion. We fight not for glory nor for wealth nor honour; but only and alone we fight for FREEDOM which no good man surrenders but with his life ... We pray you to admonish the King of England (to whom his own possessions may well suffice, since England of old was enough for seven Kings or more) that he should leave us in peace in our little Scotland, since we desire no more than is our own, and have no dwelling-place beyond our borders: and we on our part, for the sake of peace, are willing to play our part.

For centuries thereafter under special protection of the Pope and in order to maintain its independence Catholic Scotland was allied to France. In the sixteenth century there was briefly even a joint Queen and also, unique in Europe, a common nationality tending however almost to make Scotland a French province with Mary of Guise as Queen Regent ruling in Edinburgh. The Auld Alliance officially ended, however, with the Scottish Reformation in 1560.

In 1603 James Stuart, King of Scots inherited by descent the English throne and thereupon attempted to fuse his two kingdoms into a new United Kingdom of Great Britain, the name for which was probably suggested by his tutor, George Buchanan, Latinist and first Celtic expert. Francis Bacon, however, his English Chancellor, advised him that he only had power under the Royal prerogative to choose his Royal Style and Title which he did as Rex Britannicus; also that on his coinage and Embassies abroad. But he was blocked from going further. The Celtic name British was not one the English cared to answer to in deference to a Scottish monarch. To them the name British was redolent of a conquered race whose members once painted themselves with woad. The English Parliament resolutely refused to have anything to do with the name and a contemporary cartoon of the King bore the caption

'Your name British?' King James too hardly endeared himself to his English subjects by having a genealogist find him a pedigree showing his descent from one Brude, the last King of the Britons.

King James did, however, successfully introduce a new Union Jack or flag incorporating the English Cross of St George and the Scottish Cross of St Andrew to be flown on ships at sea. His declared aim was that of a complete Union, '*Unus Rex, Unus Grex, Una Lex*'. He was strongly opposed, however, by most English lawyers when he proposed the assimilation of the laws of England and Scotland into a single legal system. English common lawyers feared their takeover by the Oxford civilians in a league with the Scots. The King, however, made some progress towards uniformity of worship in England and Scotland with the introduction of his authorised version of the Bible which still bears the name of its royal scholar and patron.

So here, in advance of the EEC, was an attempt to combine two European Kingdom-states into a single British one. King James's successor, Charles I made further attempts towards uniformity of laws and worship. The Scots were more opposed to the latter than the former, even starting the Civil War by defiance of the King in the General Assembly of the Church of Scotland. Uniformity of language, however, was by now taking place naturally in the lowlands with the introduction of standard English in lieu of native Scots, with the former, however, still spoken with a Scots accent. On the restoration of the joint monarchy under Charles II (already crowned by the Scots on his father's execution) there still remained a separate Scottish Parliament and Privy Council—the latter, however, increasingly answerable to London. There occurred three vain attempts under the Stuarts, with joint commissioners, to assimilate the laws of England and Scotland.

The Scots were now becoming increasingly irritated at being drawn by the English into periodic wars against their old allies the French. Both King William III and after him Queen Anne now answered almost entirely to their English Privy Council. From the Scottish viewpoint the last straw was yet another war against France in 1702, again disrupting Scottish maritime trade with France and Holland. The independent Scots Parliament thereupon passed an Act in 1703 'Anent war and peace' declaring that Scotland should not in future be drawn into any wars without its express consent. Worse was to follow the next year when they passed the Act (6 Anne. c.36) regulating the future succession to the Scottish crown upon the death of Queen Anne, now known to be incapable of bearing children. It provided for the succession to the Scottish Crown to the heir of her body 'being always of the royal line of Scotland and of the true Protestant religion, provided always that the same be not successor to the Crown of England ...'

The English reaction was hostile and immediate. Indeed it was now clear that the institution of joint monarchy for two separately identified peoples had failed as it was later to do in the case of the joint monarchies of Austria/Hungary and Norway/Sweden. For separate national identities, at the same level, cannot readily share as head or symbol the same person if he or she is in practice the head of only the dominant partner. That was now the case with Queen Ann and her English Privy Council.

The English Government favoured a successor, not from the Scottish Stuart line but from the German Protestant House of Hanover. They promptly worked towards an incorporating union, moving troops up to the north of England. Nevertheless the resultant scheme of union entered into in 1706 between selected English and Scottish commissioners was ratified the following year by both national parliaments and was not wholly a Scottish subjugation. While generally unpopular it nevertheless involved a realistic decision taken by Scottish leaders of the day faced otherwise by invasion and devastation as had occurred a century before. For there was nothing to stop the English fleet sailing up the Firth of Forth. A federal solution, perhaps including Ireland to cover the whole of the British Isles, might have succeeded, but was never on offer. And an Anglo-Scottish federation would have been very lopsided considering the Scots only comprised 15 per cent of the total population.

So it was an incorporating union. The existing English Parliament with a lower House of Commons and an upper house of hereditary peers, in theory now became the new Parliament of Great Britain. But not so in practice. For there was no written constitution nor any fundamental new law promulgated for the new United Kingdom. Such indeed was alien to the English common law tradition which prefers custom and convention to written constitutions, leaving all legislation, without restriction, to the Parliamentary majority of the day. Hence the customary public law had to remain English and the English Parliament continued in form and procedure exactly as it had been before but with the addition of some Scottish members.

From these new constitutional arrangements—or rather lack of them—the continuing use of the names England and English to cover both England and Scotland may henceforth be ascribed. Indeed the first textbook on constitutional law and convention by Bagheot was aptly enough entitled *The English Constitution*.

With the Union, however, there was now a single British monarch; the Union Jack became the new national flag and a new national royal anthem was introduced. There was already a British Army and Royal Navy and an increasing number of overseas colonies were being acquired to form the first British Empire—so successful a venture that multinational problems within the home country tended to be masked. These included several constitutional anomalies. There remained, for instance, separate Scottish royal officers, a separate Scottish state church and distinct legal and educational systems. Correspondingly there remained a separate Lord Chief Justice and Earl Marshal of England, the latter responsible for marshalling British state occasions according to English practice, including a Coronation service based on that of the Anglo-Saxons. Also an English Garter King of Arms who continues to control matters of style and title in the House of Lords which also contains Anglican bishops. These were and are all part of the English and Anglican tradition and the civil and religious ceremonies deriving therefrom.

The only British officer introduced in 1707 was a new Lord Chancellor of Great Britain who, however, could not in practice operate north of the Tweed owing to the separate Scottish legal system.

It was understandable, therefore, from the English viewpoint, when so little seemed to have changed in 1707, to continue to call the whole country not Britain (the new legal name) but England. For why should they change their name just to please a Scots minority? Most Englishmen tended, therefore, to see Scotland more as a geographical fragment of England, like Yorkshire or Cornwall. They had no internal sense of separate identity, and indeed did not need to do so when they could still answer to the name of England and English as now embracing the whole of Great Britain. So they could not comprehend why Scots needed to be so self-consciously nationalistic, unlike themselves.

So matters remained in the eighteenth and part of the nineteenth centuries with most government now removed south and with no Scottish Parliament or Privy Council or even a Scottish Secretary. However, as David Hume remarked, most educated opinion in Scotland by now supported the Union. A muted Scottish identity at a lower level did still linger on even among loyal supporters of the Union like Sir Walter Scott who wrote:

> There is no harm in wishing Scotland to have just so much ill-nature ... as may keep her good nature from being abused; so much national spirit as may determine her to stand by her own rights, conducting her assertion of them with every feeling of respect and amity towards England.

In 1853 a National Association for the Vindication of Scottish Rights resolved 'that the Treaty of Union between Scotland and England recognises the supremacy, asserts the individuality and provides for the preservation of the national laws and institutions of Scotland; that any attempt to subvert or place these institutions under English control, under the pretence of a centralising economy, would deprive Scotland of the benefit of local action and would be injurious to her welfare and an infraction of the true spirit in which that Treaty was concluded.'

In 1882 a Secretary for Scotland was appointed around whom has since grown up a provincial type of administration with separate departments of state. According to the then Prime Minister, Lord Salisbury, 'the whole object of the move is to redress the wounded dignity of the Scotch people—or a section of them who think enough is not made of Scotland.' Soon the Secretary was elevated to Secretary of State with a seat in the Cabinet. The first Secretary of State, Lord Rosebery, later to become British Prime Minister, had this to say in a rectorial address upon the need for greater and lesser patriotisms. He observed that for the English this presented no problem as it did for the Scots: 'With Englishmen love of Great Britain means the love of England—the larger and lesser patriotisms are one. He speaks, for instance, of the English government and the English army, without condescending to the terms British and Great Britain.'

Many Anglicised Scots, however, were also prepared to use England as a synonym for Britain, particularly if brought up in England and educated at English public schools.

The United Kingdom of Great Britain (and Northern Ireland) thus remains a multinational state with a strong British level of national consciousness at the higher level which until recently has been miscalled English by a majority of its inhabitants as well as by most foreigners.

It is wrong, therefore, to conclude that the British nation–state has no sense of identity to support it, or that its only identities are the internal ones of Scots, Welsh and Ulstermen: or that the English are now too civilised to experience national consciousness at all. It is rather that, as Lord Rosebery observed, the majority of English lack *a lower level* of identity to correspond with the separate territory of England. On the contrary, most identify with the whole of Britain, but under the English name. Hence they experience no *internal*, or lower level, of distinctiveness.

In the 1970s there arose a growing desire among many Scots for better identification and better preservation of Scottish institutions through some kind of quasi-federal arrangement within the British state. Such a constitutional arrangement might have been possible in earlier years if able to include Ireland and so furnish Irish Catholics and Protestants with a *shared higher* level of identity, under the originally Celtic British name. Now it was more difficult, perhaps too difficult. But at least the Scottish identity viewpoint has been made, namely that Britain and England are not synonymous and should represent different identity levels for English as well as Scots. The names Britain and British have now come into official use for the whole country. A separate English identity at a lower level has even begun to appear at international football matches with English supporters for the first time waving the English national flag, hitherto only flown on Anglican churches.

This digression into Anglo–Scottish relations now helps to show the importance of enabling individuals to identify under different national names at different levels of identification. It also helps to put an aspiring European identity into better perspective. For Scotland used to be among the most European of nations. Changes too in British nomenclature, so vital to British identification, are also of relevance to a European identity as to human attachments in general. For names are what people answer to as being their own.

The example of continuing national identities within the British Isles, now forming two separate nation–states and several nations, also gives warning against facile assumptions that free trade necessarily leads to the removal of all national distinctions and therefore to the amalgamation of nations. It is indeed as misplaced as the notion of an enduring international class of workers if everywhere there were to be introduced the social (ie state) ownership of all the means of production. These are all supposed *economic* solutions for a human problem which is basically social and *psychological*.

9

Imperial and International Identities

IMPERIAL LEVELS OF IDENTITY

Imperial group consciousness displays yet again the operation of the group attachment trait involving attitudes of *us* and *them*, this time, however, experienced as imperiousness on the part of a ruling people or state over imperial subjects. It is thus akin to class or racial consciousness. Some imperial subjects, however, may display a willing deference as of a lower towards a civilising upper class providing temporary advantages not to be found among their own people. But, as time passes and standards of civilisation are raised, there arises a desire to be free, meaning collectively free, which is the sign of rival group identification.

If multinational states are difficult enough to integrate and keep together, how much more so then for far-flung empires—at least so soon as their subject peoples become nationally or racially self-aware that they are *we*, to whom their own country really belongs.

This again is not a question of economics, but of psychological attachments. Indeed imperial consciousness is no different from any other in the social attitudes displayed. It may also transform into national consciousness if coincident with one land mass and the majority come to identify as one people. As already seen some of the older Greater Nations, like France, became so through the successful conversion of a surrounding empire into a homogeneous whole, obviously easier with a continuous land mass. The Frenchness or national consciousness of France, however, could not be extended to Muslim Algerians or Moroccans separated by the Mediterranean: once thought capable of being turned into metropolitan French with seats in the French Assembly.

France also had other overseas colonies in French Indo-China which, after the Second World War, it re-occupied from the Japanese and fought hard to retain against the Vietnamese. In 1954 they were forced to withdraw causing Cambodia and North and South Vietnam to divide in the process. The Americans later moved in to try to support a westernised regime in South Vietnam—but in turn had to evacuate. Cambodia, now renamed Kampuchea after its ancient name, was then taken over by the Khmer Rouge in a class revolution of country folk against town folk, and indeed anyone displaying middle class tendencies. Over a million are believed to have been killed as 'non persons' or 'other people' in this class revolution according to the precepts of Lenin that a people liberated from colonial control should then turn against their own upper class.

It was not, however, only west European nations which had empires at certain stages of economic development. In the ancient world there were Chinese, Persian and Roman. For 1400 years there was a black Ethiopean one with the Amharic tribal 'nation' lording it over others who were never assimilated within a single national identity. In Middle America there were the Aztec and Inca Empires exercising dominion over other tribal groups. That of the Aztecs (who called themselves Mexicas) was transformed, however, under Spanish Imperial rule into the modern republic of Mexico whose inhabitants are now of mixed race but with the Indian culture and identity strongly reasserted.

Due to difficulties of lasting identification the most successful European empires, however, have been those involving the settlement overseas of large numbers of kith and kin anxious at first to *retain* their national identification with their home countries in distant parts as the basis of fragile new communities. In contrast, however, where foreign territories with large native populations have come to be ruled by Europeans, the imperial identification has proved difficult to create and, in the longer term, impossible to maintain. All the major West European countries like France, Germany, Belgium, Holland, Denmark, Spain, Portugal, Italy—and above all Britain—had overseas native colonies. The very word native was indicative of inferiority, particularly when used of native troops. An attempt was made to nurture these native empires in the image of the various ruling nations, using the language, religion and national symbols of each imperial state. It was only a native élite educated abroad, however, who ever acquired some sense of imperial identity. Generally the imperial state relied more on deference and respect for its own imperial symbols of power with stress on oaths of allegiance. It took little in the way of postwar agitation, therefore, to bring all this quasi-class deference to an end with scores of new independent nation-states coming into being.

The latter now make up the majority of the 159 nation-states which comprise the United Nations Organisation.

The basic trouble from an identity viewpoint was that each imperial nation ruled in its own national name and under its own national flag and thus in the manner of a ruling class. Indeed it did so most effectively where it had such a ruling class at home, brought up and educated for this very imperial purpose. This was so of the Roman Empire, whether under the Caesars or the Republic, whose patrician families supplied the governors of the Roman Imperial Provinces. Yet, through lack of a continuing loyalty to Rome or identification with the Roman name as well as a growing Christian refusal to worship the Emperor as symbol of allegiance, the decline and fall of the Roman Empire became inevitable.

It has been the same with other Empires unless, like the Chinese, they could convert themselves into Greater Nations.

REFERENCE LIBRARY BELFAST

The British Empire lasted for 250 years and was the most widespread of all, holding within its civilising and pacifying thrall about one-quarter of the world's land surface and as many of its inhabitants. The United Kingdom was a relatively small country but had a sophisticated upper class trained to rule and to expect deference. It was also supported by the Royal Navy combined with the deadly cohesion of British Infantry Regiments.

From the viewpoint of imperial loyalties, a clear distinction now needs to be drawn between the first British Empire of British settlers and the second Empire of native subject peoples to which alone Lenin's theories of empire could possibly apply.

The first English settlers were the subjects of James I in what was then known as British North America. It was indeed to him that the Pilgrim Fathers on first landing addressed their loyal compact. *Pace* Lenin they were not an exploiting class engaged in the last stages of capitalism. They were religious nonconformists and small land-holders trying to wrest a living from a wilderness hunted over by Amerindians. Theirs was the first New Frontier.

It is the subsequent effect of empire and the local re-identification of these first white settlers that will now be considered: for the group identification of native peoples starting as racial and transforming into national consciousness centred on colonial boundaries has already been considered.

The first white colonists identified as English or New Englanders. Soon they were organised by the English government into thirteen colonies run from London through local governors. These colonies flew the Union flag and were guarded by the Royal Navy and Army. King James, however, was not King of America, but of England to whom the loyalties and allegiances of his New England subjects were owed. The French American colonies of Acadie and New France finally fell to Britain in the middle of the eighteenth century causing British North America to stretch from Hudson's Bay to the mouth of the Mississippi. Like other European colonies this area was run under the colonial preference system, with the colonists supplying the mother country with raw materials in return for preference in regard to her manufactured products.

Every schoolchild knows how the American War of Independence began in 1775 in protest against this system of colonial preference, against taxation without local representation and particularly against British insistence upon the land beyond the Appalachians remaining Indian. It has been a universal feature of imperial rule that the imperial state has tended to favour better treatment for the natives than local white settlers were prepared to concede. The British government, therefore, would not yield to requests for self-determination.

When war broke out the loyalties and disloyalties involved were described by the future President Adams as being one-third of the population loyal British, one-third loyal American and the other third uncommitted. Yet one-third disloyal has proved throughout history to be a significant proportion if events can sway the uncommitted in their direction. It may indeed provide an answer to Seton-Watson's question posed at the beginning of this book as to what proportion of a population requires to experience national consciousness for a new nation to be born. In the course of the American War of Independence the one-third uncommitted eventually sided with the American patriots and therefore a sufficient sense of American national identity came into being.

Yet many of the American rebels who went into action at Lexington and Bunkers Hill did so at first as misused Englishmen with the Union Jack still displayed in one corner of their new flag alongside the thirteen red and white stripes of the protesting colonies. Some of the new regimental colours of Washington's Continental Army, such as those of the New Hampshire Regiment, also incorporated the British flag. Only later in the war did the Stars (at first in a circle) and Stripes come to replace the British flag to form the famous Star-Spangled Banner.

The rebellious colonists, nicknamed Yankees, called themselves Patriots and their opponents, Tories. The latter seem at first to have been regarded more as a class faction than, as later, American traitors to be tarred and feathered and sometimes even hanged for their anti-American Britishness.

Not all of British North America, however, joined in the rebellion. British North America then included Nova Scotia with the great bastion of Halifax, the equivalent of the other British bastion at New York. Nova Scotia raised and sent south to fight on the British side regiments such as the Loyal Nova Scotia Volunteers and Royal Highland Immigrants. Also fighting for the British were the Kings Royal Regiment of New York, the New York Volunteers and the New York Loyalists. Other regiments of volunteers, all indicating preparedness to risk their lives on behalf of Britain, were the King's American Regiment, the Royal American Regiment, the King's Rangers (raised to police the Appalachians against the settlers), the Pennsylvanian Loyalists, the Maryland Loyalists and a cavalry regiment called the British Legion, hated and feared by all those now beginning to answer to the American name. Most of the Indians, including the Iroquois of the 'six nations' were firmly on the British side.

Yet the constancy of George Washington and his Continental Army (formed out of the old Militia) finally won the victory they deserved, aided by a French fleet. The British Empire had now given birth to the first of its many national offsprings—although no other successor nation had ever to fight to gain its independence. The new Americans now assumed for themselves that continental name.

From beleaguered Charleston and New York at the end of the war the now-despised British Loyalists and their families had to flee to Britain or Canada. Many were shipped to Nova Scotia where they eventually formed the province of New Brunswick. Others, including most of the Iroquois, moved into western Quebec where along with numerous other Loyalists and later new immigrants they were to form the loyal province of Ontario.

The Americans at first tried to carry their so-called social revolution and the Rights of Man into British North America led by Congress's own Canadian Regiment. They even captured Yorktown (now Toronto) and Montreal, but were repulsed at the walls of Quebec. The latter's French inhabitants had been persuaded by their British governor to oppose the

American invaders as rebellious Protestants who would subvert their French law and Catholic religion. The whole of French Canada was now renamed Quebec. But with large-scale immigration, mainly from Britain, this was later subdivided into upper and lower (French) Canada. The French-Canadians later fought shoulder to shoulder with the British to repulse the American invasion of 1812 when there were naval battles on the Great Lakes and the British temporarily captured Detroit. But the Americans were decisively repulsed at the battle of Queenstown Heights.

In identity terms the American Declaration of Independence from Imperial Britain also implied a declaration of independence of all the other British of North America from the United States. To the north of the 49th Parallel the other provinces simply carried on with their own governors under the British Flag and Crown, all sharing a British sense of identity which at that time was both colonial and imperial; but not yet locally national. With continued immigration on a wide scale, western Canada was opened up before its counterpart in the United States. Finally under the British North America Act 1867 a new North American state was brought into being called Canada, with four federal provinces, later to be increased to ten. Unlike the USA, this Canadian federation retained the British parliamentary style of government described as 'responsible government', but with a new Canadian flag retaining the Union Jack in one corner, as all other British settler Dominions were later to do.

Canada was thereafter well served by a succession of British Governors-General. While virtually an independent nation, it still proudly regarded itself as a British Dominion and part of the British Empire. The attachments and loyalties of British kith and kin, particularly of the former Loyalist immigrants from New England, remained firm.

The French–Canadians, however, never came to regard themselves as British nor, therefore, to experience much of a British imperial identity. Indeed their attachments and loyalties continued to Old France and to the French *fleur-de-lis*, preserved in the separate and largely Catholic province of Quebec. Their separate sense of identity, far from being imperial, sometimes placed the Canadian federation under internal stress. No more so than over the question of conscription to man the Imperial Forces in two world wars, which many French–Canadians chose to regard as purely British imperial entanglements. But towards the end of both the First and the Second World Wars, when faced with the growing casualties of their fellow English-speaking Canadians unable by themselves to man their forces, the federal parliament on each occasion quietly voted for universal conscription.

In 1980 the movement of the Parti Québécois to turn Quebec into a separate nation–state to match their separate French sense of identity (thereby splitting western Canada from the Maritimes) came to a head. However, this movement had already been headed off by a French–Canadian Prime Minister introducing bilingualism at federal level throughout the whole of Canada and also by substituting a new Canadian red and white flag with a maple leaf in the middle to replace the British one. This new flag has now become sufficiently popular to be flown all over the Union along with the separate provincial flags. It seems that the federal province of Quebec, apart from retaining its own French language and civil law, is now settling down to be more like other Canadian provinces. And, of course, the Canadian name is itself a French one. Canada is no longer an imperial Dominion and although still a monarchy, the Queen is now styled Queen of Canada. The metamorphosis from imperial Dominion to Canadian nation is now, therefore, complete.

By Act of the Imperial Parliament in 1900 the same British political system, with a Governor-General to represent the Crown and with a Federal government chosen from Parliament, was instituted for the Dominion of Australia. It has six federal states. Neighbouring New Zealand became a Crown Colony in 1841 after which massive White immigration from Britain was encouraged. In 1907 it became the Dominion of New Zealand.

Both Australia and New Zealand have national flags still containing the Union Jack in one corner and New Zealand still uses the British national anthem. But Australia has now adopted as its anthem 'Advanced Australia Fair'. These former imperial Dominions advanced to nationhood more slowly than Canada which became nationally aware of itself more quickly due to the French–Canadians and also because the now friendly United States made Canada less reliant upon British sea power for protection. So Canada was the first of the Dominions to resolve to stand on its own feet.

Some imperial identity continued with Canadian forces still part of the Imperial ones and with periodic imperial conferences in London. The Statute of Westminster in 1931 provided that all three British dominions should become coequal with the mother country and with full power of nationhood leaving only a vestige of British imperial authority.

However, for the British Empire to span one-quarter of the world's land surface signified British rule in places other than those settled by British kith and kin. This was the second British Empire. India was even created an Empire in itself to please Queen Victoria, henceforth styled Empress of India. She was not, however, Empress of any other British dominion. The second British Empire included island colonies like Ceylon, and also Burma, Malaysia and most of Africa. In some of the more temperate parts, large British settler communities grew up as in Kenya, Southern Rhodesia, Durban and the Cape. Here British kith and kin intended to make their permanent homes but were gradually overtaken by a reactive racial consciousness causing Blacks to regard them as other people and not true Africans at all. This transformation from colonial Black subjection or deference into a sense of coequal, if not superior, Black racial awareness leading to independence, has already been described. But it should nevertheless not be overlooked that at one time, particularly in India, there was a genuine, if temporary, period of respect for the ruling British class or race which could not have remained in control, even for a decade, let alone a century, without it. It was also a strong civilising influence.

The imperial identification of individuals does not therefore appear to be so different from any other except that, unlike national consciousness, an imperial consciousness lacks a sufficient territorial base. The bulk of a colony's inhabitants do not even visit the mother country, unless they have relatives there. Most inhabitants cannot therefore be expected to identify with a mother country they have never seen. An imperial monarch, however, who actually comes to see them is better appreciated.

Where the imperial loyalties lay for British kith and kin at the time of the outbreak of the Second World War in 1939 gives some guide to a continuing imperial identification.

With the collapse of France in June 1940 and the German occupation of most of Europe, Britain was left facing Germany and Italy alone for nearly a year. The Soviet Union then seemed almost to be on the other side having invaded and dismembered Poland along with the Germans so causing the initial outbreak of the war. But Britain was not entirely alone for, in declaring his defiance of Germany, Churchill said that Britain would continue the war, if need be abandoning the British Isles in favour of the British Empire.

Within days of the British declaration of war in 1939 every single independent parliament of the British Dominion freely voted to declare war against the enemy of the mother country as also being their own. The Prime Minister of Australia even exclaimed: 'the borders of Australia are now on the banks of the Rhine!' Yet to fight the Germans for their invasion of distant Poland was hardly in the economic interests of Australians. Only in South Africa was the vote a narrow one due to separate Afrikaner loyalties that were far from imperial and were shortly to gain their racial ascendancy. Yet even the South African flag still has the Union Jack in one corner.

Until the Soviet Union and the United States entered the war, the Germans and the Italians were held at bay due entirely to the British Empire. In Canada, safe from German bombing, a great military arsenal and a Commonwealth training scheme for airforce pilots were set up. The Italians posed the most immediate threat in North Africa. India's armed forces comprising two million volunteers manned numerous divisions to fight in North Africa and Italy, and provided the major strategic reserve force of the Middle East. Australia and New Zealand likewise provided their soldiers, seamen and airmen. Canada contributed the equivalent of a whole Field Army. From the African colonies came Black contingents like the King's East African Rifles who helped the South African Armoured Division to defeat the Italians in East Africa.

In the Soviet Union the British contribution to the Second World War is regarded as insignificant, as indeed it appeared compared to the Soviet victories and casualties on the Eastern Front. Nevertheless the Russian Steppes were less strategically important than the Mediterranean. The heartland of industrial Germany too was pulverised, not by Soviet planes, but by a largely British bombing force which caused the total destruction, by saturation bombing, of Bremen, Hamburg, Cologne and Dresden. To this the Canadians contributed 45 Airforce squadrons. Indeed, by 1944 one-quarter of the air crews attacking Germany night after night under British command were Canadians. Had it not been for the British Empire causing the Germans throughout the war to face two ways and keep large parts of their airforce in the west, the outcome might well have been different.

The foregoing is sufficient to show that imperial consciousness, being the group attachment trait focused on a mother country, can only persist among those who continue to regard themselves as one people. It is impossible to maintain among those who regard themselves as other people—particularly when they are of different colour and race—and is anyway bound to weaken when kith and kin become outnumbered by immigrants from other countries.

A multinational state faces difficulties enough in attracting and maintaining loyalty and allegiance. Those of a far flung empire, whether Roman or British, are in the long run insuperable.

THE INTERNATIONAL WORKING CLASS

The phenomenon of Black racial consciousness changing into national consciousness is similarly matched by the group consciousness of the international working-class. Such a transformation from class into nation again tends to confirm the basic proposition that all identities depend upon the group identification of individuals; also that class consciousness has no special attributes compared with any other. For it is only when people with distinctive habits become group conscious of themselves as *we* and as recognisably different from others that they can be said to be class conscious of themselves as distinct from other nationals.

Class consciousness thus depends upon a certain distinctiveness of outlook and manners as recognised even among young children. It tends, however, not to be territorial or it will become national as in the case of the Finns and Czechs. Some classes are also religiously defined when they are usually called castes—although in India the two words are interchangeable. The first International was that of the International Working Man's Association founded in London in 1864 and addressed by Marx. The identification of its members as working class was then confined to industrial manual workers. But landless peasants exploited by landowners have also throughout history been conspicuous for their collective antagonism.

The first international working class state, claiming to represent an international working class, was the Soviet Union founded within the collapsed Russian nation-state and Empire after the October Revolution. The Bolsheviks then seized power from a new liberal government which had, however, already caused the Czar to abdicate. The Bolsheviks then assumed power, however, not just in the name of the Russian workers and peasantry, but also in that of the former subjects of the Russian Empire who were also called upon to support the Revolution. Most indeed were prepared to do so in expectation of being allowed to retain or regain their separate national identities. This led to a confused situation with White Russians trying to assist national liberation movements. These had to be fought off in outlying parts by the dashing Red Cavalry Division with Stalin as its Commissar and many future Soviet field marshalls in its ranks. Its recruiting posters bore the spirited caption 'Proletarians mount up!' The Red Cavalry, however, were stopped in their tracks outside Warsaw when trying to recapture that portion of the Russian Empire which had included Eastern Poland (Germany and Austria then held the other parts). On the breakdown of the German, Austrian and Russian Empires, patriotic Poles had regained independence at their own hands and were determined not to be 'liberated' by Russians in the name of The International Working Class.

No model for coping with such a peculiarly Russian colonial situation had been provided by Marx or Engels, and Lenin and Stalin had now simply to devise their own. Lenin provided the theory and tactics of the International Class Revolution in such a colonial context, as well as the immediate dictatorship of the Russian workers. He wrote (1924):

> People who have not gone thoroughly into the question think there is a contradiction in Socialists of oppressing nations insisting on freedom of *secession* while Socialists of oppressed nations insist on freedom of *union*. However a little reflection will show that there is not, nor can there be, any other road leading from the *given* situation to internationalism and the amalgamation of nations, any other road to this goal.

So Lenin's theory was essentially an adaptation of Marx's to fit imperial situations, with a grand strategy of encouraging international working class consciousness, where appropriate, by secession or union of the International Workers in order to lead to a single human society.

In Russia this was thought by Lenin to be a *union* situation involving the amalgamation of oppressed nations, and on his death Stalin became executor of the same strategy. He was a brilliant tactician and, above all, the real architect of the Union of Soviet Socialist Republics (USSR) based on working class rather than on national or imperial consciousness. In theory the USSR was intended to be the expanding base of the International Proletariat. Its first constitution was granted in 1924. This was replaced by a new one in 1936 of which Stalin said:

> We now have a multinational socialist state which has stood all tests and whose stability might well be envied by any national state in any part of the world.

In this context a socialist state meant one ruled by the working class under a single party of the Workers with all the means of production owned by the state in accordance with Marx's original socio-economic theory. When put into effect all states and nations were thus supposed to wither away or, it would, as Lenin put it, lead to the amalgamation of nations.

This book is not concerned with querying the truth of any political or religious movement or belief so much as with studying different forms of resultant group consciousness. Most collectively conscious groups have their systems of shared belief which help to hold them together. Nevertheless it is necessary to consider briefly a different theory of group consciousness claimed to depend entirely on economically induced class consciousness solely in order to see if the results support the theory in question.

Marx's basic theory has already been mentioned in connection with group identity and warfare. To him all warfare was class warfare and classes in turn arose from control of the means of production. So all group consciousness is class consciousness. It is now necessary to see how this theory has worked out when put into actual practice by Lenin and Stalin with complete state ownership within the USSR as the start of a new universal human society.

The new Soviet state, instituted in 1924 and controlling the complete land mass of the former Russian Empire, had to avoid the appearance of being an imperial or Greater Russian one. So it was conceived to be not a nation at all but a supranational state and an organisation of workers and peasants with loyalties based not on nation but on international class. Yet within the new USSR there were still territorial nations (called *narods* or nationalities) and former colonies over which the Czar had once ruled as Emperor of 'all the Russias'. Their existence was recognised by Lenin and they were encapsulated in subservient provinces within a new federal state whose higher supporting identity was, however, to be not Greater Russian, but Proletarian.

Originally there were eleven national republics, including large Russian and Ukranian ones. Others, as already seen, were simply manufactured by Stalin out of racial or linguistic tribal groupings.

This multinational working-class state has certainly been successful in holding the country together, including all its subsidiary nationalities. But what of working-class consciousness itself once all internal social classes had been eliminated? How could a strong working-class consciousness continue when there were no other distinctive classes to be distinguished from? In short, how could there continue to be a sense of *us* without some others regarded as *them*?

Stalin himself in his report to the 17th Congress of the Soviet Communist Party in 1934 posed this very question and gave his own answer. He said that as there was now no economic exploitation nor separate classes within the USSR there was strictly now no Soviet Proletariat. It was wrong therefore to continue to refer to Soviet workers as Proletarians. In Stalin's view Marx and Engels had wrongly abstracted themselves from the international scene:

> As you see the working class of the USSR is an entirely new working class, a working class emancipated from exploitation, the like of which the history of mankind has never seen before.

Nevertheless, he went on to say that as this working class was still encircled by capitalist nations intent upon its destruction, it required to remain collectively conscious of itself as part of the international working class and, for the foreseeable future, to be on its guard. In his same address he proclaimed the worker's continuing loyalties in these terms:

> The workers of the West say that the working class of the USSR is the shock brigade of the world proletariat. This is very good. It shows that the world proletariat is prepared to continue all the support it can to the working class of the USSR. This imposes a serious duty upon us. It imposes upon us the duty of working better and fighting better for the final victory of socialism in our country, for the victory of socialism in all countries!

Hence a working-class consciousness, stimulated by state propaganda was still to be the supporting identity of the Soviet State.

Stalin's 1934 address preceded the revolution in China. If Marx's theory of class consciousness had been correct, however, this should then have caused the adjoining Soviet and Chinese states to amalgamate as part of the international working class rather than to remain with sharp dividing lines caused by other linguistic, racial and cultural identity strands.

In 1939 Germany and the Soviet Union dismembered Poland between them to revert to the 1918 situation when the Polish nation–state did not exist—but Poles as such certainly did.

In 1941 the USSR was suddenly invaded by Germany. The result was at first chaotic. The German army, almost unimpeded in places, advanced to the very outskirts of Leningrad, Moscow and Stalingrad where it was ultimately stopped in its tracks as the whole Soviet people fought like tigers with their backs to the wall. Stalin, the architect of the USSR, was now their dynamic Generalissimo—for revolutionary leaders tend to make outstanding field commanders.

Most Soviet troops, even Muslim ones, remained loyal during the invasion. But there were some defections, including that of complete units from the Soviet to the German side. There were, however, no German defections to the International Workers—despite hopeful playing in the front line of the Internationale to encourage them to cross over. The Germans even managed to recruit the dashing 15th Cossack Cavalry Corps, from within the Soviet Union, officered by White Russians bent on liberating Russia from the Soviet State. The German Army also came to include the 162nd Turcoman division of anti-Soviet Muslims which saw active service in the Italian campaign.

Supplied now from behind the Urals, the Soviet army was later able to strike back and the ensuing battles were the nearest to Armageddon the human race has ever seen. There were tank battles at Stalingrad and Kursk involving hundreds of divisions with tens of thousands of tanks on either side. In what is now known as the Great Patriotic War, the Soviet Union suffered 20 million dead. Huge war memorials now stand in the major Soviet cities, often manned with guards of honour of local schoolchildren, so that the young shall never forget.

In February 1945 at Yalta, Stalin insisted, for Soviet protection, upon the contraction of Poland and Germany and also on the removal westwards of all German-speaking peoples from East Prussia, Eastern Poland and Czecho-slovakia numbering about 10 millions. In Poland, indeed, he got back most of what the Red Cavalry had failed to 'recapture' in 1920 but which had been the subject of the Soviet–German pact in 1939. He also insisted on all Traitors of the People who had defected to the enemy being returned for punishment which was even meted out to Soviet soldiers taken prisoner through no fault of their own. The Tatars of the Crimea, many of whom had collaborated, were also removed as a complete people to Siberia.

So the Soviet loyalty of 'the working class', between 1941 and 1945, was by no means complete and there were still some Russians and other nationals who felt no real loyalty to the Soviet state, but only to their own peoples such as Ukranians and Latvians many of whom, after the war, fled to the west.

The final disbandment parade in Austria of the 15th Cossack Cavalry Corps before the British 6th Armoured Division was an astonishing sight. Their 3rd Calvalry Division rode past the saluting base before their general with fur caps and flashing sabres as if out of old Russia, clanking with medals and even complete with Orthodox priests while the divisional trumpeters on white horses played a stirring march. It was a final Cossack national occasion.

There can be no doubt, however, where the loyalties of most Soviet people lay during the Great Patriotic War. Indeed the Soviet state for the first time then came to coincide with the *esprit de corps* of a valiant people. However, it was as a nation and not as the International Working Class that the people had fought, with millions prepared to die, not for a class, but for the Soviet motherland.

After the war a new Soviet constitution was promulgated in 1977 after a decade of debate as to whether the Soviet state had indeed now become a single nation. But there was still some reticence, out of respect for Marx and Engels, about so calling it. A new Article 62 now enjoins:

> Citizens of the USSR are obliged to safeguard the interests of the Soviet State, and to enhance its power and prestige. Defence of the Socialist motherland is the sacred duty of every citizen of the USSR. Betrayal of the motherland is the greatest of crimes against the people.

Article 28 dealing with foreign policy states as its aim 'the peaceful coexistence of states with different social systems'; but also in contradiction and more menacingly 'consolidating the position of world Socialism'.

In furtherance of the latter, the Soviet Government had in 1939 annexed into the Soviet system the Baltic nation–states of Latvia, Estonia and Lithuania to be later moulded into new working-class republics with Russian as their primary language. At the end of the war too Stalin insisted that the six East European nation–states which the Soviet Army had just liberated should have governments controlled by a Communist Party of the Working Class answering to Moscow. This was at first easy to do as all senior Soviet military and political leaders were members of and trained through the communist party. The Soviet security organisation had also by now taken over from the International Comintern the task of furthering abroad the International Working Class. This they had done when, out of deference to wartime Allies, Stalin had agreed to close down the International Comintern. An 'Iron Curtain' of *us* and *them* between Westerners and Easterners then descended across Europe, even dividing Berlin in two and causing the Western military zone of Germany to be turned into a separate West German state, none of which had been contemplated at the Yalta Conference. In response the eastern portion of Germany was also transformed into a state of the German working class with international class pretensions.

The USSR has since displayed imperiousness and even threatened or used military force against most of these East European nation–states where national consciousness remains as strong, if not stronger, than class consciousness, particularly in Poland with its strong Catholic strand of identity. The Polish working class has even come into conflict with the nation–state as not being sufficiently Polish. Not much sign here, then, of international working class consciousness. Indeed it is difficult to see *by what mechanism* mere state ownership of all the means of production should lead naturally, as Lenin thought, to the diminution of national consciousness and the consequent amalgamation of nations. This, however, was what Lenin originally thought—although perhaps later modifying his views. There is no more reason why it should do so, with a consequent amalgamation of nations, than for all nation–states to disappear within the continent of Africa by mere removal of White imperial control.

National liberation occurred in most African colonies with few having to fight for independence. But once liberated the Soviet Government has tried, in certain East African countries, to encourage Lenin's next stage of class revolution against their own ruling 'classes' before such new nations have even been properly formed. In practice they have often found themselves supporting particular tribal groups claiming they are the Working Class to be assisted by Soviet armaments against their rivals.

Within the Soviet Union itself national identity still, in theory, resides only at the lower level of the national republics whose identities are simply regarded as cultural or linguistic. Under the 1977 constitution there are now fifteen national republics, each with their own official languages, including the five Muslim ones. The Russian Soviet Federal Socialist Republic is much the largest with a population of 142 million out of a total of 273 million. The second largest is the Ukraine with 50 million and there are nine national republics with populations of five million or less. It is thus a very lopsided federation although becoming less so with the increase of Soviet Muslims in relation to Slavs. Each national republic now, for the first time, also has its own national flag and soviet or parliament. For the whole union there is also now a separate Soviet national flag (with the Workers' emblem of Hammer and Sickle pushed significantly into one corner) and even a national anthem distinct from the Internationale of the International Workers.

Such symbolic changes are important as indicating, even within the USSR, the presence now of nationhood or of a classless nation, rather than of international class. With such territorial attachments it is difficult to see how it could be otherwise. The country, however, still lacks a good national name which its citizens can recognise as their own. They are not prepared or indeed encouraged to answer to the former Russian name; and the Soviet one is inappropriate as the word Soviet means a worker's council. The people, as individuals, do not therefore answer to the name of Soviets despite westerners so calling them. They prefer to be called Soviet citizens with allegiance to the initials USSR like others feels towards the USA or UK.

In an ideological article appearing in December 1983 in the newspaper *Pravda*, the organ of the Soviet Communist Party, the Kremlin's nationalities policy, criticised as 'Russification', was defended but an end called to internal racial prejudices. The article admits that such prejudice still exists as seen in the resentment by other nationalities of Russian dominance and is likewise expressed in Russian scorn for the Muslim tribesmen of Central Asia. It added:

> Changes in people's social psychology take place slowly and some citizens retain nationalistic prejudices.

The article continued:

> The spinal cord of brotherly relations among all nations and nationalities was and will remain by right the great Russian people, commanding deep respect because of revolutionary policies, selflessness in conflict and work and spiritual generosity.

It states that 82 per cent of the Soviet people now speak Russian 'the language of friendship and brotherhood' and says that there is a need to encourage minority cultures at the same time as developing Soviet culture for 'to be international in the thinking of V I Lenin, does not mean to be without a nation'.

Under international law the Soviet Union is now indeed recognised as an ordinary nation-state through its membership of the United Nations Organisation. The national republics of the Ukraine and Mongolia, however, are also separate members of UNO which may set a precedent for the future in relation to other Greater Nations with only a single vote in the United Nations Assembly. As indicative of national as opposed to class consciousness, Soviet athletes now compete in the international Olympic Games where they vie with those of the United States. The new Soviet national anthem—not the Internationale—is now played as Soviet victors ascend the rostrum to receive their gold medals and return home to a *national* hero's welcome.

The concept of being the vanguard of the working class, as Lenin and Stalin proclaimed, nevertheless still lingers on but joined now with a stronger Soviet national strand. The latter is helped by the *esprit de corps* of the Soviet armed forces in which most citizens are required to do several years national service. Russian is the universal military language and also that of the higher echelons of the Communist Party which effectively runs the country.

So the group consciousness of the Soviet people has been transformed from the group consciousness of the International Working Class into a national one; yet one which still likes to regard itself as patron of exploited working classes in other countries where such distinctive classes exist and who experience some attachment to Moscow.

It is probably wrong, therefore, to describe the USSR as having still an imperial consciousness, or of being an Empire owing to its inclusion of former Russian colonial peoples. It all depends on whether the Russians still regard themselves as an imperial ruling people or class and whether inhabitants of other national republics see themselves as subservient peoples ruled by Russian aliens from whom they now desire to be free. There is little evidence so far, however, to suggest that this is so. Indeed the peoples of the

Muslim national republics now appear to be better off than those of most independent Muslim states and also still appear loyal to the Soviet state. Soviet Armenians are certainly happier than formerly under Turkish rule. Nor must it be forgotten that the great architect of this new socialist multinational state, replacing the former Russian Empire, was not a Russian trying to induce subject peoples to identify under that national or imperial name, but an ex-colonial Georgian.

This transformation from class into nation has its parallel in the case of other class identities transforming into larger national ones like the Czechs and Finns in relation to imperial Austrians or Swedes. Whatever the cause of such transformation, however, the resultant sense of *we-ness*, once it becomes territorial, turns into national consciousness which is not just confined to a ruling class or élite. Perhaps it was Marx's misconception on this matter which now accounts for Soviet reluctance to call themselves a nation or publicly to abandon the aim of international class warfare that lies behind the current confrontation of *us* and *them* between Westerners and Easterners.

Other classless states, apart from the USSR, still like to regard themselves merely as segments of an international working class. Most inhabitants of such states, however, identifying by class or as 'the people', tend to become nationally conscious whenever they start to prefer as *us* their own national inhabitants. It seems hardly necessary, therefore, for the USA to try to destabilise such 'international' states if they are likely anyway to evolve naturally into national ones. Nor likewise for the USSR to try to destabilise European nation–states into becoming segments of an International Working Class that could never in practice survive as a universal human identity.

INTERNATIONAL ORGANISATIONS

When an imperial identity becomes transformed into several new national ones, any continuing communication between them becomes international. For the adjective 'international' literally means the relations *between* nations, or, in the case of international law, the law governing the relations *between* nation–states. *International* group consciousness is therefore something of a misnomer for individuals cannot literally identify *internationally* anymore than they can do so *multinationally* unless there is a distinctive group which happens to bear an international or supranational name as the extra focus of their identification. Most international organisations with identities of their own are therefore really striving after some kind of supranational or even antinational identity which they choose to call 'international' although in theory supposed to supplant nations.

The first International was that of the Working Man's Association founded in London in 1864 with a working-class identity and a self-awareness and dignity of its own. Later came the International Comintern directed more towards international class warfare by the prewar Soviet Government.

Group identification centred on an international organisation is thus no different from any other and still depends on the individual's group consciousness. It follows that a working-class loyalty embracing the whole of mankind is unlikely to be created, still less maintained. The missing element in a sense of distinctiveness at world level from others. There is indeed no reason to suppose that an international ruling class of workers would be better able to create a world identity where would-be world empires have failed. This is seen from the experience of revolutionary China and the Soviet Union, each more homogeneous now as classless nations, but with their respective peoples still confronting each other as *us* and *them* and far from sharing a sense of workers international brotherhood. Nor do any international religious organisations show any better sign of being able to unite the whole of mankind as opposed to their particular religious adherents.

The former British Empire, whose component nations, White or Black, are now all independent and free, have been transformed into the Commonwealth of Nations from which the name British has now been dropped. It is a multinational and multiracial organisation, with any identities largely confined to the organisation itself, but not popularly based. For the Commonwealth hardly yields an appropriate name for ordinary people to answer to as being their own nor to experience a sufficient sense of *shared* distinctiveness. All that is shared is some residual sense of Britishness or way of doing things as well as the English language and culture.

Nevertheless, the Commonwealth Organisation, as presently conceived, and operating as an institution parallel to nation–states makes for amity and cooperation between them. It also organises conferences and interchanges of various kinds and provides a meeting place for the Heads of Government of about one-third of the world's nations. A remarkable feature too is the willingness of the constituent governments still to recognise the British Monarch as symbolic Head and as relic of an identity once, but no longer, imperial. In many ways therefore the Commonwealth provides a model for other such affiliations between nation–states. But of group consciousness or loyalty and allegiance on a Commonwealth scale there is little.

The European Economic Community (EEC) represents a more definite move towards the union of old and established European nations that is at present difficult to classify. It is a multinational organisation of 12 nation states, run by a council of their national ministers to whom a European Commission answers as executive. Its formation was peculiar. In the postwar chaos of Western Europe and resultant identity vacuum the bold step was taken of creating a new Franco–German accord by linking together their heavy industries. So three European 'Communities' were formed that were not national ones but the European Iron and Steel Community, Euratom and later the EEC proper which was later still to incorporate the other two. The European Economic Community is thus primarily an economic organisation for promoting a free industrial and controlled agricultural market within its borders—the latter being of particular advantage to both France and Germany.

The European Council of Ministers meets in different locations. There is a Court of Justice at Luxembourg for interpreting and enforcing Community law. There is also a directly elected consultative Parliament which does not however have legislative powers. It is situated at Strasbourg. At present therefore the EEC may be described as an economic and social organisation parallel to its several nation–states but still dependent on them; and into which they have voluntarily pooled their sovereignty in certain fields.

The EEC does not yet call itself, nor is it regarded by others, as a Greater nation–state. Nor is it a member of the United Nations Organisation. It was however assumed by its Founding Fathers who were federalists that a new superstate or supranational organisation would eventually emerge from the working of a free industrial and controlled agricultural market so as to generate a sufficient European identity.

No strong European consciousness, however, can yet be said to have arisen among a majority of the peoples of its constituent nations. As yet a European sense of loyalty and allegiance seems mainly confined to a small élite of politicians and civil servants. Of European nationals those most prone to identify as such seem to be the Dutch, Belgians and Italians, with more provincial than national identities of their own.

It appears, indeed, that there may be some limit to the number of identity levels at which an individual's sense of attachment can readily focus. This limit may be prescribed by the requirement of distinctiveness. For group consciousness to arise a majority of individuals require to be conscious of *us* and *them* and of answering to a particular group name or names as being their own. Too many names at too many levels can therefore lead to ambiguity and be insufficiently distinctive. The requirement of seeing or conceiving others to be different also makes it hard for people speaking different languages with different cultures to identify as one—without at least some common culture and shared symbols to give some wider sense of group awareness and distinction. The USA would not be what it is with ten official languages of government.

Insofar as participatory elective parliaments are concerned, then, it is doubtful if more than one or two can ever be identified with as being one's own. So at higher or wider levels and, above all, at international or supranational level the political organisations concerned can only earn respect as bodies to the grudgingly tolerated rather than attract the loyalty or allegiance of ordinary people.

Twelve European nation–states is, however, a relatively good number to try to downgrade into federal provinces and on which to try to build a new United States of Western Europe—if such is intended. But two are already federations, five are constitutional monarchies and the British Monarch is Head of the Commonwealth. Experience so far in other parts of the world seems to suggest that before such a multinational federation could come into being, let alone be thereafter maintained, there would need to be at least some sense of identity among a majority of its inhabitants. To provide a focus for such European identification would also seem to require a European national flag and some new capital as the seat of Government, Parliament and the European Court of Justice.

Would France or England, however, ever agree to becoming European provinces? Not unless their peoples came to experience a European sense of *we-ness* or distinctiveness as compared with other neighbouring nations outside the boundaries of the new European Federation. But the nearest countries are Austria, Switzerland and East Germany normally regarded and answering to the name of Europeans. The EEC would need to pre-empt the European name from other European nations—just as the Americans have tried to pre-empt the American one within the Western Hemisphere. However, if the name of Western Europe were to be chosen to distinguish it from Eastern Europe then Greece would appear out of place. And where would the other half of the German people belong? Would Scotland too, in order to maintain its separate identity, seek separate provincial status with its own seat in Brussels?

There can indeed be no sense of allegiance or of belonging to Europe without answering to that particular name and regarding Europe as one's country. A start has been made through dropping the word 'economic' from EEC and referring to the 'European Community' in the hope that this might help to stimulate a sense of belonging. But that is not the present identity situation nor one that is bound to occur just through the workings of a free market. That is clear from the continuance of separate Scottish and English identities despite a common market since 1707. So the problem is more a psychological than an economic one. Individuals need to be able to answer to the wider national name and be encouraged to identify with the boundaries of any new federal state—but as a Greater Nation—as indeed has occurred, but in easier circumstances, within the USA and the USSR. Nor is it as yet clear whether Greater National States or Greater Nations, rather than looser Continental associations of nations, are more likely to advance international peace. Do the USA and USSR maintain international peace between them or do they rather help to maintain a dangerous state of international tension?

It is difficult to be certain.

To sum up the present identity situation, which could however change: this still appears to be *Europe des patries* in a loose association now directed in mutual economic and social programmes by a Council of ministers. The latter in turn controls the European Commission which is answerable to a European parliament elected by universal suffrage throughout Western Europe. At the 1984 European elections, however, there was a lower turn-out in most countries than in their own local government elections and significantly the election campaigns were all fought on national issues and considerations rather than on European ones. This is a good indication of where the identities still lie. Before a strong Western European identity could be said to exist, Western Europe would have to be regarded by a majority of its inhabitants as *the* Nation in contrast to others. There are nevertheless some agencies now at work of a quasi-federal or supranational character, namely, the European Court of Justice; the European Council of Heads of State and Government; and the Committee for European Political Co-operation.

As a lesson in the cooperation of independent sovereign nation–states within half a continent of formerly warring nations, its progress is nevertheless of international significance. It could even provide a model for other such continental associations in South America or Africa. It also provides a working model of a supranational Court of Justice whose decisions are actually put into effect by National Governments.

If an area is to be politically controlled, particularly by democratic means, it seems that it should be large enough to be able to provide the facilities which national peoples nowadays expect; but also small enough to be manageable. It is the latter requirement that huge continental states may find it difficult to satisfy quite apart from the problem of inspiring a sufficient sense of identification on the part of a majority of individuals.

Yet any continental state organisation requires a continental loyalty to support it.

The United Nations Organisation is now the only international organisation covering the entire world. It comprises 159 so-called 'peace loving' nation–states which is the qualification for admittance as laid down by the victorious Allies—the USA, the USSR and the UK—at the end of the Second World War. The United Nations Organisation is a valuable institution existing parallel to nation–states. It has a Director General and various derivative international agencies. Its members are national governments and it has a General Assembly of national delegates together with a security council of five 'Great Powers' rendered ineffectual, however, by a right of veto. UNO nevertheless fulfils certain vital international functions without which the world would be less secure. It still seems, therefore, to be a major instrument of peace and the most promising organisation on which to build a new system of international law and order. The organisation as such, however, is unlikely ever to attract the universal loyalty of a majority of individuals throughout the whole world. The very name United Nations or the initials UNO are hardly such as to attract the allegiance of individuals. As observed in the earlier chapter on racial consciousness, individuals cannot feel a sense of world loyalty or pride in belonging to the whole human race. For on a world scale there is no-one else to be distinguished from. *Homo sapiens* cannot experience a sense of collective pride or racial group consciousness in the absence of any other human species.

THE RIGHT OF SELF-DETERMINATION

The right of self-determination so forcefully expressed by the United States of America in their Declaration of Independence was later pronounced as a right under international law by President Wilson. It was then adopted by the League of Nations and given effect to when constructing new nations in Eastern Europe and the Middle East at the end of the First World War. This involved separation rather than the reverse process of international integration we have just been considering. Nevertheless most of these newly created nation–states have survived.

The principal of self-determination also now appears in Articles 1 and 9 of the United Nations Charter. However, as the constitutional authority Jennings (1956) observed: 'On the face of it, it sounded reasonable: let the people decide. In fact it was ridiculous because the people cannot decide until someone decides who are the people.' Popper (1974) was even more scathing when he wrote:

But . . . the utter absurdity of the principle of national self-determination must be plain to anybody who devotes a moment's effort to criticising it. The principle amounts to the demand that each state shall be a nation state: that it should be confined within a natural border, and that this border should coincide with the location of an ethnic group; so that it should be the ethnic group, 'the nation', which should determine and protect the natural limits of the state.

But nation states of this kind do not exist ... nation states do not exist, simply because the so-called 'nations' or 'peoples' of which the nationalists dream, do not exist. There are no, or hardly any, homogeneous ethnic groups long settled in countries with natural borders. Ethnic and linguistic groups (dialects often amount to linguistic barriers) are closely intermingled everywhere. Masaryk's Czechoslovakia was founded upon the principle of national self-determination. But as soon as it was founded, the Slovaks demanded, in the name of this principle, to be free from Czech domination; and ultimately it was destroyed by its German minority, in the name of the same principle. Similar situations have arisen in practically every case in which the principle of national self-determination has been applied to fixing the borders of a new state: in Ireland, in India, in Israel, in Yugoslavia. There are ethnic minorities everywhere. The proper aim cannot be to 'liberate' them all; rather, it must be *to protect* all of them. *The oppression of national groups is a great evil; but national self-determination is not a feasible remedy*. Moreover, Britain, the United States, Canada and Switzerland, are four obvious examples of states which in many ways violate the nationality principle. Instead of having its borders determined by one set or group, each of them has managed to unite a variety of ethnic groups. So the problem does not seem insoluble.

Popper's main criticism is therefore that all group conscious people cannot expect to be able to control their own destinies as nation–states within their own exclusive territories. Otherwise most nation–states would be permanently open to disintegration unless able to induce an entirely homogeneous outlook within their borders.

Self-determination has nevertheless been the principle under which all the ex-African colonies, some very small, have received their freedom as new members of UNO, each hopefully now trying to gain a national consciousness of its own. To prevent the secession of subsidiary tribal 'nations', the Organisation for African Unity in 1964 resolved that all African frontiers should be maintained as at the date of independence. In effect this imposed a guarantee of all the old colonial frontiers as new national ones which could not henceforth be altered from without or within. This principle is also buttressed by Article 2:7 of the United Nations Charter which prohibits intervention in matters which are essentially within the domestic jurisdiction of a nation–state. A UNO Resolution of 1970 reads:

States enjoying full sovereignty and independence and possessed of a representative government, effectively functioning as such with respect to all distinct peoples within their territory, shall be considered to be conducting themselves in conformity with this principle (i.e. self-determination) as regards these peoples.

So it seems that no subnation within any of the new African nation–states, or within Great Britain or the Soviet Union, can appeal to the principal of self-determination under the United Nations Charter.

Various articles of the Charter also enjoin that the territorial integrity of all nations be respected. Due to the disappearance since the Second World War of all overseas empires there now indeed appears to be emerging a world of more homogeneous and geographically cohesive nation–states. This makes for better identification within proper home countries rather than distant motherlands. Some small unviable islands, however, each proudly conscious of their own distinction, still pose problems when the exercise of their right of self-determination is by claiming continuing kinship with a distant mother-country from which they derive, to the affairs of which they make no contribution but which they nevertheless expect to defend them.

Another problem connected with the right of self-determination (and Jenning's comments) is that of testing for entitlement through a mass referendum, and whether such should be confined to the candidate or a wider constituency. In the Northern Ireland context should such a referendum be confined to the people of Northern Ireland alone; or include the whole of the British electorate of which they claim to be part? Or should the electorate be that of the whole of Ireland?

A related problem arises within a nation-state or province with strong minority loyalties or identities which are consistently over-ridden, in the very name of democracy, by the majority who feel their position otherwise threatened by the minority's foreign attachments.

These are all problems of identification of which any new system of International Law would have to take cognisance.

TOWARDS INTERNATIONAL LAW AND ORDER

Neither the United Nations nor the Commonwealth Organisation have so far been able to stop international wars between their constituent members. Nor is there, as yet, any effective agreed international code of law known to apply in advance of a crisis and by whose decisions national governments are prepared to abide as regulating international conduct. The Security Council of Great Powers each with a right of veto has also been unable to maintain peace, hardly surprisingly when they are often the main exponent of war-like confrontation. Only a pre-agreed code of international law backed by inter-pretive decisions of a supranational Court is likely to induce international order in advance of major crises, and eventually to substitute international law for lawlessness.

There has been only one instance so far of the United Nations Organisation engaging in actual enforcement. This was to prevent the invasion of Korea by China from the north; but not in furtherance of any pre-agreed international code of law. It was a political decision taken in the Security Council only due to the absence of the USSR which had temporarily withdrawn. Several nations, under American leadership, then successfully fought the Korean war. But this was hardly an example of the enforcement of a pre-agreed system of international law and order.

The connection here between new trends in international law and group consciousness is plain to see, and the group attachment trait therefore needs to be taken into account in any new international legal system. A new *jus gentium* needs to be based upon some new concepts.

Juridical laws are not like scientific ones but are cultural contrivances drawn up by committees and then approved by national governments as a basis of legal conduct in future international crises *before* the latter occur. This then gives international statesmen, as national leaders, the chance to hide behind such laws from their own national constituents, yet in their longer term interests. While UNO or a Supranational Court is unlikely ever to attract universal loyalty it could nevertheless gain widespread respect. The qualification for membership of UNO might then be changed to that of acceptance of the new International Legal code rather than the meaningless qualification of being 'peaceloving'. The only stable subject of international law to which such a code could be applied must, however, remain nation-states. For *international* law, meaning the law between nations, cannot be applied to religious or racial groups or social classes.

There are, as yet, no reliable means of law enforcement. These have still to come. Nevertheless there is a slow but steady movement towards some system of law and order and a growing wish to defuse the present ideological confrontation between East and West—the most dangerous divide of *us* and *them* the world has ever seen.

Some modest steps have indeed now been taken towards law enforcement using United Nations or independent multinational forces operating in a purely peace-keeping or policing role. These forces may only use their arms in self-defence or in resisting any attempts by forceful means to prevent them from discharging their duties. Such a confined role, however, can only be carried out under clear mandate and with the host country's consent. Those nations too with a special interest in the local situation have to be debarred as military contributors.

A multinational force organised by several national governments to keep peace in Beirut has, however, proved ineffective. For a multinational force is always subject to recall by its contributor nations whose leaders have to contend with their own electorates back home, in the event of casualties. During the Beirut operations, notable for the Shi-ite suicide car bombers, the clamour back home proved too much for national leaders who recalled their respective contingents one by one.

This operation, however, was not under UNO auspices.

Other multinational forces have been recruited by the United Nations Organisation, and with Egyptian and Israeli approval have effectively carried out a peace-keeping role in the Sinai Desert. Such a temporary multinational force, however, faces all the difficulties inhibiting *esprit de corps* that were found in similar temporary formations during the Second World War. The previous study of *esprit de corps* at Field Army level is here directly in point, particularly the difficulty of achieving a sense of identity in the temporarily formed binational 'American' 5th and 'Canadian' 1st Armies.

The UNO multinational force in Southern Lebanon faced the difficult military task of holding a line between the Israelis and Southern Lebanese. It was not allowed to shoot back except in self-defence, which in the circumstances meant not really shooting at all. At the time of the 1984 Israeli invasion the United Nations forces were therefore simply overrun with hardly a shot and the occupying Israeli army merely entrenched themselves around them. Only some Nepalis held out for a time to satisfy regimental honour.

Group consciousness is, of course, the great impediment to the working of any new system of international law and order. But it can also be used in its enforcement. This is due to its potential for stimulating *esprit de corps* among soldiers whose loyalties can then be focused upon their units *regardless of country*.

It should, therefore, be possible to recruit an International Corps with full supporting arms to exercise not just a policing role but a more robust and active peace-keeping function. It could even contain subsidiary national brigades thus using national identity at a lower level as an aid to national recruitment, while still encouraging a supranational *esprit de corps* at the higher level. This was indeed the identity situation with national battalions recruited from abroad, to fill the ranks of the International Brigades fighting on the government side in the Spanish Civil War. Another parallel is the outstanding *esprit de corps* of the Gurkha Brigade. So an International Corps recruited for international service could be made to attract a fine *esprit de corps* and the respect of millions. It could be trained for amphibious warfare with full naval and air support so as to be capable of providing a permanent International Task Force. This could be used to hold an international dividing line or even to retake, on a small scale, illegally captured territory thousands of miles away—as the British Task Force was able to recapture the Falkland Islands. But it would have to be kept under the strict control of the United Nations Organisation and only launched in furtherance of clear breaches of pre-agreed international law.

Epilogue

As indicated in the first chapter, this study of group consciousness concerns a particular field of psychology in which individuals are seen to express feelings of *us* and *them* in different contexts and at different levels. So far as historical examples have been given (and the contemporary have usually been preferred) this has only been to try to discern the main identification strands. It was never the intention to give a complete historical account or analysis of these events. So the resultant 'potted history' may seem superficial and is consciously incomplete. In some instances the strengths ascribed to particular identity strands may have been misplaced. Nevertheless the universal and endlessly repeated pattern of identification and of *us* and *them* is plain to see. Also the conclusion that it is a psychological and probably therefore an inborn faculty which is being observed.

Into this psychological field economic factors have sometimes intruded, particularly in the formation of socio-economic classes which are one example of *us* and *them*. But even here it is really the psychological consequences and observed differences in life style which are the more important. Social identification seldom seems to depend upon economic factors alone, unless leading to differences in lifestyle. While economic history can reveal much in this respect it cannot show how nations originally achieved a sense of nationhood and thereafter maintained it even in the face of other nationals whose economic circumstances are identical.

Economic factors alone do not therefore account for the creation of group consciousness or the maintenance of nations.

The present subject of study has thus been in the psychological rather than the economic field, with the conclusion that group consciousness is biologically rather than economically based and spiritual rather than purely materialistic.

The subject of biological race or taxonomy occupies, like economics, yet another field. It only happens to coincide with group consciousness where members of a particular biological variant, or a segment thereof, suddenly become aware of themselves as distinct from others, taking racial distinction as their hallmark. Such racial group consciousness then falls within the field of psychology rather than of taxonomy.

Another separate field is that of the Arts which should not be determined solely by national or class consciousness. The artist may take as his theme that of human identities and the clash between them and the individual, as in Tolstoy's *War and Peace*; but great art should not just be directed towards *furthering* group consciousness whether on a national or a class basis.

Finally, but not least important, comes the question of religious belief which gives meaning, social ceremony and moral support to the daily lives of millions, especially in time of stress. Religious beliefs again occupy a separate field. Nothing contained in this book need offend anyone's religious faith. Group consciousness and the religious impulse in man only happen to coincide when the attachment trait of religious believers is aroused against those of contrary faith and hence into *identifying* religiously. Normally, the different religious customs and beliefs of different nations (or even classes within nations) need cause no antagonism. But they may all too easily be stimulated into so doing. Religious fundamentalists are the worst in this regard with their inflamed sense of *us* and *them* and that God is behind their atrocities. Most religious beliefs, however, have little to do with loyalty or group consciousness. Yet religious leaders cannot always escape its consequences.

This book has been concerned not only with the deliberate fabrication of loyalties as proof of the presence of an inborn trait, but also with their *unintended* operation which is just as telling. Religious identities as such have not usually been the intention of saints. The concept of God the Father and His children forming a Brotherhood of Man might have been expected to provide a surer guide to peaceful coexistence. The trouble in practice has been that this concept has tended to become confined to a religious *us* as opposed to infidels.

So the present study of group consciousness is a psychological one occupying a separate field of its own.

Such a psychological study has inevitably drawn upon the works of others, including Trotter, who did not regard sociology as a separate science but as applied psychology or the psychology of man in association. He also saw the importance of human group behaviour in war as well as peace, and, unlike Marx, regarded human gregariousness as an inborn factor of evolution. Many of his conclusions, however, can no longer be supported, particularly his Freudian concept of fixed instincts requiring 'release' and his belief in Darwinian natural selection now operating at the level of nations.

Only a basic attachment trait however or faculty, which can be part of our evolutionary inheritance. Its particular slant or direction is not inborn and therefore remains subject to moral choice and control. In itself group consciousness can have no moral content nor are feelings of loyalty and allegiance always the most admirable of characteristics. Often they are, but occasionally, as under Hitler and Mussolini, they have been fearfully misused in furtherance of the nationalistic state, and with an arrogant disconcern for the feelings and even the lives of others. There is little in practice to choose between hateful feelings engendered by 'hate education' whether promoted on grounds of nation, class, race or religion—for all are just varieties of group consciousness.

Indeed the words national, class, racial, or religious consciousness or awareness are but similar to describe different examples of group identity which are all capable of transformation from one type into the other. Previous chapters have shown how classes, races and religious groups can all be turned into nations; and how certain groups of people, like the Jews and Sikhs, have at times worn all these different guises.

Marx's scientific theory that all social antagonism is due to economically induced class consciousness is thus seen to be dangerously incomplete. It could be adapted by substituting for class consciousness the more generalised words group consciousness of which class is but one example. But if the concept of class warfare and the eventual victory of an international working class remains crucial to Marx's theory, it is clearly unattainable, for the more it succeeded the more it would loose its distinctiveness. Class warfare is also based on hatred and movements born of hatred take on the characteristics of what they oppose.

Group consciousness in whatever form should not now be raised upon a pedestal as the sole determinant of human conduct. There are people who, for one reason or another, are seldom collectively aware and are hence bereft of loyalties and allegiances—not always for the better. National consciousness is not always in the forefront of people's minds. Individuals are usually more concerned with personal and domestic problems. In Western democracies, when seeking the individual's vote, politicians appeal largely to economic issues like jobs or housing as affecting his or her domestic situation. But, in so doing, they also often lay claim to represent *the* Nation at large. National identity itself, however, is not usually in issue. The ritualised *us* and *them* of a two-party political system giving the electorate the relief of changes of political scene, simply takes national identity for granted. A healthy nation may indeed be one which does not always need to be asserting its nationhood; but only when its sense of identity is threatened or humiliated.

It is perhaps less surprising then that economists, in propounding their theories, tend to overlook national and other identities and, above all, industrial ones upon which industrial production ultimately depends. Industrial relations depend on group psychology. To put their economic theories into practice also requires a national finance minister to take into account a currency whose very presence is due to national distinction. The need, too, to promote more exports than imports is to promote employment as a matter of national social concern.

Without wishing to deny the importance of economic factors in many fields it is only group consciousness with which this book is concerned and to the formation of which economic factors contribute little. In relation to racial, religious and linguistic group consciousness, they play no part at all.

The problems of group identity and of multilevel identification thus confront every country throughout the world, whatever their economic systems, and regardless of whether they identify as 'Westerners' or 'Easterners'.

It is hoped by now that the biological aspects of the group attachment trait may have lost their menace and be appreciated as an advantage rather than as a disadvantage. It is not a preprogrammed instinct or drive requiring Freudian 'release' in a particular direction. It is purely a faculty which being readymade, does not then need to be culturally implanted. It already exists at birth, fortunately free from the parents' own prejudices and antagonisms. Coming generations of children can therefore be educated out of being national chauvinists, religious bigots or racial antagonists. No such hateful attitudes are ever inherited however habitually disposed the infant's parents were in such directions. Thus no child of an Irish Protestant is genetically programmed to hate Irish Catholics or vice versa. They are merely brought up to do so. Nor is any Greek child born to hate all Turks. Again they are only schooled in this direction. Nor are White children in multiracial societies encoded to hate their Black compatriots or vice versa. Their upbringing and social milieu so incline them. Yet racial distinctions, if compounded by differences of language, class or culture may all too easily be stimulated into group hatred. Yet even this tendency may be culturally overriden.

By the same token human warfare deriving from group identity and antagonism is not in itself encoded in the human genes. But is likely to occur if not guarded against.

This is not to underestimate the strength and persistence of group consciousness, once formed. It is only to emphasise that no actual loyalties are ever inborn, and that each new generation of children is capable of being brought up to share more benign types of identity at more suitable levels—if only public opinion can be brought to bear using all the modern means of communication. We are indeed the first generation to be able to see what is happening on the other side of the world on the day it occurs and thus have our compassion aroused for fellow human individuals rather than as enemy stereotypes.

What finally emerges then from this study of group consciousness is the survival of moral choice, and the importance of the upbringing of children. Also the need to introduce international law and order to curb the more lethal tendencies of the human primate. Far from the destruction of morality being involved there thus emerges the question of moral control and the need for man to save himself from his greatest enemy of all—*Homo sapiens*. There is indeed no-one else who can do so. It is up to the present generation to understand and redirect group identification into safer channels. That is not to further all types of group consciousness regardless of slant or size or focus, but to encourage better identities and a better respect for the identities of others.

Nor is the conclusion disregardful of the individual self. For group consciousness can only be experienced by individuals. National consciousness causing national identity is a matter of individual feeling or sentiment. If the loyalty of a majority of individuals comes to be withdrawn, any existing identity simply disappears. It is not the state organisation which, in the long term, always rules regardless of their subject's views. It is the individuals, on the contrary, whose loyalty and allegiance are needed to support it.

If anything, since Marx's day, the history of the present century has been one of regression and mass slaughter in the name of nation, religion, class or race. In Europe alone millions have been killed by self-styled sapient man. The Second World War accounted for 47 millions. To study group consciousness is not therefore to 'take leave of one's senses'; but, on the contrary, to try to control them.

The moral aim must surely be to reduce social antagonism and warfare and eventually to supplant international lawlessness with a new code of supra-national law. This is merely the continuation of a process already achieved within most national territories; but which must now be extended.

Group consciousness in the individual and the loyalties and allegiances it involves may therefore be stimulated for good or for ill. In getting people to cooperate together in industrial enterprises, it is seen to be good. In arousing a sense of social conscience and of social duty it is likewise benign. Hence, a feeling of national identity or of national awareness is by no means immoral. It is only dangerous when allowed to become too chauvinistic, too restrictive or too hateful of others. Likewise with class or racial consciousness within a national framework; or even religious consciousness if turned sectarian against those of other creeds.

The words nationalist, racialist or classist, tend to be used of the exponents of various matching 'isms' and as signifying the element of external antagonism. Another such word is 'communalism' meaning religious antagonism. The words 'socialist' or 'communist' however usually signify a spirit of internal amity or cooperativeness to political adherents, but the reverse to others regarding themselves as threatened. The words, however, are just other 'ists' appended to the words 'social' or 'commune' without clearly indicating how particular social attitudes at different levels need to be encouraged. The same may be said of the word humanist.

Neither Marx the theorist nor Lenin the tactician confused the state with the community nor regarded the former as an end in itself. It was communal cooperation they envisaged as the ideal with the virtue of working for others and not only for self. But nowhere do they explain how people on a large scale can be induced to cohere or cooperate in the absence of a national state structure or without some degree of group consciousness to engender loyalty and allegiance. Yet a sense of nationhood is not the same as a sense of humanity.

The proposition that national, class, religious, racial or linguistic identities of *us* and *them* all spring from a group attachment trait needs to be tested against all the above 'ists' and 'isms' to show that no single one can be true to the exclusion of all others.

Concern and affection for other humans as individuals is what the words humanity and humane really mean, or as one human being to another within an enclosing spirit of decency. Something of this spirit, once preached in the Sermon on the Mount, needs to be allowed to permeate *all* identities with the conviction that *we* and *they* do not need to be antagonists.

Class has only recently yielded first place to race as a main focus of human antagonism. Yet, even here, as in the case of national identity, there may be pride and loyalty in belonging to a particular race or class whose loyalties have sometimes proved truer to national interest than those of others.

It is important then to realise that *we* and *they* do not need to be antagonists; nor need *they* be made into enemies, foes or fiends (the German for enemy). Human societies can acquire feelings of interdependence and identity without being *against* anyone. Identity does not require xenophobia.

It is feasible then to have loyalty and respect for one's own people while respecting the same feelings in others, but with a desire nevertheless to protect and improve one's own. The Empires are now gone. So too the Herrenvolk or Master Race. Nor is there room for some new Master Class of Men.

The Brotherhood of Man needs to be *cultivated* and based on a deeper sense of humanity.

References

Ainsworth, M D S *Infancy in Uganda: Contribution to Infant Care and the Growth of Attachment* (John Hopkins Press: Baltimore MD 1967)

Ainsworth, M D S 'Some contemporary patterns of mother-infant interaction', in *Stimulation in Early Infancy*, Ainsworth and Bell (eds) (Academic Press: London & New York 1969)

Bowlby, John (ed) *Attachment and loss*, Vol 1 (Pelican Books 1971)

Carpenter, G 'Mother's face and the newborn child', in *Child Alive*, Lewis, R (ed) (Temple Smith: London 1975)

Darwin, C *Origin of Species* (John Murray: London 1859)

Darwin, C *The Descent of Man, and Selection in Relation to Sex* (Appleton: New York 1871)

Darwin, C *The Expression of the Emotions in Man and the Animals* (John Murray: London 1872)

Dennis, W 'Does culture appreciably affect patterns of infant behaviour?' *J Soc Psychol*, Vol 12, pp 305–17 (1940)

Durkheim, Emile *The Rules of Sociological Method* (8th edn) (The Free Press: New York 1964)

Eaton, Theodore H, Jnr *Evolution* (Thos Nelson & Son 1970)

Evans-Pritchard, E *The Nuer* (Clarendon Press: Oxford 1940)

Fitzgerald, Garret 'The 1982 Richard Dimbleby Lecture', *The Listener*, 27 May 1982

Freud, S 'Why War?', in *The Complete Psychological Works of Sigmund Freud* (Standard edn) Vol 22 (1933)

Goodall, Jane Van-Lawick *In the Shadow of Man* (Collins 1971)

Goodall, Jane Van-Lawick *The Quest for Man* pp 131 and 221 (Phaidon 1975)

Halsey, A H 'The Social Order', Reith Lectures, *The Listener*, p 208 (1978)

Harlow, H F 'The nature of love', *Amer Psychol*, Vol 13 pp 673–85 (1958)

Harlow, H F 'The development of affectional patterns in infant monkeys', in *Determinants of Infant Behaviour*, Foss, B M (ed) (Methuen 1961)

Hartley, E L, Rosenbaum, M and Schwartz, S 'Children's use of ethnic frames of reference', *J Psychol*, Vol 26 pp 367–86 (1948)

Jahoda, G 'Development of Scottish children's ideas and attitudes about other countries', *J Soc Psychol* No. 58 pp 91–108 (1962)

Jahoda, G 'Children's concepts of nationality', *J Soc Psychol* No. 35 pp 1081–92 (1963)

Khleif, B B 'Insiders, outsiders and renegades: towards a classification of ethno-linguistic labels', in *Language and Ethnic Relations*, Giles, H *et al.* (eds) (Pergamon Press: Oxford 1979)

Koestler, Arthur 'The Brain Explosion', *The Observer Review*, 15 Jan 1978

Lambert, W E and Klinebert, O. 'A pilot study of the origins and development of natural stereotypes', *Internl Soc Sc Jnl*, No. 11 pp 211–38

Leach, Edmund *Social Anthropology* (Fontana 1982)

Lienhardt, Godfrey *Social Anthropology* (2nd edn) p 58 (OUP 1960)

Leakey, Richard E and Lewin, Roger *Origins* (Macdonald & Jane: London 1977)

Lorenz, Konrad *On Aggression* (Methuen 1970)

Morgan, Lewis *Ancient Society* (Henry Holt & Co: New York 1877)

Morris, Desmond *Manwatching; a field guide to Human Behaviour* (Triad/Granada 1978)

Mortimer, Edward *Faith and Power* (Faber & Faber 1982)

Muscovici, Serge 'Society and theory in social psychology', in *The Concept of Social Psychology*, Tajfel, H. (ed) (Academic Press: New York 1972)

Plaget, J and Weil, A 'The development in children of the idea of the homeland and of relations with other countries', *Internl Sc Bull*, Vol 3, pp 561–78 (1951)

Popper, K R *Conjectures and Refutations* (Routledge and Kegan Paul 1974)

Pushkin, Isodore and Venness, Thelma 'The development of racial awareness and prejudice in children', in *Psychology and Race*, Watson, Peter (ed) (Penguin Educn 1973)

Radke, M, Trager, H G and Davis, H 'Social Perceptions and attitudes of children', *Genetic Psychology Monographs*, Vol 40, p 327 (1949)

Reynolds, Vernon *The Biology of Human Action* (Freeman & Co 1976)

Rivers, William Halsey *Instinct and the Unconscious* (2nd edn, Cambridge 1922)

Robertson, J and Bowlby, J 'Responses of young children to separation from their mothers', *Coun Cent Int Enf*, Vol 2, pp 131–42

Robertson, J *Young Children in Brief Separation* (Film and Guide booklet) (Tavistock Inst of Human Relations, London 1967)

Sadat, Amwar *In Search of Identity* (Collins 1978)

Schaffer, H R *The Growth of Sociability* p 60 (Penguin 1971)

Seton Watson, Hugh *Nations and States* (Methuen: London 1977)

Shepher, J 'Mate selection among second generation Kibbutzin adolescents and adults', *Arch. Sexual Behaviour* Vol 1, p 293 (1971)

Sheriff, Muzafer and Carolyn *Groups in Harmony and Tension* (Harper: New York 1953)

Spencer, Herbet *Principles of Ethnics* (Williams: London 1892)

Stavrinides, Zenon *The Cyprus Conflict: National Identity and Statehood* (Limmasol 1975, privately printed)

Steiner, George 'What is Swiss?', *Times Lit Supp*, 7 Dec 1984

Sumner, W G *Folkways* (Ginn & Co: Boston 1907)

Tajfel, H 'Experiments in a vacuum' in *The Concept of Social Psychology: A Critical Assessment*, Israel, J and Tajfel, H (eds) European Monographs in Psychology, No. 2 (Academic Press: London 1972)

Tajfel, H 'Social Identity and Intergroup Behaviour', *Social Science Info* 13, 2, pp 65–93 (1974)

Tajfel, H *Differentiation between social groups: studies in the social psychology of intergroup relations* (Academic Press: London 1978)

Tajfel, H *Intergroup Behaviour*, Turner and Giles (eds) p 144 (Blackwell: Oxford 1981)

Tajfel, H (ed) *Social Identity and Intergroup relations* (CUP: Cambridge 1982)

Taylor, A J P 'Nations in History', in *The Crown and the Thistle*, MacLean, C (ed) (Constable, 1977)

Turner, J C *et al.* 'Social comparison and group favouritism', *European Jnl Soc Psychol* Vol 9, pp 187–204

Turner, J C 'The experimental social psychology of Intergroup Behaviour', in *Intergroup Behaviour*, Turner and Giles (eds) p 77 (Blackwell: Oxford 1983)

Trotter, Wilfred *Instincts of the Herd in Peace and War* (21st edn) (OUP 1953)

Waal, Frans de *Chimpanzee Politics* (Jonathon Cape 1982)

Weber, Max 'Race Relations', reprinted in *Selections*, Runciman, W G (ed), Matthews, E (trans) (CUP: Cambridge 1978)

Weinstein, B 'Language Strategists: redefining political frontiers on the basis of linguistic choices', in *World Politics* 31, p 345

Index

Aborigines, Australian,
and identification, 30
Aggressivity, 101, 102, 103
and international sport, 102–3
Ainsworth, M D S, 17
Amazulu, 31
American identity, 130–1
Anglo–Scottish identities, 121, 127
Apartheid, 34
Arab identity, 52, 57, 58, 115
Assad, President, 115
Australia, national identity, 133

Bangladesh, national identity, 62
Baur, Chris, 22
Belgium, language identities, 45
national consciousness, 120
Black racial awareness, 35, 36, 133, 135
Bowlby, J, 17
British Empire, 130–4
British regiments, 86–95
identity formation, 89
and regimental loyalty, 91–2
Bushmen, group identification, 31, 97

Canada, national identity, 132–3
Carpenter, G, 17
Children, identities of, 24–8
first attachments of, 16
social attachments of, 16–28
wider attachments and allegiances,
19–24
Chimpanzees, group behaviour of, 41
China, People's Republic of,
language identity, 52
national identity, 116
Chomsky, N, 18
Christianity, and religious identity, 55,
63
Class awareness, 21, 22, 23, 135–42

among adults, 22
Class consciousness, 10, 98, 99, 116
Colour consciousness, in children, 20
Commonwealth of Nations, 143
Communist Manifesto, 98
Cyprus, religious identity, 63–70
Greek–Cypriot identity, 64
Czechoslovakia, national identity, 50

Darwin, Charles, 19, 33, 41, 98
Dennis, W, 17
De Valera, Eamonn, 75, 76
Disloyalty, 44, 70
Durkheim, Emile, 13

Eaton, T, 33
Engels, F, 98, 99
Eskimos, group identification, 31, 38
Esprit de corps, 79–95, 96
amalgamation of regiments, 95
in American Army, 117
army identities, 93–4
arousal of, 81
British regiments, 86–95
Divisional identities, 93–4
Gurkha Brigade, 81–3
Indian regiments, 83–6
in multinational forces, 149–50
in Soviet Army, 141
significance of drill, 88–9
in Swiss Army, 119
in Yugoslav Army, 118
in Zulus, 31
Ethnic, definition of, 3–5, 79
Ethnocentrism, definition of, 3
European Economic Community (EEC),
143–6
Evans Pritchard, E, 29, 30
Falklands Campaign, 23, 105–9
and national identity, 105–9

Finland, language identity, 47, 48
Fitzgerald, Garrett, 25, 76, 78
Football, and national allegiance, 24
France, imperial consciousness, 128–9
    national consciousness, 114
Freud, Sigmund, on warfare, 100–5

Gandhi, Mahatma, 61
Germany, language identities, 48–9
    national identity, 115
Goodall, Jane Lawick, 39, 41
Greeks, ancient Greek identity, 44–5
    Enosis, 66–8
    national identity, 64–7
    Orthodox Christianity, 64, 66
    religious identity, 66
Group antagonism, 96–7, 99, 102
Group attachment trait, 128
    of children, 16–28
    inborn, 13–14, 18, 25, 26, 42, 110, 152
Group consciousness, characteristics of,
    6–10
    definition of, 5
    international, 142–6
    and international law, 149
    positive and negative aspects, 110–13
    racial, 32–8
Group identity, 2, 9
    transformation between types, 152–3
    and warfare, 96–109
Gurkha Brigade, *esprit de corps*, 81–3

Halsey, A H, 113
Harlow, H F, 17
Hartley, H L, 20
Homo sapiens, loyalty to whole, 42
    sub-races of, 34
Herder, Johann von, 48
Herodotus, views on identity, 44, 45
Hindus, and the Indian Army, 83–6
    religious identity, 61
Hitler, A, 48–9
Holland, colonial language identities,
    46–7
Humboldt, Wilhelm von, 48

Identification, definition of, 6
    at different levels, 10–11
    transformation into other forms, 11,
    152–3
Imperial identities, 128–35
Imperiousness, 35

India, Hindu identity, 61, 121
    imperial identity, 133
    language identity, 133
    partition of, 61–2
Indian Army, *esprit de corps*, 83–6
    class recruitment, 84
International law, 148–50
    and group consciousness, 149
International organisations, 142–6
    Commonwealth of Nations, 143
    European Economic Community,
    143–6
    United Nations Organisation, 129, 141
    146–8
International working class, 135–42
    see also Soviet Union
Iraq, national identity, 59
Ireland, Easter Rising, 74–5
    Home Rule Bill, 73–4
    language identity, 52, 70
    religious identity, 70–8
    Ulster loyalists, 75–8
Islam, and religious identity, 55–63
Islamic, *see* Muslim
Israel, state of, 60

Jahoda, G, 23
Jennings, Sir Ivor, 146
Jews, group consciousness, 38, 49
    history of, 11
    national identity, 60
Judaism, and religious identity, 55
Juvenile identities, artificial, 24–8

Khlief, B B, 47
Kingansell v *Police* 1979, case of, 4–5
Kinship patterns, 29
Koestler, Arthur, 104

Lambert, W E, 23
Language, and identity, 44–53
Language acquisition, 18
Leach, E, 29
League of Nations, 50, 59
Leakey, Richard, 100
Lebanon, national identity, 59, 116
Leinhardt, G, 29
Lenin, V I, 98, 130, 136, 141
Lewin, Roger, 100
Lorenz, Konrad, 101, 102
Loyalty, 26, 29
    to the Faith, 54

transformation, 90
to the whole human species, 42–3

Makarios, Archbishop, 67, 68
Malinowski, B, 29
Mandla v *Dowell Lee* 1984, case of, 3–4, 62
Mao Tse Tung, 98, 99, 100
Marshall, S L A, 88
Marx, Karl, 11, 136, 153
    on warfare, 97–100
Military group consciousness, *see Esprit de corps*
Military loyalty, 86
Moorehead, Alan, 89
Morgan, L, 29, 98
Morris, Desmond, 100
Mortimer, E, 62, 63
Mother tongues, 44–53
Multinational states, 113–21, 128
Muscovici, S, 25, 26
Muslim, Republics of Soviet Union, 51
Muslims, foundation of Islam, 55, 56
    and the Indian Army, 83–6
    Ottoman Empire, 57
    Ummah, 55, 56, 57, 58
    and religious identity, 61

Nation, definitions of, 1
National consciousness, 1, 2, 23, 44
    and imperial consciousness, 128
    and religious identity, 54
National identity, 111, 113
    and the Falklands Campaign, 105–9
    greater and lesser, 121–7
Nationalisation, 111
Nationhood, 70, 113–15
New Zealand, national identity, 133
Northern Ireland, religious identity, 70–8
    self-determination, 148

Orthodox Christian Church, 64, 65
Ottoman Empire, 57

Pakistan, national identity, 62, 63
    partition of, 62
Palestine, national identity, 59–60
Pan-African consciousness, 37
Patriotism, 88
Play, importance of, 19
Popper, Sir Karl, 146–7
Prehistoric co-operation, 31–2

Punjab uprising, 62
Pushkin, I, 20

Quebecois, identity of, 45, 132

Race Relations Act 1976, 4, 5
Races of humankind, 33–4
Racial consciousness, in the United States, 117
Racial group consciousness, 32–8, 44, 110–12
Radcliffe-Brown, A R, 29
Radke, M J, 20
Religion, and group consciousness, 132
Religious fanaticism, 55
Religious identities, 54–78
    and national consciousness, 54
Reynolds, Vernon, 99–100
Rivers, W H, 29, 68
Robertson, J, 19
Rousseau, J J, 32, 97

Sadat, A, 23
Scandinavia, language identities, 47–8
Schaffer, H R, 17, 18
Scotland, language identity, 124
    national identity, 122–7
    union with England, 125
Scott, Sir Walter, 126
Self-determination, right of, 146–8
Seton-Watson, Hugh, 1, 113, 130
Shepher, J, 40
Sheriff, Carolyn and Muzafer, 27
Sikhs, history of, 4, 11
Slavs, racial and language identity, 50
Slovaks, language identity, 50
Social attachments, in higher social animals, 39–42
Social identity, definition of, 6, 25–7
Soviet Union, class consciousness, 135–42
    German invasion, 138–9
    language identity, 50–1
    national consciousness, 117, 138–42
    transformation into nationhood, 141–2
Spain, language identities, 45–6
    national consciousness, 114
Spencer, Herbert, 3
Sport, international,
    and aggressivity, 102–3
Sri Lanka, national identity, 120

Stalin, Joseph, 98, 136, 137, 138
Standards of proof, lawyers, 15
Statehood, 70, 113–15
Stavinides, 2, 67, 69
Steiner, G, 119
Stereotyping, 9, 18
Switzerland, national identity, 118–19
Syria, national identity, 59

Tajfel, H, 2, 11, 25, 26, 35, 102
Taylor, A J P, 1
Tribal consciousness, 29–32
Tribal identity, 58
Trotter, W, 101
Turkey, language identities, 46
Turner, J C, 2, 25, 26
Turner, Sir Richard, 83
United   Kingdom,   national   identity,
    122–7

United Nations Charter, 147
United Nations Organisation, 129, 141,
    146–8
United   States   of   America,   national
    identity, 116–17

Waal, F de, 41
Warfare, and group identity, 96–109
    Freud on, 100–5
    Marx on, 97–100
Weber, Max, 35, 48, 49
Weinstein, B, 46
Working-class consciousness, 137–8
World consciousness, 43

Yugoslavia, national identity, 117–18

Zulus, group identification, 31